SEXUAL CULTURES: New Directions from the Center for
Lesbian and Gay Studies
General Editors: José Esteban Muñoz and Ann Pellegrini

Black Gay Man
Essays
Robert F. Reid-Pharr, Foreword by Samuel R. Delany

Passing
Identity and Interpretation in Sexuality, Race, and Religion
Edited by María Carla Sánchez and Lisa Schlossberg

Passing

Identity and Interpretation in Sexuality, Race, and Religion

Edited by
MARÍA CARLA SÁNCHEZ AND LINDA SCHLOSSBERG

NEW YORK UNIVERSITY PRESS

New York and London

NEW YORK UNIVERSITY PRESS
New York and London

© 2001 by New York University
All rights reserved

Library of Congress Cataloging-in-Publication Data
Passing : identity and interpretation in sexuality, race, and religion /
edited by María Carla Sánchez and Linda Schlossberg.
p.   cm. — (Sexual cultures)
ISBN 0-8147-8122-5 (cloth : alk. paper) —
ISBN 0-8147-8123-3 (pbk. : alk. paper)
1. Passing (Identity)   I. Sánchez, María Carla, 1968– II. Schlossberg,
Linda, 1969– III. Series.
HM1068 .P37 2001
302.1—dc21   2001002805

New York University Press books are printed on acid-free paper,
and their binding materials are chosen for strength and durability.

Manufactured in the United States of America

10 9 8 7 6 5 4 3 2 1

Contents

Introduction

Rites of Passing

Linda Schlossberg

> Visibility is a trap.
>
> —MICHEL FOUCAULT, *Discipline and Punish*

Theories and practices of identity and subject formation in Western culture are largely structured around a logic of visibility, whether in the service of science (Victorian physiognomy), psychoanalysis (Lacan's mirror stage), or philosophy (Foucault's reading of the Panopticon). At the most basic level, we are subjects constituted by our visions of ourselves and others, and we trust that our ability to see and read carries with it a certain degree of epistemological certainty. For instance, we commonly use a vocabulary of vision to signify cognition, understanding, and truth: a well-written article is perceptive, clear-sighted, focused, visionary. (Those individuals we disagree with, on the other hand, are myopic and shortsighted). Because of this seemingly intimate relationship between the visual and the known, passing becomes a highly charged site for anxieties regarding visibility, invisibility, classification, and social demarcation. It disrupts the logics and conceits around which identity categories are established and maintained—even as it may seem to result in the disappearance or denial of a range of "minoritized" or queer identities.

1

If passing wreaks havoc with accepted systems of social recognition and cultural intelligibility, it also blurs the carefully marked lines of race, gender, and class, calling attention to the ways in which identity categories intersect, overlap, construct, and deconstruct one other. Cultural historians of the body, for instance, have noted the ways in which Jews and homosexuals are similar in that they share the dubious honor of being largely invisible or un-readable,[1] which leads, in the cultural imagination, to paranoid fantasies of stealth queers taking over higher education, or powerful Jews secretly con-trolling the federal government. The cultural anxieties surrounding physical illegibility in turn have produced a wealth of pseudoscientific literature de-voted to identifying the Jewish and homosexual body—bodies that have overlapped, given the historical tendency to articulate signs of Jewish racial difference in terms of sexual and gender deviance. At the same time, the Nazis' pink triangle and Star of David can be seen as an anxious overcom-pensation for the fact that these two identities are not immediately readable or recognizable in visual terms.

Similarly, literary critics have noted the way in which racial and gender passing often coincide in African American literature. Nineteenth-century novelists often exploit the plot device of the escaped "tragic mulatto" slave who disguises him- or herself by cross-dressing, and the light-skinned black man, in Harlem Renaissance literature, is typically coded as feminine, deli-cate, and emotional.[2] Furthermore, the passing subject's ability to transcend or abandon his or her "authentic" identity calls into question the very no-tion of authenticity itself. Passing, it seems, threatens to call attention to the performative and contingent nature of all seemingly "natural" or "obvious" identities.

In recent years the term *performance* has emerged as a key word for think-ing about identity. This volume will ask how passing lends itself to the per-formance of various identities, and will explore the ways in which the pass-ing subject's strategies of signification differ across various historical and na-tional contexts. In addition to contributing to ongoing discussions about race and racialization, the theorizations of passing collected in this volume have much to add to the critical conversation surrounding queer identity, a conversation structured by the twin issues of the closet (Eve Sedgwick) and performativity (Judith Butler). Much current scholarship in the field of lesbian and gay studies concerns itself with the way in which identities are articulated and elaborated: to be recognized as gay, queer subjects must perform themselves as such, through bodily self-inscription, speech acts, or public displays of affection. A public or readable queer identity can be said, therefore, to consist of the active or willful negation of passing. But because an accurate reading of the queer body can, in many social and political contexts, result in obviously terrible consequences (even unto death), passing becomes a form of passive resistance, one that protects the gay subject from hostile interpretations. Passing thus can be understood at the most basic level as an attempt to control the process of signification itself. As the essays here reveal, however, this control is often illusory or fleeting at best.

Passing, Interpretation, and Narrative

One of the aims of this volume is to explore the various ways in which passing can be experienced and expressed. Like queer identity itself, passing can be experienced as a source of radical pleasure or intense danger; it can function as a badge of shame or a source of pride. Passing as practice questions the commonly held assumption that visibility is necessarily positive, pleasurable, even desirable. Indeed, rather than simply functioning as a cop-out or a ruse, an ingenious method of protection or self-defense, passing can also, it seems, be experienced as a uniquely pleasurable experience, one that trades on the erotics of secrecy and revelation. At the same time, passing can be fundamentally conservative: although it may often represent social progress for an individual, it generally holds larger social hierarchies firmly in place. Hence the real moral and even political anxieties engendered by what seems to be a private act. This contradiction, we would argue, suggests that there may be something fundamentally "queer" about the phenomenon of passing itself. Passing's ability to be both playful and serious asks us to reconsider our interpretive strategies and forces our most cherished fantasies of identity to self-deconstruct.

Passing is not simply about erasure or denial, as it is often castigated but, rather, about the creation and establishment of an alternative set of narratives. It becomes a way of creating new stories out of unusable ones, or from personal narratives seemingly in conflict with other aspects of self-presentation. The passing subject's need to create a coherent, plausible narrative to account for his or her past suggests, on a very basic level, that every subject's history is a work in progress—a set of stories we tell ourselves in order to make sense or coherence out of a frequently confusing and complicated past. The risk and pleasure of narrative thus seems intimately connected to the risk and pleasure of passing.

If, as we are suggesting, identity is primarily a form of storytelling, then the stakes of the story are different depending on the social location of the narrator. For people of color, gays and lesbians, members of the working class and poor, and people of marginalized religious faiths, the allure of rewriting identity cannot be disconnected from the very real emotional and material advantages of doing so. Obviously, the creation of a coherent narrative or stable history, a mappable trajectory, becomes all the more tempting in such cases, particularly for racialized subjects whose histories have been violently erased. This is among the many reasons that passing, as a subject of close critical study and historical analysis, has been most forcefully undertaken in the field of African American studies. This makes intuitive sense, of course, given that the ability to pass as white was historically the precondition for achieving and maintaining the status, at the most basic level, of being a citizen and human being (a fact made manifest by the ratification of the U.S. Constitution in 1787, in which African slaves were counted as three-fifths of a person for purposes of apportionment). For racially marked subjects, passing can mean the difference between life and death, community and isolation, status as property and status as subjects.

At the same time, the more abstract notion of political and social "invisibility" must be taken into account when we consider the complications of passing (as Ralph Ellison's *Invisible Man* famously suggests). Historically, in the United States, racial readability has been translated into social immobility and, ironically, social invisibility. "Visibility," in this context, functions as metaphor rather than objective phenomenon: to be marked is to be marked out. When Patricia Williams writes that "white people see all the worlds beyond me but not me. They come trotting at me with force and speed; they do not see me. I could force my presence, the real me contained in those eyes, upon them, but I would be smashed in the process," she calls attention to the tensions between being visibly marked as black and being socially "invisible" as a black woman.[3] This is the gap between being visible and being seen. For Williams, it is precisely her heightened visibility (or readability) as a black subject that—paradoxically enough—causes her to be invisible as a social subject with rights and desires.

Passing is further complicated by the fact that to be "unmarked" is to occupy a position of privilege, in which the subject hides behind an apparent transparency. White individuals, for instance, are in a constant state of passing as having no ethnic or racial identity at all, as having "nothing to say" about race, or as somehow existing outside the volatile world of "racial tensions." Indeed, white racial identity seeks to make itself visible only when (as in the case of White Aryan Resistance or the KKK) it perceives itself as being under siege financially (from Jews) or sexually (from blacks), or when the ability of people of African American racial heritage to pass as Caucasian calls a white person's own seemingly unblemished whiteness into question.

Similarly, heterosexual culture continually passes itself off as being merely natural, the undisputed and unmarked norm, rather than as a set of highly visible and frequently commodified practices (for example, marriage ceremonies; the commercialization of Valentine's Day) with its own compulsive behaviors and codes. As Judith Butler argues, the continual presentation and representation of gender "as we know it" produces "a set of corporeal styles, which, in reified form, appear as the natural configuration of bodies into sexes which exist in a binary relation to one another."[4] Heterosexuality thus passes as the "natural" by obsessively disguising the factors and learned behaviors that occasion its own production. The gay and lesbian liberation slogan "It's not a lifestyle, it's a life" might better be replaced by "It's all a lifestyle."

The notion that identity is performative, however, has different consequences for the passing subject. A convincing performance of, for example, "whiteness" or "straightness" or "womanliness" requires not just culture but skill; the seams must not show. We should note briefly that, generally speaking, as Bill Clinton's infamous "Don't Ask, Don't Tell" military policy illustrates, the ability of homosexual subjects to pass as straight is comforting to the dominant social order ("I don't care what they do, as long as they do it in the privacy of their own home"), while the ability to pass for white is anxiety-producing and disrupts a system of social stratification based on racial hierarchy. There are exceptions, of course: the fact that a gay scout-master might pass for straight would be upsetting to some parents who would not want their children to fall under even closeted homosexual influence; the husband and wife next door who pass for white in their suburban neighborhood may not occasion anxiety if, of course, no one is able to read them as "black." Yet it remains a provocative fact that the dominant social order often implores gay people to stay in the closet (to pass), while subjects who pass for white are encouraged to "come out" or reveal themselves as authentically "racial" subjects—at times by both minority groups *and* the dominant social order. (Witness the anxious reactions following the death of writer and *New York Times* critic Anatole Broyard in 1990, who, for much of his professional life, passed for white.)[5] Furthermore, as Ann Pellegrini has argued, passing for white can involve completely rejecting and disavowing one's family or community, while passing for straight can be a way of maintaining membership in one's family of origin.[6] These glitches in analogical thinking force us to recognize that passing's motivations and results are never predictable.

The first three essays in the volume, by Judith Halberstam, Daniel Itzkovitz, and María Carla Sánchez, concern themselves with the conjunctions between passing and narrative: which kinds of life stories are culturally intelligible, and how those narratives fit into the cultural production of identity as a whole. In "Telling Tales: Brandon Teena, Billy Tipton, and Transgender Biography," Halberstam looks at representations of Teena and Tipton in literature and film, arguing that within the enterprise of transgender biography, a desire to "narrate lives" may encounter opposition in the form of self-representations that "willfully defy narrative." Halberstam reveals how "female masculinity" intersects with other facets of subjectivity (race, class, and regional identity) to form a complex identity and relation "between people, within a community, or within intimate bonds." Many of those intersections, Halberstam suggests, are elided in the project of traditional biography (transgender or otherwise), broaching the question of how identity formations either do or do not make narrative "sense."

Similarly, Daniel Itzkovitz's "Passing Like Me: Jewish Chameleonism and the Politics of Race" explores how the modernist impulse to identify a contradictorily "essential" and "elusive" Jewishness contributed to the development of twentieth-century American "rhetorics of racial and national identities." Parodic and even "chameleonic," Jewishness emerges as an identity that can all too easily pass as something else, one that, paradoxically, becomes all the more "real" in its ability to be hidden or mistaken for something else. In his reading of modernist literature, Itzkovitz juxtaposes the early-twentieth-century impulse to identify Jewishness against contemporary depictions of blackness; each, he finds, was used "to navigate the uneasy limits of whiteness." All three of these terms—*Jewishness, blackness,* and *whiteness*—combine in the developing understanding of modernity and of the modern racial subject.

María Carla Sánchez's essay on early Mexican American literature, which focuses on the work of nineteenth-century novelist María Amparo Ruiz de Burton, asks what it means to pass both into a different social class and into a particular literary genealogy. Juxtaposing the "whiteness demonstrations" of early writers with the indigenous and working-class values of contemporary Chicano studies, Sánchez examines the ideological and linguistic sleights of hand necessary to reconcile competing claims to identity and history. The politics of literary history, often expressed through a familial desire to imagine various authors as ancestors, are played out in efforts to maneuver authors into contemporary identity categories or constituencies—categories into which they may not precisely fit. As many early writers were concerned with the new, post-Mexican-American War social order in which they lived, the politics of who speaks (and for whom and as what) becomes crucial in understanding this particular meeting of literary past and present.

Brad Epps's trenchant exploration of the politics surrounding U.S. immigration law serves as the focus of "Passing Lines." Examining the various racial and sexual identities, characteristics, and associations that can disqualify one for United States asylum or citizenship, Epps reveals how endemic passing becomes to the process of entering the country (such entry itself the result of a passage, and merely one among a number of "rites of passage" that must be experienced). Homosexuality, once a valid disqualification for citizenship by means of its inclusion under the category of "medical exclusions," was dropped as a psychiatric disorder by the American Psychiatric Association in 1973. Yet, Epps argues, even as legal language seemingly becomes more inclusive, the "passing lines" do not vanish but merely shift. As he writes, "There is something queer about the fact that even as homosexuality, as an excludable category, disappears, another category, that of HIV and AIDS, appears." The metonymic relationship of HIV-AIDS to homosexuality allows state-sanctioned discrimination to flourish more subtly, even as it creates another identity category—that of the person with AIDS— that must be disguised in order for citizenship and "naturalization" to be granted.

In the volume's next essay, "From Victorian Parlor to *Physique Pictorial*," Michael Bronski traces the development of the physical culture movement in the United States and Britain. He argues that the spectacle of the beautiful, well-defined male body could function simultaneously as a source of artistic inspiration for homosexual aesthetes and as a recognizable emblem of conventionally heterosexual, masculinist, and racialist discourse. Bronski suggests that the increasing popularity and commercialization of the body-building culture in the first half of the twentieth century—a culture immensely popular with both heterosexuals and gay men—made it increasingly difficult to recognize and categorize the "typical" invert's body, a body that had been previously coded, in the late-nineteenth and early-twentieth centuries, as "spectacular" and easy to see in its supposed effeminacy and weakness. As such, his essay traces a historically specific manifestation of the anxieties that surface when homosexual subjects are no longer perceived as being visibly marked out and easily identifiable.

Seizing upon an issue that in academic discourse often seems to be undervalued or dismissed out of hand, Peter Hitchcock presents a genealogy of class passing, and, more specifically, of "slumming." Arguing that "for as long as there have been classes, there has been slumming," Hitchcock examines different textual narratives of slumming and locates in the act of passing the revelation of "what is living and what is dead in class relations." Beginning with Nero—the figure he calls "the Ur-Slummer"—and proceeding through readings of texts by Friedrich Engels, Jack London, and George Orwell, Hitchcock reveals slumming to be both a critical investigation of class hierarchies and, all too often, a reinforcement of them.

Similarly, in "The Self-Made Man: Male Impersonation and the New Woman," Sharon Ullman investigates a theatrical phenomenon that in many ways undermined, and in other ways significantly buttressed, fin-de-siècle essentialist concepts of masculinity and femininity. Male impersonators—women who performed onstage as men—were a surprisingly popular element of the vaudeville repertoire in the late-nineteenth and early-twentieth centuries. Through a careful examination of unpublished archival materials related to turn-of-the-century performance, Ullman reevaluates this theatrical phenomenon so as to "[demonstrate] the ways in which the discourse surrounding such onstage activity was deployed to negotiate the gender difficulties created by the call for women's political equality offstage." Although many of these performers disavowed any connection to or sympathy with the suffrage movement—instead asserting a

9

traditional, stereotypical, and what we would now call "essential" femininity as their true identities—the performers and the anxieties engendered by the act of "male impersonation" itself necessarily became embroiled in the larger political issues at stake. "What it is that 'makes a man' had obviously become a subject of some debate," writes Ullman. "Could a man truly be 'self-made' by anyone—even a woman?"

A jump ahead to the end of the twentieth century finds us still within the realm of gender passing and theatrical performance, although the terms of the debate have significantly shifted. In "Mimesis in the Face of Fear," Karen McCarthy Brown analyzes her personal interviews with members of the "voguing" Ballroom Houses of Newark, New Jersey, in order to understand "the mimetic dimensions of the Ballroom scene" and the way this type of pleasurable, yet intensely serious, ritualized behavior interacts with phantom desires "for religious and familial belonging." Quoting a Ballroom House member who insists that "the Ballroom is very contradictive," McCarthy Brown finds gender essentialism flourishing in a manner that most of the members experience as liberating. Perhaps, she argues, this apparent paradox stems from the rampant homophobia and racism that, occurring outside the confines of the houses and the ballroom, disallow any sort of cross-gender identification at all.

The volatile combination of racism and religious intolerance also comes under scrutiny in Patrick O'Malley's "The Church's Closet." Examining the anxieties surrounding nineteenth-century English Catholicism and the increasing popularity of ritualism within the Church of England itself, O'Malley finds national, sexual, and religious identities figured as at risk by Catholicism's apparent ability to pass as and into normative English (read: Protestant) life. What was referred to in the nineteenth century as "the Church's closet"—the confessional—comes to emblematize the secrecy and supposed promiscuity of Catholicism (for, as O'Malley points out, who knows what goes on behind that curtain). O'Malley finds Catholics, Protestants, and Jews entangled in a series of discursive exchanges that attempt to define the porous limits of English national identity.

Miriam Peskowitz's recollection of her astonishing visit to "Moses' Wilderness Tabernacle" closes the volume, in some ways, by coming full circle; her mix of the personal and the theoretical (or what bell hooks has called "theorizing through autobiography") recalls the concerns raised by Halberstam's essay on biography at the beginning of this collection. Relating her experience of visiting "The New Holy Land," a touristic rendition and re-creation of biblical villages in northwest Arkansas, Peskowitz movingly considers the desires for group identification that underlie not only all passings but often the mundanities of everyday, "nonpassing" lives. When she is asked by her tour guide to join the group in asserting her faith in Jesus Christ, Peskowitz—who is Jewish—wonders what is at stake in such requests, what results will ensue if she gives an affirmative or negative reply. Is there no way, she wonders, to reveal the immense ironies of her situation without courting social discomfort, or, at least, emotional danger?

And haven't such questions been asked countless times before? Given the current volatile climate in which debates concerning identity now find themselves—from political campaigns to attain even basic civil rights for gays and lesbians, to the contentious battles over affirmative action in higher education and the workplace—it seems likely that the issue of passing will continue to surface (and surprise us) in new and unexpected ideological arenas. Who we are and who we appear to be remain matters not merely of academic interest but also of survival. We hope the essays collected here will help to complicate the terms of a debate that itself shows no signs of disappearing or passing away.

Notes

I am grateful to María Carla Sánchez and Ann Pellegrini for their help with this introduction. For their advice, support, and encouragement, María and I also would like to thank Marjorie Garber, Henry Louis Gates, Jr., Barbara Johnson, Cecilia Feilla, José Esteban Muñoz, Elaine Scarry, Ryan Schneider, and Eric Zinner.

1. See, for instance, Sander Gilman, *The Jew's Body* (New York: Routledge, 1991).

2. On this, see Phillip Brian Harper, *Are We Not Men? Masculine Identity and the Problem of African-American Identity* (New York: Oxford University Press, 1996), esp. 13–26.

3. Patricia Williams, "On Being the Object of Property," in *The Alchemy of Race and Rights: Diary of a Law Professor* (Cambridge: Harvard University Press, 1991), 213–236.

4. Judith Butler, "Performative Acts and Gender Constitution: An Essay in Phenomenology and Feminist Theory," in *Writing on the Body: Female Embodiment and Feminist Theory,* ed. Katie Conboy et al. (New York: Columbia University Press, 1997), 401–417; 407.

5. See Henry Louis Gates, Jr., "The Passing of Anatole Broyard," in *Thirteen Ways of Looking at a Black Man* (New York: Random House, 1997), 180–214.

6. Private communication.

1 Telling Tales

Brandon Teena, Billy Tipton, and Transgender Biography

Judith Halberstam

Introduction

The names "Brandon Teena" and "Billy Tipton" have become synonymous with a cluster of questions and concerns about passing, gender identities, memory, history, and transgender biography. Brandon Teena was a young woman who passed successfully as a man in a small town in Nebraska and who was brutally murdered when some local men decided to take their bloody revenge for what they considered to be a grand deception. Billy Tipton was a jazz musician who was only discovered to have a female body after his death. Since Tipton had married several times and was survived by a wife and adopted children, the revelation of his biological sex created a minor sensation. In the case of each of these transgender subjects, their lives were dismantled and reassembled through a series of biographical inquiries. This paper situates transgender biography as a sometimes violent, often imprecise project, one which seeks to brutally erase the carefully managed details of the

This chapter originally appeared in "Queer Autobiographies," a special issue of *a/b: Auto/Biographical Studies* 15.1 (spring 2000), edited by Thomas C. Spear.

life of a passing person and which recasts the act of passing as deception, dishonesty, and fraud.

I will be asking here what kind of truths about gender we demand from the lives of people who pass, cross-dress, or simply refuse normative gender categories. None of the transgender subjects whom I examine here can be definitively identified as transsexual; none can be read as lesbian; all must be read and remembered according to the narratives they meticulously circulated about themselves when they were alive. "Telling Tales," addresses thorny questions about the ethics of biography, about who has the right to tell tales about whose life, and it explores and fleshes out the postmodern category "transgender."

Transgender History

For the last five years or so I have been working on topics under the organizational heading of "female masculinity." However, very recently it has become obvious to me that this term lends itself to an interrogation of the politics and history and cultures of what we call "transgender" subjectivities. While "transgender" has served as a kind of umbrella term in recent years for cross-identifying subjects, I think the inclusivity of its appeal has made it quite unclear as to what the term might mean and for whom. Some theorists, such as Bernice Hausman, have dismissed transgenderism as a form of false consciousness which circulates through the belief that genders can be voluntary and chosen, and she concludes that "the new gender outlaws are just newer versions of the old gender conformists" (197). Others, like female-to-male transsexual theorist Henry Rubin, read transgender politics as a postmodern critique of the commitment to the "real" that he thinks is implied by transsexualism. Still others, like Biddy Martin, identify transgenderism as a faddish celebration of gender crossing which assigns non-cross-identified queers to the ignominy of gender conformity. But as I will show in this paper, we have hardly begun to recognize the forms of embodiment that fill out the category of transgenderism, and before we dismiss it as faddish, we should know what kind of work it does, whom it describes, and whom it validates. "Transgender" proves to be an important term not to people who want to reside outside of categories altogether but to people who want to place themselves in the way of particular forms of recognition. "Transgender" may, indeed, be considered a term of relationality; it describes not simply an identity but a relation between people, within a community, or within intimate bonds.

I will engage here with the somewhat paradoxical project of transgender history—paradoxical because it represents the desire to narrate lives that may wilfully defy narrative—but I will begin by establishing the terrain of female masculinity and registering where and how it overlaps with what has been called transgenderism. At least one of the reasons that I began thinking through and about female masculinity in the early 1990s was the desire to mark a place for cross-identifying women which did not fold neatly into community and medical models of transsexuality. As female-to-male transsexuals became more numerous and more visible in urban queer communities, there was inevitably a reshuffling of categories and etiologies. Young people coming out in the 1990s may be forgiven for not quite knowing what their experiences of cross-identification may mean. If "lesbian" in this context becomes the term for women who experience themselves as female and desire other women, and if "FTM transsexual" becomes the term for female-born people who experience prolonged male-identification and think of themselves as male, then what happens to those female-born people who think of themselves as masculine but not necessarily male and certainly not female? We do use the term "butch" for this last category, but I try to extend the term "butch" beyond its 1950s context and its inevitable coupling with "femme," and I locate it in a larger terrain: female masculinity. Jay Prosser's *Second Skins: The Body Narratives of Transsexuals,* in particular, has been enormously useful in thinking through the relations between the terms "transgender" and "queer" and elucidating the continuities and difference between butch and FTM.

I will use Prosser's work here in order to map the theoretical terrain of

transgender studies. Prosser's formulation of the role of narrative in transsexual transition has established itself in opposition to what he understands
to be a queer and, indeed, postmodern preference for performativity over
narrativity. In *Second Skins*, Prosser asks what the effect of a theory of gender
performativity has been upon our understanding of transsexuality; he also
argues that for all our talk about "materiality" and "embodiment," it is precisely the body that vanishes within ever more abstract theories of gender,
sexuality, and desire. Prosser points out that in *Gender Trouble*, Judith Butler
implies that the transgender subject symbolizes the "gender trouble" to
which every subject is heir; in other words, the split between sex and gender
which is so readable within the transgender or transsexual body reveals the
constructedness of *all* sex and gender. Gender normativity, within this
schema, is a place of self-deception inasmuch as the "straight" subject imagines his or her gender to be consistent with his or her sex and the relation between the two to be "natural." Prosser comments:

> *While within this framework, this allocation is a sign of the devaluation of straight
> gender and conversely queer's alignment of itself with transgender performativity rep-
> resents queer's sense of its own "higher purpose," in fact there are transgendered tra-
> jectories, in particular transsexual trajectories, that aspire to that which this scheme
> devalues. Namely, there are transsexuals who seek very pointedly to be nonperforma-
> tive, to be constative, quite simply, to be. (32)*

This is a complicated passage but I think it can be rendered as: many transsexuals do not want to represent gender artifice, they actually aspire to the
real, the natural, to the very condition that has been rejected by the queer
theory of gender performance.

    While I am totally sympathetic to Prosser's argument that the transsexual
has been used in queer theory as a symbol for the formulation of a subjectivity that actually threatens transsexual claims to legitimacy, I do think
there are problems with Prosser's formulation of a transsexual desire for realness and with his sense that gender realness is achievable. After all, what actually constitutes the real for Prosser in relation to the transsexual body? The

penis or vagina? Facial hair or shaved legs? Everyday life as a man or a woman? The primary example of a transsexual desire for realness that Prosser examines involves Venus Extravaganza from *Paris Is Burning,* a figure whom Butler discusses at length in *Bodies That Matter.* Prosser critiques Butler for making a distinction between transgender transgression and transsexual capitulation to "hegemonic constraint," and he notes that as long as Venus remains gender ambiguous then she can represent the transgression of the "denaturalization of sex;" but because she expresses a desire to become a white woman and live in the suburbs, Butler talks of the "reworking of the normative framework of heterosexuality." Prosser, on the other hand, not only wants to release the transsexual from the burden of representing subversive sexuality and gender, but he also wants to draw attention to the fact that Venus Extravaganza is killed by a transphobic john *not* because she is a woman but because she is mid-transition—not quite a woman. Prosser notes ominously: "Butler's essay locates transgressive value in that which makes the subject's life most unsafe" (49).

In the argument between Prosser and Butler I believe a distinction needs to be made between "realness" and the "real," a distinction which would have been meaningful to Venus, who lived in the world of balls, voguing, and realness. Realness in *Paris Is Burning* is, in the words of Dorian Corey, "as close as we will ever come to the real." It is not exactly performance, not exactly an imitation, it is the way that people—minorities excluded from the domain of the real—appropriate the real and its effects.[1] Realness, the appropriation of the attributes of the real, one could say, is precisely the transsexual condition. The real, on the other hand, is that which always exists elsewhere and as a fantasy of belonging and being. Venus accordingly expresses her desire for the real in the form of things she will obviously never attain—suburban respectability. Similarly, the FTM expresses his desire for a manhood which on some level will always elude him. This need not be the downfall of transsexual aspiration, however; indeed, it may be its strength. Needless to say, the fantasy that many queers may entertain of gender realness is extremely important as we challenge the limits of theories of performance. Prosser suggests that transsexuals become "real" literally through authorship, by writing themselves into transition. "Narrative," Prosser notes, "is not only the bridge to embodiment but a way of making sense of transition, the link between locations: the transition itself" (9). Gender discomfort can be alleviated by narratives which locate the oddly gendered subject in the world and in relation to others. While I cast the relationship between the transgender subject and narrative in slightly different terms in this paper, I find Prosser's understanding of the role of narrative in transsexual self-authorization to be crucial. What happens, I ask, when the transgender subject has died and is unable to provide a narrative of his complex life? What is the difference between transsexual autobiography and transgender biography?

One way in which queers and transgenders have put themselves in the way of gender realness is to inhabit categories of their own making. While some people suggest that categories (gay, lesbian, transsexual) are themselves the site of regulation, trouble, and repression, I would argue that—to use one of Butler's terms—categories represent sites of "necessary trouble."[2] Queer theory has long been preoccupied with the relationship between identity and regulation; post-Foucault, we recognize that to embrace identities can simply form part of a "reverse discourse" within which medically constructed categories are lent the weight of realness by people's willingness to occupy those categories.[3] However, it may be that we have allowed this Foucauldian insight to redirect discussions of identification away from the subjects of categories themselves. The term "reverse discourse" in *The History of Sexuality, Vol. 1* identifies and rejects the traditional formulations of gay and lesbian political struggle as essentially oppositional. Since certain sexual liberation discourses recapitulate the very terms of the homo/hetero binary which oppress minority sexual subjects in the first place, then these discourses become part of the installation of the sexual hierarchy that they seek to oppose. However, Foucault also understands emancipation struggles as strategically and historically necessary; furthermore, a "reverse discourse" is in no way the "same" as the discourse it reverses. Indeed, its desire for reversal is a desire for transformation.

We may not want to reject *all* reverse discourses *per se,* but we may want to limit the ways in which we invest in them as end points (coming out, for example). Foucault, and Butler for that matter, clearly believe that resistance has to go beyond the taking of a name ("I am a lesbian") and must produce creative, new forms of being by assuming and empowering a marginal positionality. Furthermore, the production of categories is different in different spaces—expert produced categories ("the homosexual," "the invert," "the transsexual") are ultimately far less interesting or useful than the sexual vernaculars or categories produced and sustained within sexual subcultures. The naming of sexual vernaculars and the production of community histories can be traced back to the work of Gayle Rubin, who has spoken eloquently about the limits of expert discourses (such as psychoanalysis) on sexuality, and the importance of questions of "sexual ethnogenesis" or the formation of sexual communities.[4] Scientific discourses have tended to narrow our ability to imagine sexuality and gender; in general, the discussions that take place in medical communities about embodiment and desire may be way behind the discussions taking place on email lists, in support groups, and in sex clubs. Doctors, for instance, use categories in a very different way from the manner in which people cruising for sex partners use categories. Accordingly, we should take over the prerogative of naming our experience and identifications.

Nowhere has the effect of naming our identifications been clearer in recent years than in relation to the experience we call "transgendered." Transgender is for the most part a vernacular term developed within gender communities to account for the cross-identification experiences of people who may not accept all of the protocols and strictures of transsexuality. Such people understand cross-identification as a crucial part of their gendered self, but they may pick and choose among the options of body modification, social presentation, and legal recognition available to them. For instance, you may

19

find that a transgender male is a female-born subject who has had no sex-re-assignment surgery, takes testosterone (with or without medical supervision), and lives mostly "as a man" but is recognized by his community as a transgendered man in particular. The term "transgender" in this context refuses the stability that the term "transsexual" may offer to some folks and embraces more hybrid possibilities for embodiment and identification. At the same time, the term "transsexual" is itself undergoing reconstruction by publicly identifiable transsexuals; Kate Bornstein, for one, has made a career from the reshaping of the public discourse around gender and transsexuality.[5] In other words, transsexual is not simply the conservative medical term to transgender's transgressive vernacular; both transsexuality and transgenderism shift and change in meaning and application *in relation to each other* rather than in relation to a hegemonic medical discourse.

While some people will argue against using the term "female masculinity" for transgender subjects, for female-born people who go on to live as men, the work performed by this term is useful in terms of recording the histories of transgender subjects. In relation to the female-born person who passes as male (with or without hormones) for most of his life, the term "female masculinity" registers the distinction at least between *his* cultivated masculinity and a male's biological masculinity and addresses the question of the transgender man's past history as female. For these subjects, of course, we need a transgender history, a method of recording the presence of gender ambiguous subjects sensitive enough not to reduce them to either "women all along" or "failed men." Transgender bodies, ultimately, seem to be both illogical and illegible to any number of "experts" who try to read them. At the same time, transgender lives often seem to attract enormous attention from biographers, filmmakers, talk show hosts, doctors, and journalists, all of whom are dedicated to forcing the transgender subject to make sense. While one would not wish to assign the transgender life to the inauspicious category of nonsense, we should be wary of overly rational narratives about lives filled with contradiction and tension. Ultimately, we must ask questions about history and documentation, as well as the sometimes dangerous project of scrutinizing lives which were organized around gender passing.

The lives and deaths of Brandon Teena, a Nebraskan teenager who was murdered by local boys when they discovered that he was a woman living as a man, and Billy Tipton, a jazz pianist who was discovered posthumously to have a female body, have suffered the untimely and rude effects of over-exposure. While obviously my efforts to examine the flurry of representation surrounding Brandon Teena and Billy Tipton and other transgender figures actually adds to this effect, the production of counter-narratives seems all the more important in a media age when suppression of information is virtually impossible (nor would I necessarily argue for the suppression of information under any circumstances). In the cases of Billy Tipton and Brandon Teena, however, it serves some purpose to examine the motives behind various representations of transgender lives. In general, we can identify three different and often competing sets of motivations for the representation of a transgender life by non-transgender people:

1) *The project of stabilization*—in this mode of production, the destabilizing effects of the transgender narrative are defused by establishing the transgender narrative as strange and uncharacteristic and even pathological;
2) *the project of rationalization*—here the biographer or film maker or writer finds reasonable explanations for behavior that seems dangerous and outrageous: an economic motive, a need to be in hiding, the lack of community are some rationalizing narratives;
3) *the project of trivialization*—the transgender life might be dismissed within such a narrative as non-representative and interesting but without any real effects upon gender normativity.

The term "transgender" can be used as a marker for all kinds of people who challenge (deliberately or accidentally) gender normativity. Jazz singer Little Jimmy Scott, just to give one example, is a male vocalist whose high counter tenor voice causes him to be heard as "female." His voice has been

described as "angelic," and he has influenced many famous female jazz vo-
calists, such as Nancy Wilson. The term "transgender" can be applied here
not to remove Jimmy Scott from the category "male," but rather to prevent
him from being heard as "female." In interviews he strenuously objects to
criticisms of his voice that liken it to a woman's, and he insists, in a way, that
his voice, his transgender voice, extends the category of maleness rather than
capitulates to the strict dictates of gender normativity. In this context, the
term "transgender" appears as an adjective to describe a voice rather than as
an identification category which describes Scott's gender identity or sexual
orientation. In what follows, I will use "transgender" as a descriptive term
for several different forms of non-normative gender presentation. While
Jimmy Scott has recently given interviews about the medical condition (Kall-
man's Syndrome, a hormonal dysfunction) which gave him his high voice
and his androgynous appearance, other people who present their gender
ambiguously may not be given the opportunity to explain what motivates
their gender variance. Transgender history should be a discourse which
allows the gender ambiguous to speak. Too often, I will claim, the histories
of women who pass as men, or the narratives of transgender men, attempt to
rationalize rather than represent transgender lives in the glory of all their
contradictions.

Ghost Writing: The Case of Billy Tipton

*Many ghost writers believe they are the real authority on their subject and not the
ghost themselves.*   —*Jackie Kay,* Trumpet

Early on in *Trumpet,* a haunting novel by British author Jackie Kay, the widow
of the celebrated jazz musician Joss Moody comments: "The only thing that
feels authentic to me is my past" (37). Shortly after her husband dies, the secret that she and Joss have kept meticulously over the years of their marriage
leaks out to the press: Joss Moody was born a woman. As Millicent Moody
mourns the death of her beloved husband, she also has to fend off journal-

ists, try to repair the damaged relationship with her son, and protect the memories of her life with Joss from the vicious re-writings to which they are now subject. "I am the only one," she says, "who can remember him the way he wanted to be remembered" (40).

In *Trumpet,* as even a short summary of the novel makes clear, Joss Moody is modeled on the life and death of the American jazz musician Billy Tipton. When Tipton died in 1992, paramedics called by his son were shocked to find breasts beneath the man's clothing. Tipton's son and wife claimed to have no knowledge of his secret. Unlike Tipton's wife, Millicent Moody in *Trumpet* is depicted as having full knowledge of the "facts" of her husband's embodiment. For Millicent, her husband's breasts and female genitalia were "our secret," a secret not all that different from the many secrets kept between spouses: "Lots of people have secrets, don't they? The world runs on secrets. What kind of place would the world be without them?" (10). The revelation of the "secret" of the passing man or woman, however, seems to occasion a very particular kind of curiosity and has produced sometimes cruel and disrespectful revisions of life narratives. The revelation of Billy Tipton's "secret," for example, prompted speculation and investigation of the so-called "true" identity of Billy Tipton.

In her highly publicized biography of Tipton, Diane Middlebrook comes dangerously close to claiming that Tipton's life as a man was simply the result of his overwhelming ambition to perform as a musician. This rubric then forces Middlebrook to view his relationships with women as elaborate deceptions; she depicts Tipton accordingly and variously as a "magician" (147) weaving a "tangled web of deceit" (176), as lacking "self-esteem" (222), as someone who preyed upon innocent and naive women. Describing one wife, Betty, who was young when she married Tipton, Middlebrook writes, "Billy made a shrewd choice in choosing Betty as a partner, and it is the shrewdness that diminishes Billy's moral stature" (177). Suddenly, the objective and scholarly biographer has turned into judge and juror; the life hanging in the balance is measured by impossibly high standards.

While obviously transgender and transsexual critics may also be guilty of manipulating the subject matter of transgender lives, more often than not the transgender or transsexual researcher will reveal his or her own investment in the subject matter at hand.[6] Other analysts and biographers and historians, like Middlebrook, remain hidden from view, content to allow the spotlight to shine on the strangeness and duplicity of the transgender subject. For this reason, Middlebrook's academic biography of Billy Tipton is subtitled "The Double Life of Billy Tipton," and Kate Summerscale's biography of butch lesbian Joe Carstairs names her life story "eccentric" in its subtitle. Eccentric, double, duplicitous, deceptive, odd, self-hating: all of these judgments swirl around the passing woman, the cross-dresser, the non-operative transsexual, the self-defined transgender person, as if other lives—gender normative lives—were not odd, not duplicitous, not doubled and contradictory at every turn. When Middlebrook tries to reveal herself to the reader's gaze, she oddly places herself in the position of a duped wife and writes:

What if I had met Billy at age eighteen, Betty's age when they became lovers? In 1957 I was as ignorant about the specifics of sexual intercourse as most of my girl-friends, and I did not know much about male anatomy. Would I have discovered Billy's secret? (175)

This isolated moment of self-revelation in a text completely trained upon the eccentricity of Tipton tells us much about the biographer. It tells us that she identifies with and is in sympathy with Billy's wives, rather than Billy; it tells us that her particular perspective may allow her unique insight into the lives of those women who chose to ignore and accept Billy's anatomy while loving and honoring his chosen gender. This biography, indeed, was commissioned by his last wife, and it is written for her (or at least on her behalf), to her, and in concert with her desires. What would the biography look like if the biographer identified with Billy? Should such an identification be a precondition for writing such a biography? Why is the life of Tipton the life on show when the lives of his wives share in the "eccentricity" that so fascinates Middlebrook? Those wives also lived double lives, also made choices, shrewd choices; how is it that the scandal of the transgender body drains attention away from the extraordinary qualities of other conflicted lives?

Returning again to Jackie Kay's novel, we find a character closely mirroring Middlebrook. In *Trumpet*, a biographer is hot on the trail of Joss's secrets and she tries to bribe both his son and his wife to give her information about Joss. In the last half of the novel, Kay details the struggle between journalist Sophie Stones and Joss's son Colman over the documenting of Joss's life; it is in this section of the novel that Kay forcefully brings to a crisis questions about naming, identity, and narrative. In the characterization of Sophie Stones, moreover, it is impossible not to read parallels between her and Middlebrook. While Middlebrook's biography of Tipton, *Suits Me: The Double Life of Billy Tipton,* was, we may recall, commissioned by his last wife, Kitty—almost to exonerate her from the supposed crime of impersonation so successfully enacted by her late husband—in *Trumpet*, Joss's wife steadfastly refuses to have anything to do with a biography of Joss, and Millicent comments in outrage: "the idea that I could cooperate with a book about my life, that I could graft myself into this life that they think I had. . . . My life is up for grabs. No doubt they will call me a lesbian. They will find words to fit onto me. Words that don't fit me. Words that don't fit Joss" (153–4). Kay depicts the biographer as a stranger who seeks intimacy with the dead for the purposes of telling a good story: "The public might hate perverts," she tells herself, "but they love reading about them" (264). In order to tell the story of the cross-dresser or the transgender subject, the biographer must convince herself that her own life is normal, beyond reproach, honest. But Kay shows that biography as a project is inevitably bound to deception and manipulation in its own way—how else does the biographer get loved ones to inform upon their former father/husband/son? How else to create a position from which to judge? At one point, however, Sophie Stones questions her own motivations, and asks herself: "I wonder what I would have felt if I had been Mill Moody. Would I have fallen for Joss Moody too?" (126). This question is an uncanny echo of Middlebrook's own questions about her motivation for rewriting Tipton's carefully constructed life. In both cases, the biographer is presented as a person who has no identification with the subject of the biographical project; in both cases, the biographer can only wonder about the desire directed at the transgender subject.

In a flurry of investigative zeal, Kay's novel shows us that a life carefully written by its author—and owned and shielded by loved ones—may suddenly stand exposed as a lie. The beauty of Kay's narrative is that she does not try to undo the life narrative of a passing man; rather, she sets out to honor it by weaving together a patchwork of memories from Joss's survivors (mainly his wife's), and making that patchwork into the authentic narrative. When Millicent asserts, "I am the only one who can remember him the way he wanted to be remembered," she rejects the attempts made by the press to revise, reform, and rescript her husband. Although the blurb on the back cover of *Trumpet* refers to the love between Millicent and Joss as something built "out of a complex, dazzling lie," the novel itself quietly side-steps the equation between passing and lying and instead investigates the particularity of desire: "I didn't feel like I was living a lie," Millicent thinks. "I felt like I was living a life" (95).

While Tipton was born a white midwesterner, Kay's character, Moody, is black British: "His father was African, his mother Scottish" (17). Joss and Millicent adopt a black son together, Colman, who later in life wonders how his parents pulled off their masquerade. In the wake of the revelation of his father's sex, he struggles with the complex legacy of ambiguity that Joss leaves him: "I didn't feel Scottish. Didn't feel British either. Didn't feel anything. My heart is a fucking stone" (51). He remembers how Joss could not tell him stories about his grandparents, but instead told him to "make up" his own bloodline, to imaginatively create his own family tree. He remembers the accidental resemblance between his father and himself: "I am the same kind of colour as my father. We even look alike. Pure fluke" (50). And Colman takes pride in the ways in which he and his father are related despite the lack of a biological link. Finally, Colman struggles to make sense of his masculinity, modeled so clearly upon his father's and destabilized now by the revelation of female body parts. Is his own masculinity a lie, he wonders. Does his own identity dissolve in the wake of his father's death?

The voices that tell the life and death of Joss Moody in *Trumpet* are various, just like the lives he lived, like the lives we all live. His wife's memories approximate most closely the life he made and narrated for himself. His son's struggle with his father's legacy creates a complex and contradictory story of fatherhood and forgiveness. But there are other voices as well: a doctor, a registrar, a funeral director. The doctor and registrar both play their part in the construction and destruction of identities: the doctor crosses out "male" on the death certificate and quietly inserts "female"; the registrar agrees to record Joss as "Joss Moody" on the death papers and not "Josephine." Both continue to write the narrative of Joss as Joss himself might have wanted it written. So, too, does the funeral director preserve Joss's right to script his own life by dressing the body in suit and tie. The director observes: "There are as many different deaths as there are different people" (103), and he carefully guards the genre of death that Joss has chosen. But the biographer is a different story—indeed, has a different story—and it is the battle between competing narratives about Joss that speaks to the ethics of biography.

By taking aim at the project of narrating a life built around passing, Kay's novel also produces important questions about the project of transgender history and biography. The danger of biography, Kay's novel suggests, lies in the way "[m]any ghost writers believe they are the real authority on their subject and not the ghost themselves" (262). Kay warns us here to listen to the ghost. In her beautiful sociological study of haunting, Avery Gordon also advises us to listen to the ghost, to hear the unspoken and to see the invisible; she remarks: "The ghost is not simply a dead or a missing person, but a social figure, and investigating it can lead to that dense site where history and subjectivity make social life" (8). Obviously, the ghost for Gordon is not quite the same as the ghost for Kay, yet both texts share a sense of the mechanism of haunting as an articulate discourse. They both also suggest that haunting is a mode within which the ghost demands something like accountability: to tell a ghost story means that one is willing to be haunted. "Following the ghosts," Gordon says, "is about making a contact that changes you and refashions the social relations in which you are located" (22). The error of the willful biographer lies in her refusal to be changed by her encounter with the ghost she chases; the method of the transgender historian must be one that welcomes encounters, confrontations, and transformations.

Kay's novel raises thorny questions about biography, about precisely the kind of biography that Middlebrook has written: should identification be a prerequisite for writing up someone's life? Is a biography that tells tales and reveals secrets an act of violence? Should there be an ethics of biography? Kay herself points to the danger of biography and warns us to listen to the ghost. And unlike the ghost writer who cares nothing about the ghost, Kay grants her ghost the last word. In the novel's final section, Joss returns from the dead in a letter he leaves for his son to finally tell his own story. This simple but effective gesture of giving Joss the last word summarizes Kay's particular interest in the Tipton legend and its retelling. She comes to praise, to memorialize, to elegize Tipton/Moody and countless transgender men, and not to bury them.

Falls City, Nebraska: A Good Place to Die?

In little towns, lives roll along so close to one another; loves and hates beat about, their wings almost touching. —Willa Cather, Lucy Gayheart

While Tipton died a so-called natural death in 1992 only to have his life rearranged by the discovery of his "secret," Brandon Teena, one year later, was exposed and then killed precisely because of his secret. The tragic facts of the case are as follows: on December 31, 1993 three young people were shot to death, execution style, in a town named Falls City in rural Nebraska. Ordinarily, this story would have evoked only mild interest from mainstream America and a few questions about the specific brutalities of rural America; however, one of the three victims was a young white person who had been born a woman but who was living as a man and had been dating local girls. The other two victims, Brandon's friend, Lisa Lambert, and her friend Philip DeVine—a disabled African American man—appeared to have been killed because they were in the "wrong place at the wrong time" (although this too is debatable.) I will allude here to a few of the multiple narratives that collect around the name Brandon Teena and lay out some of the battles about gender identity, regionality, class, sexuality, and violence that have been produced by this incident. A close investigation of the life and death of Brandon reveals that more than transgender politics are at stake in the narratives that emerge from this case; also at issue are questions about urban versus rural queer identities, as well as a more general discussion of white masculinities and the geographies of gender. As a supporting text for the discussion of this case, I will use Susan Muska and Greta Olafsdottir's independent film *The Brandon Teena Story*. However, it is worth noting that this film is just one of a slew of media representations of the case in recent years: the story has been fictionalized in a novel by Denitia Smith called *The Illusionist*, and it has been written up as a true crime mystery called *All S/He Wanted* by Aphrodite Jones. Diane Keaton had been trying unsuccessfully to produce a feature film about the case, starring Drew Barrymore, but fortunately she was beaten to the punch by independent filmmaker Kim Peirce, whose feature *Boys Don't Cry* was released in 1999 to much acclaim (and won the Academy Award for Best Actress). At the same time, queer media artist Shu Lea Cheang has created a web site for the Guggenheim simply called "Brandon," which she describes as a "multi-artist, multi-author, multi-institutional collaboration."

In *The Brandon Teena Story*, Susan Muska and Greta Olafsdottir attempt to place the narrative of Brandon's life and death firmly in the countryside of Nebraska, so much so that Nebraska itself takes on the role and presence of a character. We see prolonged shots of the rolling Nebraska countryside, road signs welcoming the traveler to Nebraska's "good life," and scenes of everyday life and culture in small town America. The filmmakers make it clear that their relationship to Falls City and its communities is ironic and distanced; the camera peers voyeuristically at the demolition derby, the local line-dancing and karaoke bar, and at the lives of the people touched by the Brandon story. In a significant scene providing "local color," the camera pans the backs of local men watching a demolition derby; as the camera's gaze sweeps over them, the men are rendered in slow motion as they turn and gaze back with hostile stares of non-recognition. Interactions between the camera and its subjects register the filmmakers as strangers to the material realities of the rural Midwest, and mark the objects of the gaze as literally haunted by an invisible camera. These interactions place the viewer at a considerable distance from the actors on the screen. This distance allows for the emergence of multiple versions of the Brandon Teena Story, but also pins the narrative of homophobic and transphobic violence firmly to the landscape of white trash America and forces modes of strenuous disidentification between viewer and landscape.

The landscape of Nebraska thus serves as a contested site upon which multiple narratives unfold, narratives which refuse to collapse into simply one story, "The Brandon Teena Story." Some of these narratives are narratives of hate, some of desire; others tell of ignorance and brutality; still others of isolation and fear; some allow violence and ignorant prejudices to become the essence of white poor rural identity; still others provoke questions about the deployment of whiteness and the regulation of violence. While the film itself encourages the viewer to distance herself from the horror of the heartlands and even to congratulate herself for living in an urban rather than a rural environment, ultimately we can use Brandon's story to begin articulating the stories of working-class white rural queers, and to map the immensely complex relations that make rural America a site of horror and degradation in the urban imagination.

For queers who flee the confines of the rural Midwest and take comfort in urban anonymity, this film may serve as a justification of their worst fears about the violent effects of failing to flee; closer readings of Brandon's story, however, reveal the desire shared by many Midwestern queers for a way of staying rather than leaving. While some journalists in the wake of Brandon's murder queried his decision to stay in Falls City, despite having been hounded by the police and raped by the men who went on to murder him, we must consider the condition of "staying put" as part of the production of complex queer subjectivities. Some queers need to leave home in order to become queer; others need to stay close to home in order to preserve their difference. The danger of small towns, as Willa Cather described it (also in reference to rural Nebraska), emerges out of a suffocating sense of proximity: "lives roll along so close to one another" she writes, "loves and hates beat about, their wings almost touching." This beautiful but scary image of rural life as a claustrophobic space all too easily violated depends absolutely upon its opposite image, the image of rural life as wide-open and free-ranging, as "big sky" and open plains. Cather captures perfectly the contradiction of rural life as the contrast between wide-open spaces and sparse populations on the one hand and small town claustrophobia and lack of privacy on the other.

The life and death of Brandon Teena provoke endless speculation about the specificities of the loves and hates that characterized his experiences in Falls City, and any straightforward rendering of his story remains impossible. Some viewers of *The Brandon Teena Story* have accused the filmmakers of an obvious class bias in their depictions of the people of Falls City; others have seen the film as an accurate depiction of the cultures of hate and meanness produced in small, mostly white towns. Any attempt to come to terms with the resonances of Brandon's murder will ultimately have to grapple with both of these proposals. One way in which *The Brandon Teena Story* deploys and perpetuates a class bias in relation to the depiction of anti-queer violence is by depicting many of its interview subjects in uncritical ways as "white trash." In their introduction to an anthology titled *White Trash: Race and Class in America*, Matt Wray and Annalee Newitz define the term "white trash" as both a reference to "actually existing white people living in (often rural) poverty" and also as a term designating "a set of stereotypes and myths related to the social behaviors, intelligence, prejudices, and gender roles of poor whites" (7). The editors offer a "local politics of place" to situate and combat and explain such stereotypes.

One way in which the *The Brandon Teena Story* is able to grapple with the lives beneath the stereotypes (of white trash, of gender impersonation) is by allowing some of the women whom Brandon dated to explain themselves and articulate their own extraordinary desires. In the media rush to uncover the motivations behind Brandon's depiction of himself as a man, most accounts of the case have overlooked the fact that Brandon was actively chosen over more conventionally male men by the women he dated, despite the fact that there were few social rewards for doing so. One girlfriend after another in the tape characterize Brandon as a fantasy guy, a dream guy, a man who "knew how a woman wanted to be treated." Gina describes him as romantic and special and attentive, while Lana Tisdale calls him "every woman's dream." Brandon, we might conclude, lived up to and even played into the romantic ideals that his girlfriends cultivated about masculinity. Brandon's self-presentation must be read, I believe, as a damaging critique of the white working-class masculinities around him; at the same time, however, his performance of courtly masculinity is a shrewd deployment of the middle-class and so-called "respectable" masculinities that represent an American romantic ideal of manhood. In the accounts that the women give of their relations with Brandon we understand that he not only treated them in ways they could not expect from local boys, but also acknowledged the complexity of their self-understandings and desires.

In order to understand the kinds of masculinities with which Brandon may have been competing, we can turn to the representations of the murderers themselves. While some accounts of the Brandon Teena case have attempted to empathize with the men who murdered Brandon (John Lotter and Tom Nissen) by revealing their traumatic family histories and detailing their encounters with abuse, the film tries to encourage the men to give their own reasons for their brutality. The conversations with Nissen and Lotter are fascinating in the way they allow the men to coolly describe scenes of rape and murder, and also because Lotter, in particular, articulates an astute awareness of the violence of the culture into which he was raised. Nissen, however, shows little power of self-reflection; the film represents him as ultimately far more reprehensible than his partner in crime. For one second, the camera focuses upon a small tattoo on Nissen's arm but does not allow the viewer to identify it. In Aphrodite Jones's book on the Brandon Teena case, she provides information that situates this tattoo as a symbol of white supremacy. Tom Nissen, we learn, was involved off and on throughout his early life with a group called "White American Group for White America."[7] While Nissen's flirtation with a brutally racist white supremacist group need not surprise us, it does nonetheless flesh out the particular nexus of hate that came to focus upon Brandon, Lisa Lambert, and Philip DeVine. Nowhere in the documentary nor in media coverage of the case, however, does anyone link Nissen's racial politics with either the brutalization of Brandon or the execution of the African-American, Philip DeVine. In *The Brandon Teena Story*, Philip's murder is given little screen time and none of his relatives or family appear. In an even more egregious omission, Peirce's *Boys Don't Cry* actually edits out the DeVine story altogether. At the end of the film, credits update the viewers on the lives of Lana, Lotter, and Niessen, making note of the deaths of Lisa and Brandon, while Philip is simply not mentioned. Peirce perhaps thought that her film, already running close to two hours, could not handle another subplot, but the story of Philip DeVine is important and it is a crucial part of the drama of gender, race, sexuality, and class that was enacted in the heartland. Race is not incidental to this narrative of mostly white, Midwestern small towns, and by omitting DeVine's story from *Boys Don't Cry*, Peirce contributes to the detachment of transgender narratives from narratives about race, consigning the memory of DeVine to oblivion.

Many accounts of white power movements in America connect them to small, all-white towns in the Midwest and to economically disadvantaged white populations. While one would not want to demonize rural poor white Americans as any more bigoted than urban or suburban white yuppy populations in the United States, it is nonetheless important to highlight the particular fears and paranoias that take shape in rural all-white populations. Fear of the government, fear of the United Nations, fear of Jews, Blacks, and queers mark white rural masculinities in very particular ways that can easily produce cultures of hate. In small towns where few people of color live, difference may be marked and remarked in relation to gender variance rather than racial diversity. As Newitz and Wray point out in the anatomy of white trash, some degree of specificity is necessary when we try to describe and identify different forms of homophobia and transphobia as they are distributed across different geographies.

In "Get Thee to a Big City: Sexual Imaginary and the Great Gay Migration," anthropologist Kath Weston begins a much needed inquiry into the difference between urban and rural "sexual imaginaries." She comments upon the rather stereotyped division of rural/urban relations which "locates gay subjects in the city while putting their presence in the countryside under erasure" (262). Weston also traces the inevitable disappointments that await rural queers who escape the country only to arrive in alienating queer urban spaces. Ultimately, Weston proposes: "The gay imaginary is not just a dream of a freedom to be gay that requires an urban location, but a symbolic space that configures gayness itself by elaborating an opposition between urban and rural life" (274). Weston wants us to recognize that the distinction between the urban and the rural that props up the gay imaginary is a symbolic one, and, as such, it constitutes a dream of an elsewhere which promises a freedom it can never provide. However, we also want to be specific about which queer subjects face what kinds of threats, from whom, and in what locations. While in the city, for example, we may find that the gay or transsexual person of color is most at risk for violence from racist cops; in rural locations we may find that even the white queers who were born and raised there are outlawed when they disrupt the carefully protected homogeneity of white, family-oriented communities. We may also find that while the brutalization of a transgender sex worker of color raises little outcry in the city from local queer activists, the murder of a white boy in rural North America can stir up an enormous activist response which is itself symbolic of these other imaginary divisions.

I believe that an extensive analysis of the Brandon Teena murders can serve to frame the many questions about identification, responsibility, class, regionality, and race that trouble queer communities today. Not only does Brandon represent a martyr lost in the struggle for transgender rights to the brutal perpetrators of rural hetero-masculine violences, he also serves as a marker for a particular set of late twentieth-century cultural anxieties about place, whiteness, and rural existence. Fittingly, Brandon has become the name for both gender variance and the fear of transphobic and homophobic punishment; he also embodies the desire directed at non-normative masculinities. Brandon represents other rural lives undone by fear and loathing, and his story also symbolizes an urban fantasy of homophobic violence as essentially Midwestern. But violence, wherever we may find it, marks different conflictual relations in different sites; and homicide, on some level, always depicts the micro-realities of other battles displaced from the abstract to the tragically material. While at least one use of any Brandon Teena project must be to connect Brandon's gender presentation to other counter-narratives of gender realness, I also hope that Brandon's story can be a vehicle for discussions about class, violence, geography, and queer migration. On some level Brandon's story, while cleaving to its own specificity, needs to remain an open narrative—not a stable narrative of FTM transsexual identity nor a singular tale of queer bashing; not a cautionary fable about the violence of rural America nor an advertisement for urban organizations of queer community. Like the narrative of Billy Tipton, Brandon's story permits a dream of transformation.

The stories of Brandon Teena and Billy Tipton, their own stories, the stories that are told about them, and the stories that the people around them help to produce, bring to a close several outmoded narratives about gender and embodiment in the United States at the end of the twentieth century. Neither Brandon nor Billy fit comfortably into the sexological categories of inversion from the early twentieth century; nor do they represent new transsexual discourses involving bodily transformations. Brandon and Billy have little to do with modern gay and lesbian identities nor are they indicative of future renderings of gender, class, and embodiment. Perhaps they are the unresolved tales of gender variance that will follow us

35

from the twentieth century to the twenty-first century: not resolved, not neat, not understood. Perhaps the only way to honor the memories of Tipton and Teena is to remember them as they wished to be remembered: not as heroes or demons but as examples of what Avery Gordon calls "complex personhood." At the very least, Gordon tells us, "complex personhood is about conferring the respect on others that comes from presuming that life and people's lives are simultaneously straightforward and full of enormously subtle meaning" (5). When we read transgender lives, complex and contradictory as they may seem, it is necessary to read for the life and not for the lie. Dishonesty, after all, is just another word for narrative.

Notes

The author thanks Thomas Spear and Linda Schlossberg for editorial help.

1. For more on the relationship between realness and minority subjects, see Chandan Reddy, "Paris Is Burning" in *Burning Down the House: Domesticity and Postcoloniality*, ed. Rosemary Marangoly George (Boulder: Westview Press, 1998), 359–379.
2. Judith Butler, "Imitation and Gender Insubordination" in *inside/out: Lesbian Theories, Gay Theories*, ed. Diana Fuss (New York: Routledge, 1991), 14. Butler writes, "I'm permanently troubled by identity categories, consider them to be invariable stumbling blocks, and understand them, even promote them, as sites of necessary trouble."
3. On the term "reverse discourse," see Michel Foucault, *The History of Sexuality, Volume 1: An Introduction*, trans. Robert Hurley (New York: Vintage Books, 1980).
4. Gayle Rubin with Judith Butler, "Interview: Sexual Traffic," in *differences*, Special Issue, "More Gender Trouble: Feminism Meets Queer Theory," 6:2–3 (1994): 62–100. Rubin writes, "When I started this project I was interested in the whole question of sexual ethnogenesis. I wanted to understand better how sexual communities form. . . ." (94).
5. See, for example, Kate Bornstein, *My Gender Workbook: How to Become a Real Man, a Real Woman, the Real You, or Something Else Entirely* (New York: Routledge, 1998).
6. See, for example, Susan Stryker, "My Words to Victor Frankenstein Above the Village of Chamounix: Performing Transgender Rage" in *GLQ* 1.3 (1994): 237–254. See

also Jacob Hale, "Consuming the Living, Dis(Re)Membering the Dead in the Butch/ FTM Borderlands" in *GLQ* 4.2 (1998): 311–348.

7. See Aphrodite Jones, *All S/He Wanted* (New York: Pocket Books, 1996), 154.

Works Cited

Gordon, Avery. *Ghostly Matters: Haunting and the Sociological Imagination.* Minneapolis: University of Minnesota Press, 1997.

Hausman, Bernice. *Changing Sex: Transsexualism, Technology, and the Idea of Gender.* Durham: Duke University Press, 1995.

Kay, Jackie. *Trumpet.* New York: Pantheon, 1998.

Martin, Biddy. "Sexualities Without Genders and Other Queer Utopias." *diacritics* 24.2–3 (1994): 104–121.

Middlebrook, Diane Wood. *Suits Me: The Double Life of Billy Tipton.* Boston: Houghton Mifflin, 1998.

Muska, Susan, and Greta Olafsdottir, *The Brandon Teena Story* (1998. USA), distributed by Zeitgeist Films.

Prosser, Jay. *Second Skins: The Body Narratives of Transsexuality.* New York: Columbia University Press, 1998.

Rubin, Henry. "Do You Believe in Gender?" *Sojourner* 21.6 (1996): 7–8.

Summerscale, Kate. *The Queen of Whale Cay: The Eccentric Story of "Joe" Carstairs, Fastest Woman on Water.* New York: Viking, 1997.

Weston, Kath. "Get Thee To A Big City: Sexual Imaginary and the Great Gay Migration" in *GLQ* 2.3 (1995): 253–278.

Wray, Matt and Annalee Newitz, eds. *White Trash: Race and Class in America.* New York: Routledge, 1996.

Jewish Chameleonism and the Politics of Race

Daniel Itzkovitz

In his memoirs, Waldo Frank describes the complex feelings about race he experienced while traveling through the South with Jean Toomer in 1922: "I felt with the Negro. This empathy was startling. Lying in dark sleep I would dream I was a Negro, would spring from sleep reaching for my clothes on the chair beside the bed, to finger them, to smell them . . . in proof I was white and myself."[1] At the time of Frank's racial panic, he and Toomer were on their now famous southern tour, collecting information for *Holiday*, a novel Frank was planning about interracial desire and lynching. On the trip they played the role of light-skinned Black "professors from the North," with Frank (a "swarthy Jew") and Toomer (who was of mixed racial heritage) each going "as a Negro."[2] In most writing about their relationship Frank is commonly represented as a foil to Toomer's progressive anti-essentialism, bent on fixing and fetishizing the latter's African American ancestry.[3] But Frank's

Reprinted from Daniel Itzkovitz, "Passing Like Me," *South Altantic Quarterly* 98: 1–2 (winter/spring 1999). Copyright © 1999 by Duke University Press. All rights reserved. Printed with Permission.

dreams of himself as "a Negro," his dead-of-night panic and ultimate salvation in the feel and smell of his clothes (which "proved" that "I was white and myself"), tell us more about his anxieties over the stability of his own whiteness. If, for Frank, whiteness and identity are equated here—to be white means to be "myself"—his was clearly an identity under siege.

The ambiguous relationship between race and identity in Toomer has been widely discussed: his refusal to identify himself as African American became a scandalous footnote in early narratives on the Harlem Renaissance, while his extraordinary exploration of racial dislocation in *Cane* and other writings has recently returned to the spotlight, now recognized by many critics as a forerunner to the contemporary critique of racial essentialism.[4] "I am of no particular race," Toomer proclaimed in the early 1930s; "I am of the human race, a man at large in the human world, preparing a new race."[5] While Toomer's writing documents with astonishing insight the problematic of racial dislocation and the tensions among American identities in the aftermath of slavery and amidst the great northern migration, however, Frank's racial performance and panic begin to reveal the intimate connection of these issues to the unsettled place of *Jewishness* in early twentieth-century American culture.

Frank's anxious and visceral response to his own performance of blackness is a stark contrast to the Jewish blackface performance discussed by Michael Rogin in *Blackface, White Noise*. Rogin argues convincingly that early twentieth-century Jewish vaudevillians and movie stars used blackface performance to help catalyze the Jewish transition to whiteness. During a period when a radically shifting population infused racial volatility in American culture with new energy, Rogin claims, blackface "passed immigrants into Americans by differentiating them from the Black Americans through whom they spoke."[6] Performing in blackface helped Jews reinscribe the racial binary and—by virtue of their demonstrated ability to wipe off, with the cork, all racial markers—place themselves firmly in the camp of white folk. However, as his memoirs testify, Frank's performance served, albeit briefly, to undermine this distinction. He and the Jewish vaudevillians engaged in substantially different kinds of blackface performance, of course, but Frank's feelings of racial vulnerability during his southern trip nevertheless reveal something of the troubled and influential place of Jewishness in early twentieth-century American racial politics that is overlooked in Rogin's discussion.

The Jewish movement into "whiteness" must be understood in terms of an alternative formulation as well, one in which Jewishness was popularly conceptualized as existing problematically "outside" of whiteness. This act of "pass[ing] into Americans" was itself profoundly and crucially vexing for the self-conception of normative white American culture for an extended and formative period, from the first years of the massive influx of East European Jews into the United States in the late nineteenth century to the reconceptualization of the Jews as quintessential humans and representative Americans in the aftermath of World War II.[7] In this transitional state, popular notions of Jewish identity formed an elusive but meaningful triangle with white and black identity that has been largely overlooked by contemporary American cultural theorists, even those most subtly attuned to the meanings of U.S. racial and cultural politics. This critical silence has been partly due to the same factor that made Jewishness so perplexing to early twentieth-century writers: the lack of any vocabulary with which to engage the cultural meanings of Jewish American difference.

As my mapping here of the complex Black/White/Jewish triangulation should indicate, "the Jew" (however elusive his "nature") was a central figure in the early twentieth-century development of an American rhetoric of racial and national identity. While Rogin's project explores how Jews attempted to use the image of the African American in making themselves "white," my own interest here is in how popular conceptions and confusions surrounding Jewishness were used—in conjunction with notions of blackness—by modern American writers to navigate the uneasy limits of whiteness. In this version of the narrative, becoming white constituted an endlessly unfinished business and a process that was astonishingly generative. The construction of Jewish identity as performative and inauthentic by both black and white writers early in this century stands in contrast to popular conceptions of blackness and expresses pervasive American concerns about modernity. Anxieties about Jewish performativity and the struggle around Jewish difference had important implications for the evolution of a modernist cultural logic that was at once race-conscious and unable to locate the exact nature of racial difference.

Contemporary critics are not the first to struggle with "placing" the Jew in American culture. During the late nineteenth and early twentieth centuries, many commentators struggled with the baffling question of how to understand and categorize the Jews: in an astonishingly wide range of journalistic, literary, and social-scientific texts, the image of "the Jew" developed out of a set of paradoxes—Jews were both white and racially other, American and foreign, deviant and normative, vulgar and highly cultivated, and seemed to have an uncomfortably unstable relation to gendered difference—all of which made them seem at once inside and inescapably outside of normative white American culture. In this contradictory state, Jewishness would play a central role in the ongoing construction of American cultural politics, particularly in terms of its emergence from a culture characterized by two, fundamentally contradictory ideological stances: the "culture of personality," on the one hand, and post-*Plessy v. Ferguson* racial politics, on the other. While the former might be characterized by the profound white American investment in liberal possibility and individual self-creation in the marketplace without reference to history or heredity, the latter, by contrast, relied on a belief in embodied hereditary and cultural determinations of identity, creating a legal system of social and economic discrimination based on a logic of racial difference and resigned to the assumption that "legislation is powerless to eradicate racial instincts or to abolish distinctions based upon physical differences."[8]

Underlying this contradictory construction of Jewishness was an issue related less to Jewish stage practices than to a prevailing cultural anxiety over Jewish performativity—not Jews in vaudeville or Hollywood, but rather the

41

very notion of shape-shifting and the performance of an identity other than "one's own." Jews, it was commonly claimed, were a "chameleonic race" whose veins coursed with what one magazine termed "strange chameleonic Jewish blood."[9] The troubling notion of "chameleonic blood," with its paradoxical insinuation of *both* the fluid instability of Jewish identity *and* the embodied stability of Jewish racial distinctiveness, perfectly captures the difficult position of Jewishness in early twentieth-century American culture. The problem for many observers was not simply that Jews continually modified their mannerisms to suit their surroundings and thereby made themselves virtually indistinguishable from white Americans, but that even in so doing they maintained their mysterious difference, or what was called their "queer light" in one article (pointedly entitled "Why Are Jews Like That?"). "We have always been changing, modifying our mannerisms to suit each new environment," according to article author Lewis Browne. Yet he agrees with a Gentile friend's observation that all Jews seemed to have the same elusive and "peculiar" thing in common: "a queer light in their eyes."[10] While Browne thought of the Jews' constant "changing" as a benign diasporic response, his article's exploration of the nature of this Jewish "queer light" raises many more questions than it answers. Browne's Jews inhabit an incoherence that is wonderfully captured in the baffling combination of Jewish embodied difference ("You are all somehow different from the rest of us") and the continual shape-shifting ("We have always been changing") that made Jewish difference endlessly vexing—and made Jews, to many, intolerably suspect.

The use of "blood" (in the phrase "chameleonic blood") betrays a desire common to many writers of the period to fix the Jew by using a discourse of difference that would posit Jewish identity as somehow essential and immutable. However, despite numerous attempts to use the rhetoric of racial and cultural essentialism to mark an ontological distinction between Jews and other identity groups, the most common "fixation" of Jewishness was accomplished, paradoxically, through the notion of chameleonism—the idea that Jewish identity could be characterized only in terms of an always unstable shape-shifting. The Jew was most Jewish, that is, when not Jewish at all. In both canonical and non-canonical texts from the early twentieth century, "Jewish difference" is caught in the double bind of the "chameleonic race"—an "identity" marked at once by indistinguishable sameness and irreducible difference. In fact, Frank's story of his own passing for black is fascinating because it seems to replicate in negative terms a stock character of a white American modernism profoundly shaped by its nativist tendencies, namely, that of the "chameleonic" Jewish man who enters a community where he doesn't (naturally) belong.[11] A character familiar to readers of Anderson, Cather, Dreiser, Fitzgerald, Hemingway, and Wharton (among other writers of the period), the Jew edgily embodies the American success story, characterized as a prototypical Horatio Alger hero who makes his way up in the world yet cannot finally experience his success as such, remaining an outsider despite, or perhaps because of, his remarkable ability to penetrate American culture. Like Hemingway's Robert Cohn, Cather's Louie Marsellus, and Wharton's Simon Rosedale, Frank performed in a culture that was not his own, and like the literary characters, his transformation remains incomplete.

Jewish "chameleonism" (the cultural phenomenon that Adorno and Horkheimer considered an "undisciplined mimicry . . . passed down by a process of unconscious imitation in infancy from generation to generation, from the down-at-heel Jew to the rich banker"),[12] while a common theme in modern discussions of anti-Semitism and Jewish identity, is usually treated as an ahistorical, transcultural diasporic issue to be invoked without reference to national or cultural specificities. In discussing Woody Allen's *Zelig* (a film about an archetypal Jewish American chameleon) for example, Ella Shohat and Robert Stam accordingly defer to an overarching Jewish history unmarked by national differences, which they term "the enforced plurality of the Jewish experience, the long historical apprenticeship in cultural mimicry and the syncretic incorporation of ambient cultures."[13] But in a U.S. culture with a renewed investment in both the rigid fixing of racial identities and the liberal faith in individual self-creation and mobility in the marketplace, this notion of racial chameleonism and its double bind would acquire a significance of far greater historical specificity than these references suggest. During a period in which broad demographic and economic changes opened new possibilities for travel across class, cultural, and national boundaries, the specter of Jewish chameleonism and the struggle to locate and contain an elusive "Jewish difference" emerged out of the clash between this possibility of social mobility and the rhetoric of race; a white American identity dependent on both was thrown into a crisis of definition. As the aforementioned modernist texts suggest, there was a great deal at stake in fixing the elusive difference of the Jews, in part because Jewish performativity seemed to signal the dangers of consumer capital without the comfort and clarity of absolute difference that *Plessy*'s racial distinction appeared to offer. If the Jew could become white, anyone, then, could become "a Jew."[14]

All of us have at some time toyed with the Arabian Nights-like thought of the magical change of race. . . . If the jinny should say, "I have come to carry out an inexorable command to change you into a member of another race; make your choice," I should answer, probably, "Make me a Jew."
—James Weldon Johnson, Along This Way: The Autobiography of
James Weldon Johnson *(1933)*

James Weldon Johnson's strange and richly evocative musings appeared at a historical moment that was marked by the explosive collision between the ideologies of social mobility and racial stasis. His ultimate response to the demanding "jinny"—"Make me a Jew"—should therefore be understood in terms of the complicated U.S. cultural, racial, and economic politics in the early twentieth century. If Johnson's oriental fantasy bespeaks a sense that, for black Americans, racial change could happen only through the intervention of a magical "jinny," it also draws a striking association between magical race-shifting and Jews. At a moment when racial identity was imagined by many to be an immutable fact, Johnson's addition of magic and Jews to the mix provided an innovative solution to the problem of the color line.The association of Jews with race-shifting was already a familiar one, however, as indicated by the number of Jewish characters surfacing in modern novels that were ostensibly about African Americans passing for white. In addition to Johnson's own 1912 *Autobiography of an Ex-Colored Man,* novels such as Charles W. Chesnutt's *House Behind the Cedars* (1900), Jessie Faucet's *Plum Bun* (1928), Fannie Hurst's *Imitation of Life* (1933), and Walter White's *Flight* (1926) all feature Jews whose movements into mainstream U.S. culture resonate with the struggles of their passing African American characters.[15] The Jew in Johnson's novel, for instance, appears during a discussion of race among a cross-section of men on a train. Significantly, he does not identify himself as a Jew, although the "ex-Colored man" and some of the other passengers understand him to be Jewish. It is the Jew's social fluidity that immediately strikes the notoriously fluid narrator, who also does not identify his own racial affiliation. "In his discussion of the race question," the ex-Colored man notes, "the diplomacy of the Jew was something to be admired; he had the faculty of agreeing with everybody without losing his allegiance to any side. . . . Long traditions and business instincts told him when in Rome to act as a Roman."[16] Of course, "act[ing] as a Roman" is the cliché with which the ex-Colored man is likely to be labeled when he decides to blend into white New York and "neither disclaim the black race nor claim the white race." After changing his name, he would "make a white man's success" by working in the "South American department" of a New York City firm."[17] If the Jew and the ex-Colored man bear an unmistakable resemblance to one another, however, there is also an important difference between them: while the ex-Colored man's decision to pass as white is characterized as a betrayal of his true race, the Jew's skill at blending into his surroundings is attributed to both "tradition" and "instinct." His chameleonism is thus culturally and naturally determined; the "natural place" of the Jew is in passing.

Johnson's novel is hardly unique in this respect, given the prevailing image of the Jewish "performer of other identities" in early twentieth-century American culture. The commonsense notion that Jews were "highly imitative and adaptable," as one *Atlantic Monthly* author put it,[18] permeated American culture in films, high-modernist texts, popular fiction, and the press. It was such a prevalent idea that Johnson's fantasy of being turned into a Jew by a "jinny" has something of an oxymoronic quality. The wish to become a Jew might be read here as a desire to become that which could become anything—not unlike wishing for an unlimited number of wishes. A similar desire surfaces in Nella Larsen's *Passing* (1929), in a scene that overtly draws the already implicit connection between Jewish fluidity and the Jews' problematic relationship to American categories of identity. During a discussion among three light-skinned African American women, each of whom passes at some point in the novel, the conversation turns to an old friend of the threesome, Claude Jones, who "was no longer a Negro or a Christian but had become a Jew."[19] The rhetorical challenge posed by the idea of becoming a Jew emerges in the shifting categories here (in converting to Judaism, one renounces not only one's former religion, but also one's former race) and in the inexplicable revision of their assertion. Upon being questioned about the matter, one of the characters responds, "Yes, a Jew. A black Jew, he calls himself."[20]

In most white American writing on the subject, Jewish fluidity emerges less as an enviable trait than as one to be feared. Influential nativist Madison Grant distilled the popular anxiety over Jewish adaptability in his widely read tract *The Passing of the Great Race*: "These immigrants adopt the language of the native American; they wear his clothes; they steal his name, and they are beginning to take his women, but they seldom adopt his religion or understand his ideals."[21] Grant's sentiments were, of course, common, although what lurked behind such dismissals more often than not was a sense, similar to that of many black observers, that the true catalyst for this agitated commentary was the Jew's success in crossing the borders of culture (and, by extension, racial and national identity). As Lewis S. Gannett noted in a 1923 issue of *The Nation*, "The very rapidity with which the Jew adjusts himself to . . . life in America is his chief handicap."[22] This dynamic is quite clear in Melville Dewey's wonderfully perverse explanation as to "why the Adirondack Club had found it necessary to exclude Jews specifically and by name. . . . Many Jewish applicants for membership were so thoroughly refined in language and manners and such splendid types of true Americanism that no test based on personal characteristics would have sufficed to keep them out, and it was, therefore, necessary to make a rule excluding Jews as such."[23]

Distinctions between Jews and the white Americans who were opposed to them were clearly elusive, and it was not simply Jewish performativity but the slipperiness of Jewish difference—the fear that behind the performance there was no "authentic" kernel of difference—which made the situation so vexing. This dynamic is borne out by a 1907 *McClure's* article in which the noted journalist and anti-Semite Burton J. Hendrick observes that "the rapidity with which the New York Jew adopts the manners and trappings of Americans almost disproves his ancient heritage as a peculiar people. He objects to being regarded as a thing apart, and goes to extremes to make himself like the native-born."[24] One can easily discern in Hendrick's language a sincere confusion regarding the questionable substance of Jewish difference. Utilizing a common strategy, he resorts to attacking Jews' "hypocrisy" and the "extremities" of their performativity, rather than confronting his own confusion (buoyed by that shaky "almost disproves") over Jewish "peculiarity." Lacking both the apparent stability of embodiment and the clarity of any specific national or cultural distinction, Jewish American identity also lacked a stable signifier of its difference. If the Jew's "peculiarity" no longer held, then neither did any other clear difference between Jews and such whites as Hendrick himself.

The apparent ease of this slippage from Jewish to white American may be what some writers who included Jews in their passing narratives had in mind when they ironically juxtaposed the obvious possibilities for Jewish mobility with the ultimate stasis of a racially embodied African American identity. According to this logic, the Jew could slip into white American society with little trouble, yet the light-skinned black who attempted to do so betrayed his or her "true" race, which inevitably led to tragedy or, at least, disappointment. Johnson's ex-Colored man, for instance, having become an "ordinarily successful White man," then "feels small and selfish," haunted by "a vanished dream, a dead ambition," and "a sacrificed talent"; as one who has "sold" his "birthright for a mess of pottage," he is held up to universal disdain.[25] In Hurst's *Imitation of Life*, Peola must go through an astonishing series of contortions—betraying her mother, emigrating from the United States, and finally sterilizing herself—in order to pass, only to be haunted by the truth of her mother's words: "I's in her blood—she can't help it"; while Virginia Eden, "who was born Sadie Kress in Jersey City," need only change her name for her great American success to commence.[26] Understood in these terms, the phenomenon of the Jew in the black passing narrative belongs to the tradition exemplified by such works as Du Bois's *Souls of Black Folk* and Chesnutt's *Marrow of Tradition*, which reference, often with a note of cynicism, the success of American Jews as being achieved at the expense of their African American counterparts.[27] The Jewish newcomer succeeds where African Americans, long-term residents, still face poverty, racism, and a profound lack of opportunity. This is the irony that fuels Rogin's *Blackface, White Noise*.

But despite the apparent logic of this perspective, from which the Jew would be perceived as slipping into white American culture with no more difficulty than Sadie Kress would experience in becoming Virginia Eden, early twentieth-century references to the Jewish transition to "whiteness" (and especially to Jewish performativity) were rarely unambivalent. As the magazine articles cited earlier make clear, while Jews were understood to be quintessentially decentered mimics, capable of taking on new identities under conditions of political, social, or economic expedience, the problem of Jewishness paradoxically remained that of an unclear yet threatening difference. If African Americans passing for white ultimately demonstrated that black identity was an interiorized, immutable entity, present no matter how light one's skin (i.e, "it is the possibility of passing that will locate race 'deep down inside'"),[28] the status of the Jewish interior was far less certain and solid. The rhetoric of Jewish performativity imagines an interior that is as disturbingly elusive as the exterior. The inherently unstable subject position of the performative Jew—both the same as white Americans, yet somehow different—created productive tensions in American culture (as Hendrick's confusion betrays) precisely because a sense of Jewish difference remained long after "Jewishness" had been emptied as a stable signifier of recognizable difference.[29] For many writers, Jews appeared to be different only insofar as they did not perform "themselves." Successful assimilation made the Jew more Jewish, while the elusive Jewish interior fed fantasies of dangerous secrets behind the eyes of the suspect Jew—and rendered everyone suspect. The observation by an anonymous contributor to the *Atlantic Monthly* about one "Mr. Lowell," who was deeply affected by this atmosphere, captures the situation at its extreme, for he "detected a Jew in every hiding-place and under every disguise, even when the fugitive had no suspicion of himself."[30]

Although the tensions between these two different models of identity—one constituted by its immutability, the other by its mutability—provided the foundation for the racial work of American modernism, the Jew consistently emerged in white modernist texts as the (impossible) exemplification of both models. The imagined coexistence of racial difference and chamele-onism in the Jew served an important function for modern white Americans, who mobilized the rhetoric of Jewish performativity in an attempt to fix in the Jew those "unfixable" dualities associated with modernity (such as a pervasive and seemingly inescapable artificiality and inauthenticity) from which they wished to distance themselves.[31] Jews and blacks in modernist texts do not simply inhabit identity in different ways; they also serve as very different, though sometimes overlapping, borders for a tenuous whiteness. As I will discuss in the next section, while popular notions of Jewish identity partly served to mark these elusive boundaries, the logic of Jewish difference was in many ways only a displaced version of a logic of whiteness.

The *Plessy* decision of 1896, in which the "separate but equal" legal distinction was based on a presumed racially embodied one, was handed down within months of the *M'lle NY* "chameleonic blood" assertion about Jews, a coincidence all the more striking because of *Plessy's* implication that "one drop" of African American blood had the solemn weight of absolute solidity.

"Chameleonic blood," of course, connotes the opposite—an absolute fluidity that somehow maintains its mark of difference. This opposition between the popular American notion of black and Jewish identity was a cultural commonplace, and the coupling of the two identities in modernist texts made them seem mutually determining as well. Jewish "inauthenticity" became a lens through which an authentic black identity could be seen and understood; when brought together, representations of these identities often served to erase the question of whiteness entirely.

Jewish performativity presented such problems in part because it emerged from a culture that was itself quite aware of and structured around performative identities. With the vigorous development of consumer culture in the early twentieth century, widespread attention was focused on new possibilities for recreating and marketing oneself. According to cultural historian Mike Featherstone, during this period a "new conception of self . . . emerged, the 'performing self,' [which] places greater emphasis upon appearance, display, and the management of impressions."[32] Discussing the same phenomenon, Warren Susman argues that the transition to this "new conception of self" marked a fundamental shift in the development of twentieth-century American culture. During the century's first two decades, Susman claims, American society shifts from what he characterizes as a "culture of character," or one that values essentialist, depth-driven notions of identity, to a "culture of personality" based on imitative styles of being and the creation and performance of a self geared to the marketplace: "The social role demanded of all in the new culture of personality was that of a performer. Every American was to become a performing self."[33]

The very fluidity of the American "performing self," however, threatened the logic of institutionalized racial division, just as a culture based on performative identities threatened its (white) subjects with a frighteningly groundless inauthenticity. The tenuously placed performative Jew, I would suggest, was mobilized by American modernists precisely in order to contain those two threats. Sherwood Anderson's 1925 novel *Dark Laughter* provides a fascinating glimpse into how this dynamic played out. While interested in

confronting "the theme of racial conflict" by locating "the inherent difference between the Negro and the Caucasian," this tale of white masculinity
in crisis betrays less anxiety about the "inherent difference" of "the Negro"
than about the *inherent sameness* and the elusive difference of "the Jew."[34] Although the Jew in *Dark Laughter* is uncomfortably similar to the novel's white
protagonist, Anderson works hard to make the former seem reassuringly different (a move familiar to readers of *The Professor's House, The Sun Also Rises,*
and other novels in the modernist canon). Anderson attempts to articulate
the elusive difference between Bruce Dudley and the Jew who haunts him in
terms of the "real" versus the "artificial." It is *this* uncertain opposition, in
conjunction with a crude primitivism (faceless African Americans symbolize
all that is authentic, embodied, and sensual here), that fuels the novel's central tension, tensions deriving from the question of how a white American
could stave off the modern threats of technology, imitation, abstraction, and
disembodiment. The concern, stated thus, turns out to be not so much with
keeping the "chameleonic" American Jew from passing for white, but rather
with the ability of the white American to keep from becoming a Jew. Given
the logic of the culture of personality, these questions are not as different as
they might seem.

In *Dark Laughter,* language becomes the central symbol of the corruption
(the artificiality and inauthenticity) of the marketplace. Bruce's job as a newspaper reporter has made him deeply suspicious of the commercially-tainted
language of contemporary society; we are repeatedly told that he "was a little afraid of words. They were such tricky, elusive things." He is left in the
awkward position of being a writer who mistrusts the capacity of language to
get at anything substantial or true, a position underscored by his relationship
with a Jewish co-worker who has an astonishing talent for the false and ma-
nipulative language of the marketplace. Prior to abandoning his urban life,
Bruce—who can "get at the heart" of a story, but is unable to express this
"heart" in language—calls stories in to "the Jew," who writes up Bruce's articles. Such hyperarticulate linguistic abilities as those that give voice to
Bruce's stories epitomize the inauthentic and elusive capacities of language

51

("that young Jew in the Chicago newspaper office slinging words brilliantly—slinging the bunk"). Jewish bunk-slinging is "heartless" and theatrical; "the young Jew in the office," we are told, could "make words dance over the page." He manipulates language for its effects, while its meaning—the inherent, essential identity of each word—is lost; his talent for inauthentic, performative language reflects a world in which authenticity is increasingly difficult to locate. "What a life for a grown man," Bruce and his friend lament, "throwing bunk—sending others out to gather up city scandal—the Jew dressing it up in gaudy words." What a "non-gaudy" word would look like is never indicated, and when Bruce notes that "words are tender things, leading to poetry—or lies," the dividing line between "poetry" and "lies" is not clearly drawn either.[35] It is Bruce's sense of his own inevitable participation in this inauthentic language and world alike that leads him to loathe his profession and his life. Jewish linguistic excess, then, marks the dangerous extreme of consumer society, the parameters of which are otherwise unclear; everyone, Bruce fears, is implicated in this inescapable system. The Jew, however, by virtue of being named as such and marked as distinct, becomes a model for its containment. *Dark Laughter* is thus centered around a paradox: the language of consumer culture is inescapably universal because there is no clear line that distinguishes poetry from lies, yet self-definition in opposition to this false language is supposed to be made possible by calling it "Jewish." But how could one use language in the modern world so as to differentiate oneself from its dangers and from the Jew?[36]

The novel also establishes a second significant form of difference: while its jacket blurb touts *Dark Laughter*'s identification of the "inherent difference" between whites and blacks, it is in the difference between blacks and "the Jew" that its white protagonist finds a place for himself. For if the language practices of the Jew signify an extreme inauthenticity, the expressive capacity of the African American characters in this novel is understood as profoundly *authentic*. This is nowhere more clear than when black dockworkers enter the narrative. Bruce, in the process of making a Huck Finn-like escape down river as he flees the false language of journalism and advertising, dreamily admires them:

From the throats of the ragged black men as they trotted up and down the landing-stage, strange haunting notes. Words were caught up, tossed about, held in the throat. Word-lovers, sound-lovers—the blacks seemed to hold a tone in some warm place, under their red tongues perhaps. . . . Unconscious love of inanimate things lost to the whites—skies, the river, a moving boat—black mysticism never expressed except in song or in the movements of bodies. . . . The tones from the throats of the black workers touched each other, caressed each other. On the deck of the boat a red-faced mate stood swearing as though at the sky and the river.[37]

This move—a white character watching blacks tune into "things lost to the whites"—recurs throughout *Dark Laughter*. African Americans, constructed here as authentically real, sexually present, and not bound by societal constraints, reveal the possibility of an embodied, unconscious, richly communal expressivity—for Anderson, a truer relationship to language—as their words lose all utilitarian and commercial value, becoming indistinguishable from their sensual effects.[38] This "caressing" African American language stands in sharp contrast to that of the "red-faced mate" who swears at, rather than with, "the sky and the river." After drawing an uneasy borderline between Bruce and his former life, the narrative is then pervaded by the frustrating sense that he can never truly attain the crucial qualities signified by blackness.

Anderson himself felt similarly constrained in his own struggles, which were not unlike Bruce's. As T. J. Jackson Lears points out, Anderson had a vexed relationship to his own considerable abilities as a performer and "bunk slinger," a relationship that created a certain tension between his "persistent search for some reliable ontological bedrock" and his mastery of "the most up-to-date tools in the commercial rhetorician's kit."[39] Like Bruce, Anderson attempted to leave his commercial bunk-slinging behind, fleeing "a life of systematic deceit and self-hate" for one in which writing

53

could be "a preindustrial craft"; as Lears suggests, for Anderson, "the only expression of self that could truly be trusted was the preverbal ache of longing."[40] However, Anderson had a frustrated understanding of African Americans as the only ones who could attain this level of expression. While he claimed to Jean Toomer that he "wanted a voice" from the black dockworkers *he* spent hours watching in the South during the early 1920s, Anderson also had a hopeless sense of his desire's impossibility that was grounded in the notion of an insurmountable barrier between blacks and whites: "I wanted so much to find and express myself something clear and beautiful I felt coming up out of your race but in the end gave up. I did not want to write of the negro but out of him. Well, I wasn't one. The thing I felt couldn't truly be done."[41]

If these two extremes placed Anderson within an impossible situation, his novel conveys a vague sense of possibility for Bruce—marking his distance from his former life as embodied in the Jew, striving for an impossible closeness to African Americans while maintaining a safe distance from them. Although the novel provides only a vague resolution to Bruce's dilemma (concluding on the echoes of the black laughter that punctuated Bruce's attempt to find salvation in manual labor and nonmarital passion), a tenuous space does open up for him between his desire to break free of the expressive constraints of white American modernity and the impossibility of transgressing racial boundaries.[42] The Jew substitutes for Bruce at the limits of corrupt modernity, while the two extremes of Jew and black together set the parameters of possibility for him, even as Bruce and the Jew keep threatening to bleed into one another. The (non-Jewish) white man thus comes to occupy a vague but powerful space in between.

In concluding with a speculation that brings whiteness to a place where its theorization rarely surfaces, I want to suggest that this Black/Jewish cohabitation of early twentieth-century texts gets refigured at mid-century as the socio-literary phenomenon of "Black-Jewish relations." That is, the juxtaposition between black and Jew traced here continued to wield considerable cultural influence until well after World War II, but with a very different set of effects than that intimated by the often limited scope of the discourse on "Black-Jewish relations." For example, in a 1953 article Steven Marcus succinctly, if somewhat indelicately, attempted to contextualize America's Black-Jewish situation by describing what he saw as the main sticking points in comparisons of the relative solidity and stability of African American and Jewish identity:

The point of the parallel between Jew and Negro is just this: that where the Jew is becoming more and more anxious to rediscover that by now elusive quality which made him Jewish, the Negro is becoming more and more anxious to discover his kinship with the white race and with human history—for it surely is true that the Negroes themselves believe, however unwillingly, in their own "savagery." The Jew, it might be said, is hunting for his lost separateness—the Negro, for his unbestowed universality.[43]

Although most commentators in the first half of this century would probably have disagreed with Marcus's postwar perspective on the centrality of a Jewish quest for "lost separateness" (given their own era's understanding of Jewish Americans as wishing, above all, to lose their "separateness," to mask Jewish difference in order to blend in), this polarization and textual cohabitation was, as I have demonstrated here, common from the early days of American modernism. What emerges so clearly here, however, is that it is the unattainable edge of whiteness, somewhere between "separateness" and "universality," that both groups secretly desire. Despite the Jew's "loss" of difference *from* and the black's "loss" of commonality *with* white America, the most powerful (if implicit) claims being made in these texts would seem to be about whiteness itself.

In the passage from Marcus's article, as in Anderson's novel, whiteness silently asserts both its universal commonality and its supreme difference to assume an impossible, paradoxical position strikingly similar to the one imposed on the Jew. But these characteristics, deflected onto the Jew and thereby degraded, are never directly attributed to whiteness. Rather than being understood through an examination of its own distinctive qualities,

whiteness must therefore be understood in terms of a complicated positioning between the respective "lack" of blacks and Jews.[44] In *Dark Laughter,*
Bruce's escape from the Jew and flight into an African American world of
manual labor and manly friendships enables him both to maintain his place
on the uneasy edge of whiteness and to sustain his hope of achieving an impossible poetry.

Notes

I would like to thank Eleanor Kaufman, Ivan Krielkamp, Michael Moon, V. Y.
Mudimbe, John Plotz, Janice Radway, and Eve Kosofsky Sedgwick for the generous
attention each has given to drafts of this essay.

1. Waldo Frank, *Memoirs of Waldo Frank,* ed. Alan Trachtenberg (Amherst,1973), 105.

2. "If you go as a Negro, so go I," Frank wrote to Toomer in an undated letter; see
Jean Toomer Papers, James Weldon Johnson collection of Negro Literature and Art,
Beineke Rare Book and Manuscript Library, Yale University.

3. Critics have generally followed Toomer's lead in discussing the relationship.
Toomer's sense of being objectified by Frank was crystallized by the latter's introduction to *Cane;* on Toomer's dismay at this highlighting of his African ancestry, see
"Autobiographical Selection" in Jean Toomer, *Cane,* ed. Darwin T. Turner (New York,
1988 [1923]), 143–144. (Frank's introduction is also reprinted in this edition.) In a
fascinating development, Toomer eventually blamed Frank's introduction to *Cane*
for the popular conception that he was black. Charles Scruggs reports that Toomer's
friend H. W. Whitaker sent a letter (after Toomer had approved it) to a magazine ed-
itor complaining about a review of *Cane* in which its author had been misdescribed
as "a Negro": "Frank's introduction had pernicious influence for it created this
myth"; see his "Jean Toomer: Fugitive," *American Literature* 47 (March 1975): 84–96;
quotation from 84.

4. Langston Hughes exemplifies the earlier commentators on Toomer's uncomfortable relationship to the black community, ridiculing his ill-fated attempt to bring
the philosophy of his guru, Gurdjieff, to Harlem, pointing out Toomer's marriages
to white women, and lamenting his ultimate loss to "the Negroes," in *The Big Sea*
(New York, 1986 [1940]), 241–43. For more recent discussions of Toomer's life and

work, see Henry Louis Gates, Jr., "The Same Difference: Reading Jean Toomer 1923–1982," in *Figures in Black: Words, Signs and the "Racial" Self* (New York, 1989), 196–224; Michael North, *The Dialect of Modernism: Race, Language and Twentieth-Century Literature* (New York, 1994); and Walter Benn Michaels, *Our America: Nativism, Modernism, and Pluralism* (Durham, 1995).

5. Jean Toomer, *Essentials: Definitions and Aphorisms* (Chicago, 1931), xxiv.

6. Michael Rogin, *Blackface, White Noise: Jewish Immigrants in the Hollywood Melting Pot* (Berkeley, 1996), 56.

7. Leslie Fiedler observed in 1958 that "the Jew has become on all levels from *Marjorie Morningstar* and *For Two Cents Plain* to *Augie March* and *Goodbye, Columbus* the symbol in which the American projects his own fate"; see his "Leopold and Loeb: A Perspective in Time," in *The Collected Essays of Leslie Fiedler, Vol. I* (New York, 1971), 429–48; quotation from 444. In 1951 Norman Mailer similarly proclaimed us "all Jews to a degree" in his introduction to John W. Aldridge, *After the Lost Generation: A Critical Study of the Writers of Two Wars* (New York, 1985), i–vi; quotation from iii.

8. Henry Billings Brown's *Plessy* opinion, as quoted in Eric J. Sundquist, *To Wake the Nations: Race in the Making of American Literature* (Cambridge, MA, 1993), 236. For a more detailed discussion of the pervasive anxieties surrounding contested notions of "Jewish difference" in early twentieth-century American culture, see Daniel Itzkovitz, "Secret Temples," in *Jews and Other Differences: The New Jewish Cultural Studies*, ed. Jonathan Boyarin and Daniel Boyarin (Minneapolis, 1997), 176–202.

9. An observation made in an unsigned editorial in *M'lle NY* (July 1895).

10. Lewis Browne, "Why Are Jews Like That," *American Magazine* (January 1929): 7–9, 104–6; quotation from 8. Browne's essay, written in response to the classic quandary of Jewish difference, is styled as a reply to a non-Jewish friend who is baffled by the persistence of Jewish identity despite its refusal of coherent categories of difference. While walking together through a Jewish crowd in Manhattan, among bearded, Yiddish-speaking, "arguing and gesticulating" immigrants who bore little resemblance to Browne himself, his friend "suddenly demanded: 'Say, Browne: why are Jews like that?'" Browne is quick to point out that it was not so much anti-Semitism that prompted his friend's question as "bewilderment, exasperated wonder. . . . He had been amazed, perhaps a trifle appalled, at the strangeness, the peculiarity, of that mob" (7). But to clarify the specific confusion of his friend as one about Jewishness rather than immigrant foreignness, Browne has him elaborate his point:

"'I wasn't thinking of their language or their beards. Those things, I realize, are superficial. . . . Nor was I thinking of their manners, either. . . . No, it wasn't their manners that bewildered me but their manner.' My friend paused a moment, and then, fearing I had not caught his meaning, he explained: 'There was a queer light in their eyes, and a sort of tenseness in their bodies; that was what made me put my question to you. For you, too, show those characteristics to a degree. . . . You are all somehow different from the rest of us. And I'd like to know why'" (7–8).

11. In his letters to Toomer, Frank explicitly connects his performance of Blackness to his Jewish identity (see, e.g., the letter cited in note 2). Apparently, others made the same connection. Paul Rosenfeld, for instance, criticized Frank in a letter to Toomer of 21 December 1933: "Waldo has always been abnormally concerned with the Jewish problem (in 1921 he told the farmers in Peterboro he was a Catholic) and I think he has a complex on the subject" (Toomer Papers, box 7, folder 220, doc. 2898).

12. Theodor W. Adorno and Max Horkheimer, *Dialectic of Enlightenment,* trans. John Cumming (New York, 1991 [1944]), 182. See also Hannah Arendt, *Antisemitism: Part One of The Origins of Totalitarianism* (New York, 1968), 60–62 and 82; and Karl Marx, "On the Jewish Question" (1844), in *Writings of the Young Marx on Philosophy and Society,* ed. and trans. Lloyd D. Easton and Kurt M. Guddat (Garden City, NY, 1967), 216–48.

13. Robert Stam and Ella Shohat, "Zelig and Contemporary Theory: Meditation on the Chameleon Text," *Enclitic* 9 (1985): 176–93; quotation from 188.

14. An interesting parallel might be drawn between the tendency among theorists of Jewish identity and anti-Semitism not to explore the cultural specifics of Jewishness in the United States and the rare instances of Jewishness as a topic in American cultural studies. In neither case is the construction of the Jewish subject posited as being influenced by or having any impact on the non-Jewish world. On the problems inherent to *Plessy's* racial logic, see, for example, Sundquist, *To Wake the Nations,* 225–70, and Michaels, *Our America,* 114.

15. Werner Sollors also notes the phenomenon of the Jewish-mulatto congruence in his *Neither Black Nor White Yet Both: Thematic Explorations of Interracial Literature* (New York, 1997), 501 n. 67. For more on passing and the trope of the "tragic mulatta," see Sterling Brown, *The Negro in American Fiction* (New York, 1969); Hazel V. Carby, *Reconstructing Womanhood: The Emergence of the Afro-American Woman Novel-*

ist (New York, 1987); and Hortense J. Spillers, "Notes on an Alternative Model—Nei-
ther/Nor," in *The Difference Within: Feminism and Critical Theory*, ed. Elizabeth Meese
and Alice Parker (Philadelphia, 1989), 165–87.

16. James Weldon Johnson, *The Autobiography of an Ex-Colored Man* (New York, 1990
[1912]), 116.

17. Ibid., 139, 141, 142.

18. Ralph Philip Boas, "Jew-Baiting in America," *Atlantic Monthly* (May 1921):
658–65; quotation from 663.

19. Nella Larsen, *Quicksand and Passing* (New Brunswick, NJ, 1986 [1928, 1929]),
169.

20. Ibid.

21. Madison Grant, *The Passing of the Great Race* (New York, 1916), 16. Edwin J.
Kuh's dismissive and clearly defensive statement concerning Jewish chameleonism betrays a similar sentiment, while revealing the sense that money played an
insidious role in its magic: "They forget that the money which buys them a box
at the opera or an apartment at a fashionable hotel has not bought for them
culture"; see "The Social Disability of the Jews," *Atlantic Monthly* (April 1908):
433–39; quotation from 436.

22. Lewis S. Gannett, "Is America Anti-Semitic?" *The Nation*, 21 March 1923,
330–32; quotation from 331.

23. As quoted in Bernard Drachman, "Anti-Jewish Prejudice in America," *The Forum*
(July 1914): 31–40; quotation from 38.

24. Burton J. Hendrick, "The Great Jewish Invasion," *McClure's* (January 1907):
307–21; quotation from 320. Gannett's "Is America Anti-Semitic?" reflects an apparent familiarity with Hendrick's work.

25. Johnson, *Ex-Colored Man*, 54, 154.

26. Fannie Hurst, *Imitation of Life* (New York, 1990 [1933]), 261, 207.

27. Decades after the publication of *The Souls of Black Folk*, Du Bois famously deleted
his anti-Semitic remarks, but these can be found in the 1990 Library of America
edition, along with an introduction by John Edgar Wideman (see 87, 94, 98, and
123–4). Significantly for my argument here, Du Bois's original characterization of
the Jew was contradictory: despite resenting the Jewish appropriation of what
he felt rightfully belonged to African Americans—and his sense of a fundamentally false and superficial Jewish nature ("the defense of deception and flattery, of

cajoling and lying") notwithstanding—he chose to mark Alexander Crummell's depth by dubbing him "a dark and pierced Jew, who knows the writhings of the earthly damned" (147, 164). See also Charles W. Chesnutt, *The Marrow of Tradition*, ed. Robert M. Farnsworth (Ann Arbor, 1969 [1901]), 289.

28. Michaels, *Our America*, 116.

29. For a long list of the contradictory traits that were simultaneously attributed to Jews, see Israel S. Wechsler, "The Psychology of Anti-Semitism," *Menorah Journal* (April 1925): 159–66, esp. 160.

30. "Conversations with Mr. Lowell," *Atlantic Monthly* (March 1897): 127–30; quotation from 128. This passage also gives a sense of the connections to be made between the "queer light" of Jewish difference and the "queerness" of non-normative sexuality. In "Secret Temples" I explore the secrets imagined behind the eyes of the Jew, arguing that so-called Jewish inscrutability informed and catalyzed notions of hidden Jewish sexual and economic practice, which in turn helped to define (and trouble) the boundaries of normative white, American heterosexual masculinity.

31. For a useful discussion of the modern fascination with the tensions between authenticity and imitation, see Miles Orvell, *The Real Thing: Imitation and Authenticity in American Culture, 1880–1940* (Chapel Hill, 1989). Again, I'm not suggesting that Jews simply fell into the shape-shifting role in playing out the cultural dynamic between a performative and an embodied identity. If the Jew signified what was quintessentially mutable in a society coming to define itself by its potential for mobility, the "queer light" of Jewish difference signaled the tension between an identity embodied and an identity performed. Charles Musser is correct, then, to pinpoint "role playing" as central to early-twentieth-century Jewish American cultural productions. The prevalence of Jewish performers, and particularly their thematizing of this "role playing" as the performing of other cultures in early Hollywood films, leads Musser to suggest that it playfully expresses and celebrates new possibilities for Jews entering U.S. culture. He argues that, in thematizing and playing with the idea of racial performance, films such as Eddie Cantor's *Whoopee!* and the Marx Brothers' *Animal Crackers* exemplify the use of performance in the development of Jewish American social mobility; see his "Ethnicity, Role-Playing, and American Film Comedy: From Chinese Laundry Scene to *Whoopee*," in *Unspeakable Images: Ethnicity and the American Cinema*, ed. Lester Friedman (Urbana, 1991), 39–81.

32. Mike Featherstone, "The Body in Consumer Culture," *Theory, Culture and Society* I (1982): 18–33; quotation from 18.

33. Warren I. Susman, "'Personality' and the Making of Twentieth-Century Culture," in *New Directions in American Intellectual History*, ed. John Higham and Paul K. Conkin (Baltimore, 1979), 212–26; quotation from 220. Susman's work has since been interestingly complicated by Karen Haltunnen's *Confidence Men and Painted Women* (New Haven, 1982), which posits a prior nineteenth-century trope of American performativity of self.

34. Sherwood Anderson, *Dark Laughter*, with an introduction by Howard Mumford Jones (New York, 1970 [1925]). This edition's back-cover blurb declares that it locates "the inherent difference between the Negro and the Caucasian."

35. Ibid., 25, 40, 98, 116, 60.

36. This same Jewish relationship to language is the reason why Robert Cohn isn't a successful writer in *The Sun Also Rises*. Hemingway couldn't imagine such phoniness succeeding aesthetically even if it was profitable and impressed some people. Cohn's biggest problem is that he relies too heavily on language rather than on "life itself," according to Jake, who criticizes him for getting all of his ideas "out of a book": "I never heard [Cohn] make one remark that would, in any way, detach him from other people"; see *The Sun Also Rises* (New York, 1986 [1926]), 12, 45. The trick, then, for both Hemingway and Anderson, becomes learning how to be non-Jewish. For another take on the specifically Jewish relationship to language that mobilizes the same terms, but valorizes them in precisely the opposite way, see the odd short story by Dorothy Canfield Fisher, "Professor Paul Meyer: Master of the Word," in *Raw Material* (New York, 1923), 127–41. Professor Meyer, a Jewish philologist extraordinaire, testifies at the Dreyfus trial and is subsequently attacked and ridiculed by his anti-Semitic students. Facing his attackers, Meyer utilizes his most powerful weapon—his remarkable relationship to "the word": "He stood looking at his assailants, the chalk ready in his bony fingers, and from him emanated so profound a sense of their entire unimportance, of the utterly ephemeral quality of their emotion compared to the life of the consonant he was about to discuss, that little by little they were silenced" (135). Dying at the end of the story, Meyer is fittingly afflicted with "an obscure form of aphasia" (141).

37. Anderson, *Dark Laughter,* 106.

38. This and other features of the novel were viciously parodied by Hemingway in *Torrents of the Spring* (1926) and attacked by Wyndham Lewis in *Pale Face: The Philosophy of the Melting Pot* (1929). But both Hemingway and Lewis were themselves capable of fetishizing people of color and of anxiously defining White identity against Jewishness. In *The Sun Also Rises* (71) a similar contrast is drawn between Jewish inauthenticity and African American genuineness when Robert Cohn, the imitative Jewish boxer (who, we learn, always hated boxing), is shadowed by a "noble looking" Black boxer dearly constructed as the real thing. Although rarely discussed by critics of the novel, this character functions as a crucial counterpoint to Cohn. See also the claim by Theodor Adorno in *The Jargon of Authenticity*, trans. Knut Tarnowski and Frederic Will (Evanston, 1973 [1964]) that in the ideology of German nationalist authenticity "sub-language is superior language" (6).

39. T. J. Jackson Lears, "Sherwood Anderson: Looking for the White Spot," in *The Power of Culture: Critical Essays in American History*, ed. T. J. Jackson Lears and Richard Wrightman Fox (Chicago, 1993), 13–37; quotations from 16 and 20. Significantly, Anderson reported in his memoirs that as a student he had been "chosen class orator" and that his first speech was "on the Jews"; see *Sherwood Anderson's Memoirs: A Critical Edition*, ed. Ray Lewis White (Chapel Hill, 1969 [1942]), 198. Some critics, ironically, have viewed *Dark Laughter* as marking a turn in Anderson's writing toward the inauthentic. James Schevill, for instance, laments that, due to the success of this novel, "several years would pass before [Anderson] realized he had forsaken his own natural style for the glitter of artifice. . . . The sophistication is an assumed mannerism rather than natural expression"; *Sherwood Anderson: His Life and Work* (Denver, 1951), 209, 211.

40. Lears, "Sherwood Anderson," 23–24, 27, 33.

41. Anderson to Toomer, 3 January 1924 and 22 December 1922 (Toomer Papers, box 1, folder 1; see also Toomer's 29 December 1922 reply in Turner, ed., *Cane* 149). When he first encountered Toomer, Anderson was clearly looking for something from (what he viewed as) African American culture and spirit. He said in a letter of July 1920 to Jerome and Lucile Blum: "I'm going back to Alabama this winter to paint and write. If necessary, I'll be an unfaithful husband to Tennessee and run off into the woods with a black wench. I'm going after the American nigger. He's got something absolutely lovely that's never been touched. . . . I want to go after that." *Letters of Sherwood Anderson*, ed. Howard Mumford Jones and Walter B. Rideout

(Boston, 1953), 58. The erotics of shifting gender here (from "wench" to "he") fore-shadow the issues of desire, envy, purity, and white masculinity that Anderson would relate to blacks and displace to Jews.

42. While Anderson undoes J. L. Austin's performative/constative linguistic distinc-tion with a racially based one, he, like Austin, still attempts to recuperate language (for white people). See J. L. Austin, *How to Do Things with Words* (Cambridge, MA, 1962), where he distinguishes what he calls "serious" from "non-serious" utter-ances, that is, "truthful" utterances "tethered to their origin" (61) from those whose origins are obscured by theatrical or literary devices, which are "parasitic upon its normal use" (22).

43. Steven Marcus, "The American Negro in Search of Identity," *Commentary* (No-vember 1953): 456–63; quotation from 462.

44. This reading suggests an alternative model for thinking about "Black-Jewish re-lations," a genre that has thrived for decades within and outside the academy, as one which may be mobilized, in part, for the production of whiteness. For some of the most influential discussions of the last three decades, see *Blacks and Jews: Al-liances and Arguments,* ed. Paul Berman (New York, 1994); and, for an earlier set of discussions, see *Black Anti-Semitism and Jewish Racism,* with an introduction by Nat Hentoff (New York, 1969). Cornel West and Michael Lerner have recently shifted the genre with their literal rendition of an African American and a Jew speaking to one another in *Jews and Blacks: A Dialogue on Race, Religion and Culture in America* (New York, 1996).

3 Whiteness Invisible

Early Mexican American Writing and the Color of
Literary History

María Carla Sánchez

Toward the end of her memoir *We Fed Them Cactus*, Fabiola Cabeza de Baca
recalls an encounter between her father and a homesteader, in which the latter confusedly remarks that he thought Don Cabeza de Baca "was a white
man when [he] saw him."[1] Cabeza de Baca writes:

*Papá was tall and very fair skinned. His eyes were the blue of sapphire and his hair
was reddish brown. He could not have been mistaken by anyone as not being white,
yet these people who came to settle in our midst were ignorant of history. To them,
the only white people were those who spoke the English language as their mother
tongue. (149)*

Cabeza de Baca diagnoses the problem in this confrontation as "ignoran[ce]
of history," a lack of context that would allow the new settler to interpret correctly that which he sees before him. Both Cabeza de Baca and the settler emphasize the weight that the visual bears, appealing to a reading that should
be apparent ("He could not have been mistaken. . . ."). What Cabeza de Baca's
rhetorical gesture marks, however, is the passage of whiteness from physical

text (I thought you were a white man) to abstract and elusive identity (oh, so you are not a white man) and back to material basics (what the settler really wants: to borrow a milking cow from Don Cabeza de Baca). What the daughter terms ignorance is better understood by the father as a competition of epistemologies in which individual identity, national identity, and socioeconomic stature will be determined, in part, according to what can be seen on or in the body. Hence, the father takes protective measures and encloses himself and his property: "'I intend to fence my land and stay within it'" (149). The equation between identity and property highlights the extent to which Mexican Americans' status within the body politic will be conflated with their ability to manipulate an unfamiliar capitalist economic market. Yet as both generations of Cabeza de Bacas learn, identity proves much less amenable than soil to the restrictions of an old patriarchal control.

I open this essay with Fabiola Cabeza de Baca's story because it speaks to a twofold argument about identity in Mexican American literature and contemporary Chicano scholarship. In fact, my distinction here between Mexican American and Chicano stems from the same argument, one that recognizes the immense cultural context behind the use of a name. Fabiola Cabeza de Baca, like her father, identified herself as a descendant of the former *Mexicano* ruling classes in the Southwest (she calls her father *el patrón* and defines *rico* as landowner for the potentially ignorant reader).[2] In this self-identification she joins many early Mexican American writers who claim a "pure" Spanish ancestry, one devoid of indigenous, African, or Jewish presences, and understood implicitly within their own communities as "white." Whiteness in Latino communities (as in others) typically signifies a range of individual traits that perpetuate social and sometimes economic dominance: morality, gentility, intelligence, and wealth. Imbued with race, class, sex, and gender associations, whiteness operates as symbolic shorthand for genealogical connection to imperial Spain and its colonizing projects. Thus, the further back that Chicano Studies extends its reach, the more and more it finds writers unfamiliar (in all senses of the word) with the indigenous identifications and working-class ethos of the Chicano movement. As seems evident

from Cabeza de Baca's story, however, even as whiteness might signify similar traits, privileges, and identities in different cultural contexts, its *recognition* does not necessarily translate—especially if those contexts concern a
racialized national power. Or, one might say that its recognition simultaneously represents misrecognition: the settler's conflation of "white" with
"Anglo" allows him paradoxically to see and not see at the same moment, to
attach a signifying whiteness to the wrong signified. There is anxiety, then,
in this story and many others from early writings, concerning the invisibility of whiteness: that not all whiteness is created, or recognized, as equal.

This essay will begin by examining instances, like Cabeza de Baca's story,
of what I call "whiteness demonstrations" (*pruebas de sangre pura*) from early
Mexican American literature, in order to make an argument about understanding whiteness as class, and about how this conflation informs the morphology of the literature. Even more so, I suggest that this conflation fundamentally informs the practice and politics of literary history itself. I work
from the assumption that even as this literature constructs many levels of resistance to Anglo-American sociopolitical power, it also perpetuates racist
and classist narratives of white Hispanic superiority, making manifest a variety of passings: willing and unwilling, anticipated and accomplished, feared
and desired. In the midst of these passings, I argue, early writers reimagined
a social order whose most important feature was not its opposition to an
Anglo present but, rather, its ability to inflect a Chicano future. Early Mexican American literature does not merely imagine putting Anglo America in
its place, it powerfully succeeds in putting contemporary Chicanos in theirs.
As such, the conjunction of early literature and contemporary scholarship reveals critical narratives of familial desire, casting past writers as veritable ancestors; in the process, passing emerges as the primary means of disseminat-
ing literary history.

As narrative gestures toward a range of traits metonymically understood
as Spanishness, whiteness demonstrations are deployed metaphorically, to
convince white *Anglo* audiences of their shared fundamental "natures."
That metaphorical relationship is excessive, however, simultaneously de-

noting both similarity and distinction: most appeals to Anglo whiteness double as demonstrations of Mexican moral superiority. It is this excess, exposed in references to nobility, gentility, social responsibility, and other essentially moral traits, that reveals early writers' multivalent comprehension of class. In this essay I juxtapose these demonstrations and this comprehension against the stated political aims of Chicano literary scholarship, raising the question of how we assimilate early writers so that they might pass into reconstructed literary genealogies. Or, in other words, how do we pass these writers off (and who do we need to pass them off onto)? Second, I read María Amparo Ruiz de Burton's 1872 novel, *Who Would Have Thought It?*, so as to reconfigure this conflict of epistemologies within the manifested practice of racial passing. Early Mexican American authors either faced or engaged in various forms of passing: the passage of their lands and society into the strongly ethnonationalist and capitalist power structure of the Anglo-American United States; their own passage, as subjugated and displaced persons, into another social order altogether, akin to or including African Americans and Native Americans (those persons most spectacularly subject to and victimized by nineteenth-century Anglo-American state power); and the establishment of police(d) states in which the ability to pass as not-Mexican results in myriad advantages, now most notably manifest in the ability to avoid harassment by the INS (Immigration and Naturalization Service). While this may seem a quantum leap into the present day, I would argue that the competing discourses of whiteness that inform texts such as *Who Would Have Thought It?* have much to do with the quotidian structures of life on the U.S.-Mexico border.

Ruiz de Burton constructs a nightmarish allegory of Mexican life under Anglo-American rule, of the social devolution that will occur if the former elites of California, New Mexico, and the remainder of the Southwest do not find ways of allying themselves with the new (and hence, "real") "white people." In doing so, she transforms passing from the phenomenon of will, as which it is typically conceived (I want to pass, therefore I do), into the symptom of socioeconomic displacement and destruction, which it has been historically. What does it mean to pass against your will? For Ruiz de Burton and other early writers, whiteness is never solely or simply reducible to the color of a skin, and hence it is never discursively represented as such. Thus their passings cannot be reduced to questions of economic affluence and political power, for as regards Chicano critics, early writers' cultural capital remains powerfully intact. Finally, then, Ruiz de Burton raises the necessity for Chicano studies scholars, and all others who recover, recuperate, or rehabilitate their pasts, to self-critically examine how we reclaim the dead.

At the beginning of the twenty-first century, our history fascinates us: the past decade has witnessed a resurgence of scholarship on early Mexican American literature. The Recovering the U.S. Hispanic Literary Heritage project based at the University of Houston has reprinted many early works by Latino authors (including those of María Amparo Ruiz de Burton) and accompanying texts of criticism on the goals, challenges, and methodologies involved in its undertaking. Other university presses have also (re)introduced early works, from Antonio María Osio's *The History of Alta California* (1851) to Jovita Gonzalez's novels of south Texas life, *Dew on the Thorn* and *Caballero* (composed 1930s–1940s). The post-1848 Spanish-language press (Doris Meyer's *Speaking for Themselves* and A. Gabriel Meléndez's *So All Is Not Lost*), the Bancroft *testimonios* (Rosaura Sánchez's *Telling Identities*), and early Mexican American autobiographies (Genaro Padilla's *My History, Not Yours*) all provide the subjects of major studies.[3] Yet as the myriad ethnic designations in these titles reflect, care in denoting identities is intimately linked to the claiming of regionalized or classed communities.[4] Scholarship on Chicano literature and culture in general has promoted as its focus the expression, reevaluation, and celebration of Mexican American daily life and experience, especially so far as the experience represents that of a sociopolitically and socioeconomically disempowered class. As Juan Bruce-Novoa described it in 1982:

Chicano literature, as most people use the term, is that which is associated with a new consciousness of political, social, and cultural identity linked to the Chicano Movement. Some of the works sprang directly from the struggle, written by political activists like Rodolfo Gonzales, the leader of the Denver-based Crusade for Justice. Other works may have been written before the Movement, like José Montoya's "El Louie" or some of Bernice Zamora's poems, but publication was brought about by the cultural fervor of the Movement. . . . Moreover, the literature quickly became part of the Movement's ideological material, giving it the particular tone we know today.[5]

Ramón Saldívar, in his 1990 work *Chicano Narrative: The Dialectics of Difference*, succinctly describes this commitment to a shared ideology descended from the Movement. "Begin[ning] by sketching a historical profile of Mexican Americans as an ethnic working-class minority," one whose shared cultural background forms a sameness of "function" in their literary works, Saldívar elaborates on how that function operates:

Thematically, aesthetically, conceptually, and politically, the works of these women and men constitute no single literary tradition *but they do manifest a common idea of the* function *of literature as a result of the specific historical, social, and economic experience that these authors have been obliged to share.[6]*

Privileging the term *function* over *tradition* implies that Mexican American writers and their literature serve a purpose: that they play a role in the cause, with any notion of "art for art's sake" implicitly refuted. Numerous critics describe similar conceptions of Chicano literature and its audience.[7] The named "difference" of Saldívar's title refers to the cultural and ideological differences between Mexican Americans and persons of other racial and ethnic backgrounds; differences among Mexican Americans themselves, such as "internal class differences," are downplayed, here and elsewhere.[8] Yet class difference emerges as the major distinction between the majority of pre- and post-1960s writers, such a difference that, even though they are included in Chicano Studies, they cannot be called Chicano. For if Chicano Studies privileges a working-class and indigenous ethos, the early literature may fairly be said to validate its own whiteness.

Such is the case because the whiteness that emerges as mis/un/recognized in Fabiola Cabeza de Baca's story requires narrative defense not only against the homesteader but against the reader as well. Cabeza de Baca's reading audience represents a metaphorical (and likely, literal) legion of homesteaders: settlers within New Mexico and Texas territory, and also within the ideological and discursive worlds of whiteness that she and others like her have inhabited. Thus, not only does Cabeza de Baca insist upon the "obvious" reading of her father's racial identity, she delineates class lines between and among the newly neighboring groups of white people: "They were kindly, simple folks, these homesteaders. Their hospitality was boundless, and Miss Fabiola and Mr. Luis were idolized by young and old. My brother, Luis, and I loved them, but El Cuate [the ranch cook] and Papá kept aloof, never quite understanding what Luis and I saw in those uncouth people" (148). Growing up during the first decades of the 1900s, Cabeza de Baca records in this recollection a social harmony that deviates violently from the social unrest and virtual war occurring farther south in Texas between Mexican Americans on one side, and the Texas Rangers and U.S. Army on the other.[9] That Cabeza de Baca fails to mention this should cause no surprise: the description of "Miss Fabiola's" amiable relations with homesteaders ascertains her own whiteness. It is signified by a nobility inspirational of a deferential title, and by the language of harmless inferiority she uses to describe these Anglo settlers ("simple folks," "uncouth"). One might imagine that of the thousands of Mexican Americans lynched in Texas around the turn of the century, few, if any, were politely addressed as "Miss" or "Mr."[10]

The conflation of whiteness and class confirms for Cabeza de Baca and her homesteading reader the superiority of Spanishness. Markers of race (Cabeza de Baca's Spanish ancestry, her family's pale complexion) collapse into markers of culture (the respectful title, her ability to pass judgment on the homesteading character) in a manner that recalls Pierre Bourdieu's theory of the naturalization of class. Bourdieu describes "The ideology of natural taste" as "ow[ing] its plausibility and its efficacy to the fact that . . . it *naturalizes* real differences, converting differences in the mode of acquisition of culture into differences of nature."[11] Conflating class and race produces the ultimate naturalization of the former: real class differences, both of the acquisition of culture and of the acquisition of material wealth, emerge as inherent differences of race. In making this conflation and paying witness to her own whiteness, Fabiola Cabeza de Baca participates in a long history of such cultural work on the colonial frontiers. I follow F. Arturo Rosales's lead here in noting that such witness emerged in large part from belief in the "Fantasy Heritage" (the idea that certain Mexican American communities are "of pure Spanish descent"); likewise, that those who "adhered to 'Spanishness' . . . did so following their own agenda—one that predated the Anglo takeover."[12] Indeed, one might note that the Treaty of Guadalupe Hidalgo specifies the existence of "savage [Indian] tribes," presenting a danger to the United States and Mexico alike, and for whom the responsibility of military and other forms of social "management" now devolves upon the conquering state. This ratified distinction, of course, marks the culmination of centuries of Spanish and Mexican colonial enterprise against native peoples.[13] Osio's *History of Alta California* recounts a skirmish between Californio forces and Kodiak people over hunting territory within its first few pages; he later comments derogatorily on, and distinguishes himself from, mestizo Mexican soldiers sent north to fortify reserves there.[14] Within these texts, histories, memoirs, and political documents of war and conquest, there exists no question that Indians are not us.

In a similar vein, Rosaura Sánchez discusses the tendency of *testimonio* subjects to give voice to metonymic conceptions of Spanishness, especially as concerns gentility. Sánchez notes how the *testimonio* subjects deploy terms such as *gente de razón*, claim descendancy from *Castilla la Vieja*, and engage in larger (that is, nationwide) racist discourses surrounding Native and African Americans.[15] For Sánchez, this discursive partitioning "functions as a construct of identity rather than difference, that is, as an attempt to appear on the same racial plane with the Yankee invaders, as if national

71

origin and race could be wielded as a strategic discourse to combat racist representations of the conquered Californios as half-civilized Indians."[16] I would agree with Sánchez that whiteness demonstrations seek to establish identity, as we see with Fabiola Cabeza de Baca; however, I would argue that such identity, in its very metaphorical dimension, is excessive, performing both similarity and difference. We are just like you Anglos—we are not (like) blacks and Indians. My translation of this ideological orientation, which uses simile to describe Mexican and Anglo whitenesses, and makes that simile conditional when gesturing toward blacks and Indians, attempts to convey the sentiment of inequality present in many demonstrations of whiteness. For Mexican whites to ally themselves discursively with Anglo American whites represents a strategy of political, cultural, and psychic survival. But in reading their texts as "resistant" documents, it becomes clear that for many Mexican Americans, Mexican whiteness is not equal to Anglo whiteness. It's actually much better.

In *Old Spain in Our Southwest* (1936), Nina Otero-Warren announces that "the Spanish descendant of the *Conquistadores* may be poor, but he takes his place in life with a noble bearing, for he can never forget that he is a descendant of the Conquerors."[17] Cleofas Jaramillo, in *Shadows of the Past* (1941), proudly relates her family's settlement in northern New Mexico:

Thus did this family come to the hidden valley of the Arroyo Hondo—another family to help, by means of bloody battle and peaceful law, to bring civilization to wilderness—another family to help adapt the old customs of Spain to a new land, adding something to the heritage of the Spanish Conquistadores who came before them.[18]

That adaptation and addition does not include miscegenation, however, as Jaramillo notes that "there was a great deal of intermarriage between first and second cousins, in order to keep the Spanish blood from mixing. This happened a great deal among my family" (31). Such statements illuminate the restructuring of values that whiteness demonstrations allow. We may be poor, but we are noble: a conception of individual, communal, and racial worth expressed in moral terms. This morality trumps Anglo whiteness, effectively acknowledging Anglos' current possession of wealth but intimating their lack of personal merit. We brought civilization to wilderness: a gesture to the Puritan "errand into the wilderness" that provides mythological genealogy for Anglo America. More important, however, Jaramillo claims European civilization at a moment when, in mainstream culture, the only connection that Native and African Americans possess to civilization is one located in the ancient (Incan, Mayan, Ethiopian) past. Demonstrations of whiteness arrange the changing world of the Southwest into a stable taxonomy that uses moral traits to connote race/class residence. Only one element appears to be missing from such taxonomies: people seemingly neither white nor black, nor wholly "Indian."

Throughout *We Fed Them Cactus*, Fabiola Cabeza de Baca describes life on her father's estate as one in which three distinct groups interact and construct a new social order: Anglo whites, Mexican whites, and *los empleados*, the missing element. In a section entitled "Places and People," Cabeza de Baca states that "there may have been class distinction in the larger towns, but the families on the Llano had none; the *empleados* and their families were as much a part of the family of the *patrón* as his own children. It was a very democratic way of life."[19] Certainly Cabeza de Baca means to impugn the actualization of Anglo democratic rhetoric: true democracy is the willing extension of the familial domestic sphere. Then, a few paragraphs later, she describes educational endeavors in the Llano's democratic realm:

The Llano people had no opportunity for public schools, before statehood, but there were men and women who held classes for the children of the patrones in private homes. . . . Those who had means sent their children to school in Las Vegas, Santa Fe, or Eastern states. If no teachers were available, the mothers taught their own children to read and many of the wealthy ranchers had private teachers for their children until they were old enough to go away to boarding schools.[20]

The passage from inclusion to exclusion (when do the *empleados'* kids leave for boarding school?) is quick and unthinking, but Cabeza de Baca's message sounds clearly: our whiteness represents the real democracy. Yet as these demonstrations reveal, access to the means of representation proves as re-stricted as Cabeza de Baca's concept of democracy. As they existed prior to the Mexican-American War, the Fantasy Heritage and whiteness demonstra-tions attempt to demarcate the limits of whiteness on the Spanish colonial, and then Mexican frontier. As far as those limits were fantasmatic—that is, determined by relations with and disassociations from indigenous and African inhabitants that emphatically did not constitute them as political subjects—they were nonetheless foundational to the pre-1848 social order.[21]

After 1848, such demonstrations form part of a discursive competition over whiteness: the genteel whiteness of "old Spain" versus the rough and nouveau whiteness of *los Americanos*, in which *la mayoría de la raza*—ordi-nary folks with *indígeno* roots and varying degrees of *mestizaje*—become racially *classified* as a separate class. A. Gabriel Meléndez, in his study of Spanish-language New Mexico newspapers, notes:

Los periodiqueros *[journalists] turned to the "glorious" deeds of the Spanish colonial enterprise. Filled with pure* fabula, *the sixteenth-century exploits of conquistadores provided the periodiquero generation with a powerful master narrative to counter Anglo-American pretensions to primacy in the region. Essentialist in this regard, the emphasis on the colonial narratives overshadowed the complexities of social and class formation in New Mexico tied to its* mestizo, genízaro, and Indian past.[22]

As Meléndez notes, the appeal to the "golden age" of colonial Spain and Spanishness (certainly not to the Spain that lost its own war with the United States, and its remaining colonies, in 1898) allowed besieged Mexican Amer-ican communities to understand themselves as genealogically related to, rather than subjected by, empire. Spanish imperialism's own narratives of subjugation thus effectively disappear in a haze of whiteness. The discourse of that haze effectively transforms *los empleados* and *los peones* into plot de-vices: those who enable the white *fabula* to unfold.

The Bancroft *testimonios*, collected during the 1870s by Hubert Howe Ban-croft and his agents Enrique Cerruti and Thomas Savage, represent direct *Mexicano* reconstructions of, responses to, and negotiations with empire; including numerous dictated memoirs, they theoretically offer a space where *Mexicanos* of different classes can speak on equitable terms. Read as "heterodiscursive and dialogical" by Rosaura Sánchez, and as texts that "articulate an interregional and even interclass sense of individual and communal disjuncture" by Genaro Padilla, the *testimonios* gave voice to Californios who had lived through the upheaval of the Mexican-American War and its subsequent displacement of Californio society.[23] The narratives document vastly different experiences: Apolinaria Lorenzana recalls being an orphan in the San Diego mission ("Memorias de Apolinaria Lorenzana"); and Mariano Vallejo's nearly-one-hundred-year history of California ("Recuerdos historicios") includes his time as *comandante-general*, head of one of the Alta California presidios. But as both Sánchez and Padilla discuss, many of the *testimonios*, especially those of the men, record the experiences of the ruling class; likewise, the majority of the women's narratives come from those "from prominent families whose reminiscences were recorded primarily because of their relationship to influential men."[24] *Testimonio* subjects engaged in their own "othering" in their texts, particularly as concerned African Americans and Native Americans.[25] Thus, even as a heteroglossic, heterodiscursive, dialogical collection that implicitly and explicitly interrogates the contexts of its production, an all-too-familiar discourse concerning whiteness runs through the *testimonios*. Even those who held no particular position of prestige before the war testify to their whiteness, and thus their racial superiority. Eulalia Pérez, housekeeper of the mission at San Gabriel, begins her *testimonio* with the following information: "I, Eulalia Pérez, was born in the Presidio of Loreto in Baja California. My father's name was Diego Pérez, and he was employed in the Navy Department of said Presidio; my mother's name was Antonia Rosalía Cota. Both were pure white."[26]

A complete cataloging of all the appeals to whiteness (read: Spain, read: racial superiority, read: class superiority) that pervade early Mexican American literature is not only impossible, it is not the point. Whether or not various *Mexicano* communities were or were not "actually" Spanish also should emerge as less important than the immense affective and sociopolitical currency that such a narrative held, and continues to hold. For all of this would matter little were it not apparent that such demonstrations of whiteness conflict with the ethos of the Chicano movement, and that in this conflict writers are made to pass as a means of building genealogy. Case in point: In the beginning of *My History, Not Yours: The Formation of Mexican American Autobiography* (1993), Genaro Padilla recounts for his readers the process he underwent in choosing the subjects of his study. His preface records his conflicted feelings toward his subject matter:

> As I read into and around the social and historical events represented in many of the narratives, I found that I was both fascinated and troubled by some of the people I study here because they were members of the landed classes, ricos *for whom my* antepasados *might have labored, people who would have excluded my* bisabuelos *from their world. I more than once decided to abandon the project for political reasons. I would not spend my intellectual life arguing on behalf of people I probably wouldn't have liked in person.*[27]

What eventually reconciles Padilla to the (erstwhile) socioeconomic status of his subjects (including Cleofas Jaramillo) is their disenfranchisement: "But the more I read . . . the more I came to realize that by the end of the nineteenth century just about the only estate left to any of our *antepasados* was one situated in the geography of the past."[28] Bereft of most of that which Padilla understands as marking their class—political power, social prominence, and property—the writers of these nineteenth-century narratives become more amenable to his political concerns. But what are those concerns? By asserting that such early writers and *ricos* were eventually as disempowered as his own ancestors, Padilla implies that differences between them are muted enough to be set aside. The very act of noting such conflict belies Padilla's claims, of course; obviously Jaramillo and others like her were never disenfranchised of their cultural capital vis-à-vis their own communities. (*Cultural capital* is a well-worn term but nonetheless apropos here.) A multivalent comprehension of class illuminates the affective power that these early writings retain. The loss of once-held capital bears only the most arbitrary relationship to the expression of a racialized class as nature. Thus, even as the material elements of class dominance are repeatedly catalogued and mourned—"our ancestors" lost land, money, and political power—the naturalized markings of their class culture are rarely interrogated as such. Why locate the "estate . . . of our *antepasados* . . . in the geography of the past," when it is painfully clear that their cultural estate remains fairly intact in our *present*?

Inherent in the naming of "our *antepasados*," however, is the notion that the practice of scholarship is expressly about saving "our" own—"our *antepasados*"—and hence literary history becomes a family matter. The implicit familiality underlying such desire does not represent an inherently questionable sentiment, but it bears the potential for marginalizing or invalidating any writer or group who fails to fit an *unacknowledged* model of genealogical reproduction (working-class, more *indígeno* than Spanish, almost certainly heterosexual). Given that Chicanas and Latinas as a whole, especially lesbian Latinas, have histories of struggling to be recognized within larger representational realms, no fantasies of the group-as-family should remain unanalyzed. Jaramillo and Co. are initially put through a test of kinship that they fail: just as Genaro Padilla is certain that they would have excluded his ancestors from their world, he is tempted to exclude them from his by abandoning his project. As such, the former Mexican elite becomes unwittingly equivalent with contemporary Chicano intellectuals: each possesses the power of willful exclusion and subordination.

Tey Diana Rebolledo, discussing the same writers (Jaramillo, Cabeza de Baca, and Otero-Warren), begins by ceding their discomforting classist and racist tendencies but quickly moves to tracing their "strategies of resistance," so that she can offer this final summation: "Contemporary Chicanas could not ask for better ancestors."[29] Hence the paradox of twentieth-century "Hispanic" identity politics, as seen in Padilla's recounting of his decision-making process, and in Rebolledo's reassurance. Anglo North American conceptions of ethnic and national identity, as well as political and social events along the U.S.-Mexico border, have made of Padilla, Rebolledo, and Jaramillo one people, one *raza*. And perhaps, if one accepts the attestations of democracy by writers like Cabeza de Baca, they were all along. But such critical misgivings imply that *raza* should be (like) *familia*, and persons like Jaramillo are obviously not (like) *familia*.

Thus, the question of how early Mexican American writers assimilate into a Chicano literary history is one of how personae register within the body politic, and I do mean *politic*, of Chicano Studies. But because the foundational principles that gird Chicano Studies often reflect the political ideologies and activist experiences of the critics themselves, that body politic doubles as a body familial: the discursive construction of ethnic identity as familial membership. Hence the perturbed reactions to early writings, and the oft-recited disenfranchisements that quite literally fit early writers into and for a genealogy. Erlinda Gonzales-Berry and Charles Tatum, discussing the contents for the second volume of essays to accompany the Recovering the U.S. Hispanic Literary Heritage selections, introduce a section of essays devoted to María Amparo Ruiz de Burton with the following:

Initially, the so-called "shapers" of the Recovery Project—including [us]—were eager to privilege those texts that met our present day expectations: resist cultural assimilation or demonstrate working class alliances, that is, the predominant cultural nationalist ideology of the Chicano Movement.[30]

Resistance, then, represents the sine qua non of Chicano literary production. Yet these early writings demonstrate that resistance comprises a multivalent and polymorphous trait: a critique of one national power may very well be constructed through discourses that reaffirm the social abjection of fellow marginalized groups. For José Aranda, the ideological conflicts between early Mexican American literature and the ethos of the Chicano Movement "challenge the usefulness of resistance theory when applied to writers who preceded the Chicano Movement."[31] I suggest that it is not merely the utility of resistance theory that is at stake but the notion of a genealogy of Mexican American literature as a whole: a history of familial descent and inheritance. Early writings are not simply not resistant in the same ways as post-1960s writings; they're not Chicano. Hence it makes sense within literary history, at the beginning of a new millennium, to conceptualize (to begin or to continue, as the case may be) Chicano as a style rather than as an ethnic identity, a movement that was not only preceded but may very well be succeeded by something altogether different: Post Chicano? For to pass off "our" *antepasados* as directly related, or, as Ramón Saldívar termed it, sharing the same function of literature, will not work: it is the very function of early literature to distinguish between us and them, even among the present conception of "us." In that construction, early writers' class franchise resurrects itself, and will continue to do so until such conflations as I have described cease to be. Discursive power is no less real than a land grant, especially now that none of us have one. And onto whom would we be passing these allegedly powerless *antepasados* off, except ourselves? To return to Tey Diana Rebolledo's endorsement of early women writers ("Contemporary Chicanas could not ask for better ancestors"), to continue to search for our literary past as if it were our familial past suggests that we are trying to pass muster with the dead, or make the dead pass muster with us. Both are ultimately futile exercises.

The public construction of María Amparo Ruiz de Burton as a preeminent example of genteel Mexican whiteness is a process of long standing. Bancroft recounts the story of her courtship with Captain Henry S. Burton in his book *California Pastoral* (1888), while Rosaura Sánchez and Beatrice Pita note that the couple's relationship formed the subject of a series of newspaper articles in the 1930s in California.[32] One of the articles, "Enemy Lovers," describes Ruiz de Burton as the archetypal lady:

> *Those who used to know her remember her lovely, small feet with their high curved arches and her grace that was perfection itself in the dance. Her good nature overcame her native hauteur, and she was thoroughly beloved by those who best knew her. True aristocracy she possessed and all the weapons of charm, a beauty which had constancy beyond extreme youth's unstudied smiles, a sweet voice, a gracious manner, an eager interest in the interests of her companions. Her mind was richly endowed, though its cultivation began with her engagement to Col. Burton.*[33]

The hyperbolic portrait of Ruiz de Burton by Winifred Davidson, a 1930s southern California columnist, pictures her as etiquette-book ideal: as both a collection of enviable parts ("her lovely, small feet") and a unified whole (she is "good," "true," "perfection itself," "constan[t]," "sweet," "gracious" and "eager"). In fact, she represents the exact opposite of the stereotypical Mexican who remains in California as her (unfortunate, and general) descendant. Written during the Great Depression, the articles appeared at a historical moment when *Mexicano*s found themselves once again under siege in their own land. Davidson speaks to Ruiz de Burton's "indigenous nature," as it were: "her native *hauteur*" and her "true aristocracy," in Bourdieuan sense, signal traits inborn and not acquired. Radically above and beyond the populace that now represents her, Ruiz de Burton stands as a natural noble whose class is a function of her whiteness. Her hauteur and her aristocracy genealogically place her apart from contemporary Mexican Americans; the words signify a discreet existence.

Ruiz de Burton's unique place in Mexican American literature—as far as is known, the only nineteenth-century writer to have published novels in English—has bestowed a heavy burden upon her work: to represent the hopes, desires, and outrage of her Chicano progeny. As Rosaura Sánchez, Beatrice Pita, and others have demonstrated, Ruiz de Burton's work "carries out an aggressive demystification of a series of [U.S.] national foundational ideologies.[34] Yet the author was hardly "a Dolores Huerta of the United Farm Workers Union or a Gloria Anzaldúa of the borderlands in nineteenth-century clothes," as José Aranda aptly describes her (573). Rather, she can only be read unproblematically as a resistant foremother:

if one ignores her colonialist history as a monarchist and her characterization of herself as a daughter of the Enlightenment, and only if one discounts the rhetorical strategies in her novels that affirm a colonialism that would return both her and her community to a position of material and social power over people of color and the working class. (573)

Ruiz de Burton's novels, then, perform cultural work similar to many of her contemporaries (the *testimonio* subjects) and her earliest descendants (Jaramillo and Co.). I include *Who Would Have Thought It?* in this interrogation of Mexican whiteness because, unlike Aranda, I disagree that "the novel is only superficially about a Spanish-Mexican girl adopted by a New England family a decade before the Civil War. Its true subject, as Sánchez and Pita argue, is a critique . . . of the United States' colonial enterprise in North America" (573). Or rather, I respectfully submit that the "superficial," primary layer of Ruiz de Burton's allegory holds great import for comprehending the intersections of whiteness and class that pervade early Mexican American literature, intersections that, as we have seen, implicitly and explicitly critique *los Americanos*. Beginning with a story of forced passing, *Who Would Have Thought It?* dramatizes the conceptual foreclosure of the potential of *mestizaje*; it unnarrates the cultural space of *lo chicano*. Oddly enough, the first sign of this unmaking occurs when the heroine makes her entrance in blackface.

In fact, the chapter devoted to Lola Medina's introduction is entitled "The Little Black Girl," and other characters assume that she is the descendant of "'Indians or negroes, or both.'"[35] The novel opens with the return of Dr. Norval, a New England geologist doing research in California, to his home after an absence of four years. Besides bringing his findings and samples of western geologic specimens, Dr. Norval also returns with unexpected company: a ten-year-old Mexican girl named Lola. Despite explanations that the girl is the wealthy orphan of respectable Mexicans of Spanish ancestry, the other members of the Norval family—particularly Mrs. Norval, a self-described "abolitionist"—persist in referring to Lola as "the little black girl," "a nigger," and an "Indian."

The novel pursues two interrelated story lines: the social progress of Lola within a purportedly liberal Northern establishment, including a romance with the eldest Norval son; and the fortunes of the family and their circle during the Civil War. Dr. Norval's protestations notwithstanding, the darkness of the girl's skin is taken as authoritative; the text of her body ostensibly reads more reliably than his speech. Her allegedly visible African and/or indigenous ancestry ("Any one can see that much of her history," says older daughter Ruth Norval [17]) initiates a practice of racialized misreadings (not to say misleadings) that, even when explained nearly one hundred pages into the novel, continue to linguistically mark the tension between Lola and her WASP adoptive family. Her skin stained by the Indians who captured her and her mother, Lola unwillingly passes as a racialized Other. But even after her skin reverts to its unblemished original whiteness, those who most dislike Lola continue to refer to her as black, Indian, and thus inauthentically white. "Whoever heard of a blue-eyed Mexican?" asks the Reverend Major Hackwell, in a passage now wryly recognizable from Fabiola Cabeza de Baca's writing eighty years later (253). What it means to pass against one's will, then, has everything to do with contesting U.S. state power and its colonial enterprise. Passing always entails passage; yet some passages, even amidst meetings of Anglo, Mexican, African, and Native, remain unthinkable.

Ruiz de Burton begins by suggesting that the presence of racial/ethnic difference within her New England community is literally unspeakable. Mrs. Norval's words when she first sees Lola are expressively inexpressive: "'I don't mean the boxes in the large wagon. I mean the—the—that—the red shawl,' stammered Mrs. Norval" (14). Nevertheless, racial difference emerges as very speakable indeed. Her new adoptive family describes Lola as "a little girl very black indeed": she is twice referred to as a "specimen," as "a nigger girl," and is accused by Mrs. Norval of carrying "disease" (16–17, 91). Yet, as various Norval family members delight in pointing out, Lola lacks other features that they expect with dark skin. Her "red and prettily-cut lips" confuse, because "negroes' lips are not like those," while her "her little hand" and "all her features" are pronounced "pretty," "well cut," and "superb" (16–17). (One daughter places her in the animal kingdom, postulating that "the next specimen will be a baboon . . . for papa's samples don't improve" [16].) Ruiz de Burton links color to disease consistently: Lola later confides that "when the dye began to wear off, and my skin got all spotted, [Mrs. Norval] sent me away, because she thought I had some cutaneous disease, and she said that Mr. Hackwell said that perhaps I belonged to the 'Pintos,' and my skin was naturally spotted" (100).

Ruiz de Burton caustically indicts Anglo American provinciality and stupidity when she shows Lola being called a Pinto Indian or "an Aztec" (20). Yet the stupidity lies not merely in ignorance and misinformation: as with Cabeza de Baca's settler, the Anglo population of *Who Would Have Thought It?* lacks skill in the art of physiognomy. They consistently fail to recognize whiteness, especially when it passes as black. Yet it is *exactly* in that moment of passing that an ability to recognize Lola's whiteness will manifest class membership as being either part of Lola's sphere or apart from it. Ruiz de Burton compiles her signs of racialized class, both physical and moral, but the vast majority of characters cannot associate them with what appears to be obvious epidermal truth.[36] Lola confirms that such ignorant racism mortifies her; worse, however, is the thought that even those Anglos seemingly equal to her in class will prove physiognomically challenged. She tells her lover Julian that "though I didn't care whether I was thought black or white by others, I hated to think that you *might* suppose I was Indian or black" (100). Her avowal of general indifference rings false, however. Ruiz de Burton forces her heroine to pass unwillingly as black and Indian for the first third of the novel; in the face of these racist misidentifications, Lola declines to answer. She affects silence not because she is beyond her tormentors but because she is above them: "not liking your manner, she disdains to answer your question," remarks Dr. Norval on one of Lola's stony responses (20). The moral superiority of Mexican whiteness once again reveals itself; however, written on a young girl's body and in her scornful looks, it proves to be a text particularly difficult for others to read.

In fact, only Anglo Americans possess this unfortunate inability to decipher physiognomy; "savage" Indians recognize and acknowledge European superiority immediately in Ruiz de Burton's novel. The story of Lola's captivity and orphanage doubles as the story of her mother, a woman of "self-sacrificing devotion" who arranges her only child's escape at the price of her own mournful death (36). The chief of the tribe that holds Lola and Señora Medina, according to Dr. Norval, "seemed to feel the greatest respect for the *ña Hala* (which in the language of these Indians, means *my lady*), and all the Indians the same, obeying her slightest wish" (34–35). Mexican whiteness, even when literally under siege, commands social distinction from inferiors. Señora Medina brilliantly fits the nineteenth-century ideal of the selfless mother, advancing her child's prospects at the cost of her own. Likewise, her death follows the social and implied sexual subjugation she endures at the hands of the unspecified natives. "[S]he did not wish to see her family now, after ten years of such life as had been forced upon her," writes Ruiz de Burton; "she only wished to save her daughter from a similar fate, and then to lie down and die" (35). And so she does:

> In a miserable Indian hut lay the dying lady. The surroundings were cheerless enough to kill any civilized woman, but the bedclothes, [Dr. Norval] noticed were as white as snow, and everything about her was clean and tidy. "Thank God, Lolita is away from those horrid savages! Please do not forget that she must be baptized and brought up a Roman Catholic. . . ."
>
> Poor woman! That was a clear case of "broken heart." She died of sheer grief, and nothing else. (36–37)

The *ña Hala* rebuilds upper-class domesticity to the utmost of her ability: "clean and tidy" in the midst of savage territory, her linen "as white as snow" despite the fact that, as Ruiz de Burton has told us, her skin is stained black. This combination of "cheerless" captivity and sexual servitude at the hands of savages taints Sra. Medina more dramatically than her daughter; her renunciation of rescue and her death while still painted symbolize, in an admittedly heavy-handed manner, that once miscegenation occurs, white women can never be made wholly white again. In other words, oh intellectually obtuse Anglo reader, "going native" literally kills.

Thus passing becomes a matter of life and death: to pass forcibly as what you despise, to pass into a realm where the differences are now different, unintelligible and yet all-determining. Anglo inability to read well physiognomically is primarily of consequence to Lola; it is she who "suffers" in this forced passing. If her new society is composed of uncultivated, racist Anglos whose opinion she ostensibly scorns, what of it to them? All social power, including control of Lola's vast fortune in gold and gems, lies with bigoted yokels. Not all whiteness is created equal, and Ruiz de Burton questions the matchup of Anglo social supremacy and Mexican moral superiority. In making her symbol of Mexican whiteness a ten-year-old orphan, Ruiz de Burton merely emphasizes, but does not exaggerate, the extent to which a displaced minority now is subject to the whims of a foreign state power. The belief that Californios, Tejanos, *Nuevomexicanos*, and others represented "children" under the care of a paternal, yet alien government held great currency for Ruiz de Burton's displaced generation, and was most strongly echoed by contemporary Mariano Guadalupe Vallejo:

El idioma que ahora se habla en nuestro país, las leyes que nos rigen y las caras con que diariamente tropezamos, son nuevas para nosotros los dueños del suelo y por supuesto antagónicas a nuestros intereses y derechos, pero ¿qué importa eso al conquistador? ¡él quiere el bien propio y no el nuestro! Cosa que yo considero muy natural en los individuos pero que vitupero en un gobierno que había prometido respetar y hacer respetar nuestros derechos y tratranos como a hijos, pero ¿a qué bueno quejarnos? El mal está hecho y ya no tiene remedio.[37]

[The language that is now spoken in this country, the laws that govern us and the faces that we meet daily, are new to us, the rulers of this earth, and of course they are antagonistic to our interests and rights, but what does that matter to the conqueror? He wants what is good for him, and not what is good for us! Which is something I consider very natural in individuals, but which I detest in a government that had promised to respect our rights, and to make others respect them, and to treat us as children, but what good does it do to complain? The evil is done, and now there is no remedy.]

Fallen from "rulers of the earth" to "children," Vallejo and Ruiz de Burton reconceptualize their status within a new body politic. As with Cabeza de Baca, true democracy takes the form of a willing extension of familial spheres: the interests and rights of Mexican Americans should be looked after by the U.S. government, just as parents look after the interests of their young. Yet, given the treatment that that government metes out to its other official "wards"—the enslaved Africans of its paternalistic "peculiar institution," and the "savages" of its decimated native populations—Vallejo, Ruiz de Burton, and others of their ilk have everything to fear in becoming yet another charge in the social chancery system of the United States.

Hence Lola's young, orphaned, and stained self: this heroine, and the society she represents, have survived the fall, and bear its taint. But more so, every time the words *Indian* and *nigger* strike her skin, her society watches her fall, over and over again. (To watch her pass is to watch her fall.) Ruiz de Burton illuminates the conflation of the literal and the figurative when Lola's stain begins to wear off: white skin showing through patches of brown manifests the "disease" of color and makes visible the wrong inherent in this mixture. Yet when Lola returns to her pure whiteness and remains "the little black girl" in status, Anglo racial politics reveal themselves: race doesn't equal class (*al modo Mexicano*), but class does equal race. Thus, what makes Lola a savage and a nigger doesn't lie in her skin at all—at least, not anymore.

It does, however, lie in the skin of those whose origins remain unarticulated except within the "savage" confines of death: the Mexican *mestizo* population, the majority of its folk, Spanish *and* Indian, and alternately African and Jewish as well. The *mestizaje* that mythically gives birth to Mexico—Hernan Cortés's relations with a native woman, la Malinche—passes unwritten in *Who Would Have Thought It?*, vanishing in Sra. Medina's martyrlike death and Lola's timely escape. To mix Spanish and Indian in Ruiz de Burton's novel produces destruction, not birth; it stains and ostracizes, blotches and victimizes, goes away but never quite. In safely delivering her heroine at novel's end into the arms of her (Austrian/Spanish/Mexican white) father and (Anglo) husband Julian, Ruiz de Burton rejects the Mexican body as authoritative text, physically surrounding Lola with other whitenesses and civilly enforcing them, materializing a whiteness for her that is outside herself, as both social and legal reality. A discursive space where *mestizaje*, and hence, *lo chicano*, might take shape, is found only at the limits of Ruiz de Burton's political imagination, peopled by discreet communities of savages and Sambos, the fantasmatic figures of passing fancies. Thus the morphology of Ruiz de Burton's historical moment vanishes: those who never had land to lose, those lynched in Texas and California, those who launched a Chicano Movement, those who react with anger to these writings, all unwritten. In this unnarration Ruiz de Burton's cultural estate recomposes itself, nonetheless real for being the text of a novel rather than the text of a land grant. For all Mexican *mestizos*, this, also, is what it means to pass against your will.

Notes

1. Fabiola Cabeza de Baca, *We Fed Them Cactus* (Albuquerque: U of New Mexico P, 1994), 148, 149.

2. Unfortunately, I have been unable to offer consistency to the reader in the matter of italicizing or not italicizing Spanish words. Some of the writers and scholars whom I quote do italicize, and others do not. I have used italics myself, since the majority of those whom I've quoted from do so as well; but the reader is not meant to interpret anything (certainly not sloppiness!) from the occasional shift. Likewise, I have focused upon texts easily available through university libraries, and, where applicable, upon texts for which Spanish and English versions exist.

3. Antonio María Osio, *The History of Alta California* (Madison: U Wisconsin P, 1996); Jovita González, *Dew on the Thorn* (Houston: Arte Público Press, 1997); Gonzalez, *Caballero* (College Station: Texas A and M UP, 1996); Doris Meyer, *Speaking for Themselves: Neomexicano Cultural Identity and the Spanish-Language Press, 1880–1920* (Albuquerque: U of New Mexico P, 1994); A. Gabriel Meléndez, *So All Is Not Lost: The Poetics of Print in Nuevomexicano Communities, 1834–1958* (Albuquerque: U of New Mexico P, 1997); Rosaura Sánchez, *Telling Identities: The Californio testimonios* (Minneapolis: U Minnesota P, 1995); Genaro Padilla, *My History, Not Yours: The Formation of Mexican American Autobiography* (Madison: U Wisconsin P, 1993).

4. The Recovering the U.S. Hispanic Literary Heritage Project includes works by and on Mexican, Cuban, and Puerto Rican Americans among others; hence the umbrella term *Hispanic*. Both Doris Meyer's and Gabriel Meléndez's studies focus upon New Mexico and use the name *Neomexicano* in their subtitles; Rosaura Sánchez's book on

the *testimonios* concerns California and Californios; and Genaro Padilla distinguishes between Chicano and Mexican American in his title.

5. Juan Bruce-Novoa, *Chicano Poetry: A Response to Chaos* (Austin: U of Texas P, 1982), 3.

6. Ramon Saldívar, *Chicano Narrative: The Dialectics of Difference* (Madison: U Wisconsin P, 1990), 7, 10.

7. In *Criticism in the Borderlands: Studies in Chicano Literature, Culture, and Ideology* (Durham: Duke UP 1991), Héctor Calderón and José David Saldívar write that "individual scholarly research combined with the interests of a bicultural, working-class community" describes not only the works of pioneers like Américo Paredes and Jovita González, but also "helped mold Chicano studies in the seventies" (5). Tey Diana Rebolledo confirms these delineations of the contexts of Chicano literature. In the beginning of *Women Singing in the Snow: A Cultural Analysis of Chicano Literature* (Tucson: U of Arizona P, 1995), Rebolledo writes that "many Chicana writers, although not all, are from working-class families. They may be the first in their families to be educated" (x). In a more poetic vein, Rebolledo explains the need for a cultural analysis of this literature, stating that this approach "explores the meaning of living a border existence: existing in worlds that may contain you but are never completely yours" (x). However, she also later criticizes "a monolithic concept" of Mexican American culture as inherently resistant, and even says of Cabeza de Baca, Otero-Warren, and Jaramillo, that "contemporary Chicanas could not ask for better ancestors" (47). Older, foundational works of Chicano literary and cultural scholarship, ranging from Américo Paredes's *With His Pistol in His Hand* (Austin: U of Texas P, 1958) to Cherríe Moraga and Gloria Anzaldúa's *This Bridge Called My Back* (Watertown: Persephone Press, 1981) also reflect the commitment of many Chicano scholars to support voices that emerge from the ranks of the working class or working poor.

8. Saldívar, 12. Later in *Chicano Narrative*, Saldívar discusses the disavowal of Mexican and/or *mestizo* identity perpetrated by some New Mexican citizens as part of his look at the function of history in the writings of Rudolfo Anaya and Ron Arias (116–118). In this section the interrelated workings of racist and classist ideologies becomes clear, brilliantly revealing the stakes and contexts of shaping Chicano literature in one particularly classed form.

9. I refer to the series of armed conflicts along the border, beginning in the 1890s

and culminating toward the end of the Mexican Revolution, which involved Mexican and U.S. citizens, Anglos and Latinos. These conflicts aggravated existing tensions between the two groups and ended with an estimated five thousand *Mexicanos* dead. For an account of these conflicts explicitly set within the context of writing Mexican American history and culture, see José E. Limón on ethnologist, folklorist, and army officer John Gregory Bourke, *Dancing with the Devil: Society and Cultural Poetics in Mexican-American South Texas* (Madison: U of Wisconsin P, 1994).

10. See Wayne Moquin and Charles Van Doren, *A Documentary History of the Mexican Americans* (New York: Bantam Books, 1971), 253. Obviously, the contemporaneous existence of lynching of both African and Mexican Americans points to their similar symbolic and political statures within Anglo American societies of that time.

11. Pierre Bourdieu, *Distinction: A Social Critique of the Judgement of Taste*, trans. Richard Nice (Cambridge: Harvard UP, 1984), 68.

12. F. Arturo Rosales, "'Fantasy Heritage' Reexamined: Race and Class in the Writings of the Bandini Family and Other Californios, 1828–1965," in Erlinda Gonzales-Berry and Chuck Tatum, *Recovering the U.S. Hispanic Literary Heritage*, vol. 2, (Houston: Arte Público Press, 1996), 981–982. Whether or not specific communities actually were in large part descended from Spaniards is a matter of debate. What is more important for the purposes of this essay (and far more interesting) is the existence of this narrative of origins, and the various means of its deployment. Also, although Rosales's essay focuses upon Californios and the writings of the Bandini family, I would argue that the "Fantasy Heritage" flourishes in the works of non-Californios as well.

13. See Article XI of the Treaty of Guadalupe Hidalgo. Here I consult the text as reprinted in Iris H. W. Engstrand et al., *Culture y Cultura: Consequences of the U.S.-Mexican War, 1846–1848* (Los Angeles: Autry Museum of Western Heritage, 1998): 120–121.

14. Osio on the Kodiak confrontation, 39–42. His comments on mestizo Mexicans associate them with the arrival of social discord: "An infantry company from Tepic and seventy-five men from the Mazatlán squadron were dispatched. They arrived toward the end of the year 1819. From the moment that the troops from Tepic set foot on the beach of Monterey, robberies, excesses peculiar to coarse men, and depraved practices entirely unfamiliar to the californios began to be experienced" (53). Osio continues briefly in this vein.

15. *Gente de razón* literally means "people of reason" and is used to signify decency, respectability, and "good breeding." Hence it reveals the ideological connections and conflations made among the possession of reason, morality, and residence within a particular social class. *Castilla la Vieja*, or "old Spain," refers to the heyday of Spain's imperialism.

The *testimonios* obviously are not writings in the same sense as something like Fabiola Cabeza de Baca's memoirs. I use them here interchangeably with published writings, both because of their importance to Mexican American literary history and because of the similar constructions of whiteness that the dictated and the "written" texts contain. In searching for a pattern of such constructions, discussing differences in the conditions of production for these texts would require more consideration than I can provide here. It is also a subject explored at length by Rosaura Sánchez and, to a lesser extent, Genaro Padilla, to whose works I point interested readers.

16. Sánchez, 59.

17. Nina Otero-Warren, *Old Spain in Our Southwest* (Chicago: Rio Grande Press, 1962), 9.

18. Cleofas M. Jaramillo, *Shadows of the Past (Sombras del pasado)* (Sante Fe, New Mexico: Ancient City Press, n.d.), 15.

19. Cabeza de Baca, 60.

20. Ibid., 61.

21. Such fantasies are "purely" Spanish in one sense, however: their relation to Spain's own historical obsessions with *sangre pura*, and the ability of families to keep their bloodlines free from miscegenation with Arabs and Jews.

22. Meléndez, 108–109.

23. Sánchez, 32; Padilla, 10.

24. Padilla, 117.

25. See Sánchez, 57.

26. Eulalia Pérez, *An Old Woman and Her Recollections*, in Carlos N. Hijar et al., *Three Memoirs of Mexican California* (Berkeley: Friends of the Bancroft Library, 1988), 74.

27. Padilla, x.

28. Ibid.

29. Tey Diana Rebolledo, *Singing in the Snow: A Cultural Analysis of Chicana Literature* (Tucson: U of Arizona P, 1995), 32, 47. It should be apparent by now that the majority of the writers on whom I concentrate are women. This reflects a confluence of circumstances: that many of these women wrote in English, and hence that their works are in print, and that many of the critics I mention here have written about them; and also, that I find their work interesting. It is not meant to imply in any way that women writers were more invested than their male counterparts in the types of racist and classist discourses I examine here. It would be foolhardy, however—and frankly, bad scholarship—to ignore unpleasant tendencies in writers in order to "rescue" or recover them.

30. Erlinda Gonzales-Berry and Chuck Tatum, introduction to *Recovering the U.S. Hispanic Literary Heritage*, vol. 2, (Houston: Arte Público Press, 1996), 14.

31. José F. Aranda Jr., "Contradictory Impulses: María Amparo Ruiz de Burton, Resistance Theory, and the Politics of Chicano/a Studies." *American Literature* 70 (3):551–579.

32. Rosaura Sánchez and Beatrice Pita, introduction to María Amparo Ruiz de Burton, *The Squatter and the Don* (Houston: Arte Público Press, 1992), 10.

33. Winifred Davidson, "Enemy Lovers," *Los Angeles Times Sunday Magazine*, October 16, 1932, 5.

34. Sánchez and Pita, introduction to María Amparo Ruiz de Burton, *Who Would Have Thought It?* (Houston: Arte Público Press, 1995), viii.

35. María Amparo Ruiz de Burton, *Who Would Have Thought It?* (Houston: Arte Público Press, 1995),17.

36. Significantly, the two characters who do believe in Lola's whiteness from the beginning are Dr. Norval and his son Julian, both well educated in European cultures, well traveled, and with a "most unnatural liking of foreigners" (11). Although initially they occupy the same economic class as Ruiz de Burton's other Anglo characters, their education and taste reveal that they *possess* class, which the others lack.

37. Mariano Guadalupe Vallejo, *Recuerdos históricos y personales tocante a la Alta California*, in Rosaura Sánchez et al., *Nineteenth Century Californio Testimonials*, CRITICA Monograph Series (Berkeley: Regents of the University of California, 1994), 139. Translation mine.

4   Passing Lines

Immigration and the Performance of American Identity

Brad Epps

> Migration is an awareness of death.
>
> —ALBERTO SANDOVAL SÁNCHEZ

Movement and Its Limits

Contemporary critical discourse in the United States is rife with signs of movement: labile subjects, multidirectional identities, transgressive plays, and plural positionings; displacements, disseminations, and destabilizations; goings and comings, usually, but not always, out.[1] Its tone, often as not, is ludic, privileging a variety of parodic ploys, some more "sophisticated" and "serious" than others. The nomad, the schizophrene, and the cyborg are some of its most imposing roles. The immigrant may well be another, but one whose painful reality, whose historicity, seems more resistant to rhetorical restylization. Or perhaps, more insistent *in* restylization: for with the immigrant, bodies, words, gestures, attitudes, and deeds are objects of governmental speculation, national and international regulation, and, as I hope to make clear, diverse individual and collective (re)stylizations, fashionings, or performances. The immigrant's technical skills, psychosomatic condition, spatial relations, and performativity are not, of course, beyond a certain postmodern theorization, but they also have a practical importance whose ultimate, but by no means only, measure is death. Such organizations as Americas Watch, Amnesty International, and the American Friends Service Committee point to practices of physical and verbal abuse that hound immigrants and immigration. Together, they give a more somber twist to the differences between a land of freedom and a land of persecution, complicating their borders and, as it were, lessening their distances. Still, differences and distances persist, on and around the border, motivating a welter of acts that are not limited to those of the government or, for that matter, to those of the organizations that monitor and criticize it. These other immigration acts outstrip organized activity and established agencies and implicate individuals and groups: the ways they move, talk, and look, the stories they tell, the lines they pass.

It is with an eye to the acts and agency of immigrants themselves that I will consider, in the pages that follow, the rhetoric and reality of mobility; the contested significance of immigration, refuge, asylum, and citizenship; and some aspects of the history of immigration, before passing, finally, into the problem of passing proper. I do so with some ambivalence, for while I can sympathize with the desire to "transcend or redefine the conventional boundaries that have constrained our study and understanding"[2] of national differences; or with the urge to "develop new images, new coordinates, a series of new and more effective maps";[3] or with the call "for a position that is less *theoretical* than *theatrical*" that would allow one to "rejoice in the shared etymology of the terms: a space to see and be seen,"[4] I will be insisting on the *difficulty*, here and now, of such utopian moves: transcendent, innovative, and ever so theatrical.

Boundaries continue to constrain, and to constrain, furthermore, through the development of new and effective maps and of spaces (in which) to see and be seen. The causes for hope and celebration may be numerous, but so are those for caution, sadness, frustration, anger, and continued activism. As border patrol officers and related agents use increasingly advanced equipment, detailed maps, powerful methods of surveillance, and anxious ways of determining, as Debbie Nathan puts it, who has "the Look" of legality and who does not, the signs of movement that suffuse contemporary critical discourse encounter all sorts of obstacles.[5] No doubt, the existence of impediments, of concrete walls, barbed-wire fences, armed guards, and bureaucratic irregularities, of a generalized sense of suspicion, "nativism, xenophobia, and even hysteria,"[6] motivates, however indirectly, many of the utopian-inspired moves cited above. Activism, and the criticism with which it is associated, can scarcely dispense with utopian gestures. But it is important, I believe, to keep the "no place" of utopia (*ou-topos*) in touch, however tensely, with places whose reality is not always, or for everyone, susceptible to conceptual doubt and creative displacement.

(Im)migration is a phenomenon of movement, obviously, but of movement that does not dispense with obstacles, restrictions, foreclosures, and blockages, with places doggedly in place. All of the speculation in the world on multinationality, transnationality, postnationality, and so on does not gainsay the current division of the world into nations whose borders continue to be marked, quite profoundly, by violence and death. Alberto Sandoval has good reason to say that "migration is an awareness of death."[7] I would add only that migration is also an unawareness of death, a forgetting, bracketing, or denying of death on the part of many nonmigrants and even, at times, on the part of many migrants themselves. Some such forgetting may be fortunate, necessary even to something remotely similar to happiness, but it may also be quite perilous. So much, after all, depends on the subject in question, not merely whether one is, or has been, a migrant or nonmigrant, but also what kind of (non)migrant one is. Whatever the rhetoric of conventions, treaties, and protocols, not all (non)migrants are equal; national origin, class position, political affiliations, race, ethnicity, sexuality, religion, education, health, and a lengthy etcetera make a significant difference.[8]

I will have a great deal to say about these signs of identity, all arguably constructed, and yet I would like to note, here at the outset, that Sandoval's linkage of migration and death is linked, for me at least, to Cornel West's assertion that "death is not a construct."[9] I take West's assertion at its most scandalously naive, a willful, humanist-inflected rejection of a cocksure academic constructivism that is hardly devoid of essentialist turns of its own. Death *is* a construct, of course, inasmuch as it is the site and subject of intense symbolic investment from ritualized mourning to melancholy monumentalization. Death is a construct, moreover, inasmuch as it is realized, all too often, through the deployment of the very categories—such as race, gender, and ethnicity—that West himself recognizes as constructed. But death is *not* a construct in a more devastatingly simple sense, a sense that perhaps escapes those accustomed to privileging thought as anything but simple. Be that as it may, the scars and bruises, the beatings, killings, and deaths, together with the impediments to movement, are critical to any reflection on immigration.

No less critical, however, are the ways in which movement is sustained and bodies protected. The acts and agencies of (im)migrants, as I have indicated, are on this score fundamental. This may seem self-evident, but the very fact that "immigration act" typically refers to governmental initiatives rather than to the initiatives of immigrants themselves should not be discounted. Accordingly, I will be arguing for an understanding of immigration that holds that borders are never simple geopolitical facts, nor are their crossings. This is in no way to deny the spatiotemporal dimensions of immigration, for border crossings may indeed be understood as set in space or occurring in time, as a place or an event, or indeed as both. They involve, inevitably, geography and history. And yet they also involve performative maneuvers, speech and body acts by which subjects, especially when subjected to the objectifying gaze of an official examiner, situate and narrate themselves. The purpose of such "self-situating" narratives is to allow the narrator to go unnoticed, to stay alive, or even to prosper, to allow him or her to gain entry, to get by, to pass.[10] Attending to the more involute and intimate aspects of geography and history, to personal positionings and stories, to the institutional and noninstitutional intersections of humanity and nationality, I will be recasting border crossings as passing lines—in the sense of telling tales—in order to consider how "our" coming together, how any sense of community let alone of humanity, is crisscrossed with all sorts of obstacles, pitfalls, and exclusions; how it is centered and decentered by larger, and smaller, realities. One of these realities is citizenship: it is in that light that I, a citizen of the United States, will be focusing on the United States.

(We) Refugees, Immigrants, Citizens

Immigration is one of the primary conditions of possibility of "our" coming together, of the gathering or grouping of the "we." If the most manifest signifier of immigration is nationality, its other signifiers include race, ethnicity, class, education, religion, morality, politics, sexuality, health, and language itself. Discrete and tired as these signifiers may be, they are already mixed together: in the United States a test in the English language and American civics, for example, has been employed by the Immigration and Naturalization Service (INS) for essentially the same exclusionary—or inclusionary—purposes as a test for HIV.[11] It is with an eye to such in-mixings in and around immigration, as well as to the in-mixings that are immigration, that among the aforementioned signifiers, I will be paying particular attention to race and ethnicity; sexual orientation; and mental and physical health. Let me quickly add that even as these signifiers, or subjects, are mixed together, they are also kept apart. The U.S. government, for instance, would scarcely admit that its AIDS policy—if "policy" can designate practices marked by confusion, misinformation, and *ad hoc* applications—is shaped by racial and sexual prejudice. Given the discourse of liberal democracy, this is not so surprising. And yet, a denial of interconnections, indeed at times an exacerbated sense of unconnectedness, may also be found among some of the groups of people most directly implicated in immigration today (i.e., tensions between Cubans and Haitians). I will return to questions of connections, in-mixings, and alliances later on, how they fold in and out of questions of citizenship, but first I want to stay with the question of immigration *per se*.[12]

By immigration I mean not merely a coming to stay but also a coming to leave, perhaps even a coming, staying, and leaving all together, as in the case of circular or seasonal migration.[13] Immigration encompasses, necessarily, emigration, but also involves issues of refuge, asylum, expatriation, repatriation, (permanent) residence, naturalization, and citizenship. Various types of visas, green cards, passports, and other identification papers constitute its official materials, but personal stories and collective histories—on all sides, including that of the government(s)—are in many respects no less significant, for they often bear, directly or indirectly, on the acquisition of official identification papers.[14] Conventional wisdom distinguishes between immigrants, on the one hand, and refugees and asylum seekers, on the other: the latter departing involuntarily, under duress, and presumably with the intention of returning, circumstances permitting. The differences can be quite important, and yet are by no means clear-cut. Although immigration is a global phenomenon, it is in the so-called developed societies or, if you will, the "labor-importing post-industrial democracies"[15] that it assumes some particularly prickly dimensions, not the least of which are the relations between politics and economics. In accordance with the United Nations Convention relating to the Status of Refugees (1951), refugees and asylum seekers are characterized, so to speak, by a "well-founded fear of persecution."[16] Persecution, not surprisingly, tends to be understood in strictly political terms, as if economic inequality, scarcity, and exploitation were devoid of violence and neatly removed from political strife. Mexicans—currently the largest national group of immigrants to the United States—are typically presented as motivated by economics rather than politics, crossing the border in search of the "good life" rather than survival.

Recent events in Chiapas and other parts of Mexico muddle such perceptions, but the distinction between economics and politics, immigrants and refugees, has in a sense been muddled all along. Or perhaps it has always been all too clear: for U.S. foreign policy, particularly during the Cold War, has dictated official distinctions and designations in extraordinarily commanding ways. For example, Cubans, Poles, Chinese, and Soviets, fleeing communist regimes, were typically granted refugee or asylum status, while Guatemalans and Salvadorans, fleeing repressive regimes supported by the United States, were not. As Norman and Naomi Zucker put it, "Immigrants can be selected, asylees cannot. High numbers of immigrant visas can reward cooperative governments; high numbers of asylum grants can punish the uncooperative. Every grant of asylum is an explicit criticism of conditions in the sending country."[17] Of course, asylees can also be "selected," their "cases" often being subjected to intense scrutiny, typically, if not always, involving someone from the legal profession. But before a case is scrutinized, argued, and evaluated, a number of things must be established. Detention, interdiction, deportation, and denial of due process have been the lot of many a would-be asylum seeker, at least when the U.S. government has been wary of offending the foreign regimes it has supported or, more pointedly, of sending the "wrong message" to American citizens. According to this logic, if the United States supported Guatemala and El Salvador it would hardly be fitting to recognize refugees and asylum seekers from those nations for what they were: refugees and asylum seekers. That Salvadorans, Guatemalans, Haitians, and others were not granted refugee status alongside Cubans, Poles, Chinese, and Soviets indicates to what degree foreign policy gave the lie to the rhetoric of democracy and human rights.[18]

At the same time, even if Salvadorans, Guatemalans, and Haitians had been granted refugee status, the distinction between economics and politics would have remained largely in place. The Zuckers note that such a distinction is often specious, and that economic and political factors tend to be intricately intertwined. And yet, even they, concerned as they are about the plight of refugees, maintain that distinction. "It is not poverty alone," they assert, "but the presence of poverty together with the denial of human rights that causes large-scale refugee displacements. Human rights and economic development must be linked."[19] Linked, indeed, but perhaps quite a bit differently: for the Zuckers, concerned as they are with securing the rights of refugees, present poverty, as do so many others, as if it were not in and of itself a problem, even a denial, of human rights. What is thereby purchased is the illusory integrity of the capitalist system, where private property undergirds, and vitiates, a certain far from insignificant conception of human rights.[20] That human rights might entail a redistribution of wealth, a recognition of the wrongs of poverty, exploitation, and scarcity in a world of plenty, is itself, just possibly, a *fearful* proposition. After all, it threatens to turn the standard definition of refugee and asylum seeker (on the basis of a "well-founded *fear* of persecution") on its head and to turn it, moreover, against the very nations that present themselves as the champions of democracy and human rights. My point is not that there is no distinction whatsoever between refugee or asylee and immigrant (wars, civil strife, and generalized violence *are* critical factors) but that the distinction, accepted at face value, is deeply flawed. The immigrants who come to the United States, Canada, Western Europe, Australia, and Japan in search of so-called economic opportunities—and who often aid the economies of the receiving countries themselves[21]—push against the easy validity of such a distinction, rendering visible the flaws with their very presence.

Absence and invisibility are likewise at issue, for effective border controls mean—at least according to a material, militarized logic difficult to refute—fewer immigrants, fewer "illegal" immigrants, but also fewer immigrants who may then become eligible, subsequently, for often begrudging declarations of amnesty. More effective border controls may also generate, however, more effective means of crossing, of passing, a more extensive and seasoned network of support and advice on all sides of the border. Support and advice range from gossip, hearsay, and word of mouth to published materials such as Loida Lewis's *How to Get a Green Card: Legal Ways to Stay in the U.S.A.*[22] Borders, as I have said, are never simple geopolitical facts, nor are their crossings, whether by land, sea, or air.[23] And this is so even, if not especially, when the border crossings are apparently most isolated and individual. For in every crossing, however solitary, there is something that implicates everyone, something that folds "us" into each and every individual, something whose complexity is also called complicity.[24] Briefly put, it is the complicity not only of the North in the South, or of the West in the East, or of the haves in the have-nots but also of the citizen in the (im)migrant, refugee, or asylum seeker: some of the many institutionally coded ways of figuring human beings in, out, and across national borders. There are, to be sure, many individuals or groups of individuals who discount complicity of any sort. Such are, for instance, the citizens who understand citizenship as a naturally exclusive right—in the United States, *aliens* become citizens through a process of *naturalization*—and who do not see themselves as responsible *in any way* for citizens of other nations, even when the latter are effectively denied the most rudimentary rights of citizenship in their countries of origin or residence. And then there are those citizens who do not see themselves as responsible *in any way* for citizens of their "own" nation, let alone for non-citizens.

In certain respects, citizenship, as generally practiced, consists precisely in refusing, denying, or ignoring such responsibility, or complicity, and in *naturalizing* the ideology of individualism, by which what might be called the borders of the I are defended. From a radical perspective, citizenship itself might be said to constitute a splintering of humanity, understood globally, and hence as actually at loggerheads with *human* rights. We might recall, at this juncture, the situation of Jews under Hitler or, for that matter, of Haitians under Duvalier, and the refusal of the United States, materialized in closed ports and interdictions at sea, to allow many of those implicated to enter the country, let alone to aspire to citizenship.

Citizenship—no less than human rights or, for that matter, democracy— is arguably less a solution than a question that should be kept open, deepened, and revisited.[25] With respect to the aforementioned cases, more U.S. citizens may criticize the refusal to admit now than did at the time, but hindsight is often as generous as it is ineffective. What remains true, now as then, is that nationality is rarely a more pressing question than when immigration is at stake, and that immigration is typically conceptualized in terms of admission and exclusion or restriction. History shows how persistent such terms are. My use of such terms as *complicity* and *responsibility* does not escape this dilemma, and is clearly more sympathetic to admission than to exclusion. Let me quickly add, however, that I do not by any means consider admission to be the *only* responsible outcome, and that indeed greater responsibility may require addressing the economic, political, and cultural conditions that motivate people to seek admission into another nation in the first place. In the cases of Haiti, Guatemala, or El Salvador, for example, American foreign policy, supporting ruthless regimes in the name of strategic anticommunism, is, as I have already indicated, hardly an irrelevant factor. Still, the tension between admission and restriction or exclusion cannot be ignored, and bears further attention.

The restrictionists, at odds with the admissionists, may also be isolationists, even nativists, affirming a central core of identity and power that Benedict Anderson deems characteristic of an older national imagining.[26] And yet, some of the same people who affirm a central core of identity and power also affirm what Anderson calls the modern imagining, a firm and full demarcation of the borders. There are, in other words, communities that complicate Anderson's imagining of old and modern imaginings. An extreme example may be found in certain American militia groups that resist the center and repudiate the full, flat, even operation of sovereignty (or at least of any sovereignty other than their own). For even as they resist and repudiate established national imaginings, they reassert, as if with a vengeance, the lines of national demarcation, either maintaining, extending, or, not so paradoxically, retracting them. The image of armed extremists may seem out of place in inquiry that purports to be civil. And yet, such a self-professed civil-minded individual as Peter Brimelow, author of the "national bestseller" *Alien Nation: Common Sense about America's Immigration Disaster*, articulates a position that is incendiary in its own right. "Many modern American intellectuals," Brimelow writes, are "just unable to handle a plain historical fact: that the American nation has always had a specific ethnic core. And that core has been white."[27] The phonetic affinity between "American nation" and "Aryan nation" may be accidental, but Brimelow's assessment, as dogmatic as it is demagogic, is hardly idiosyncratic.[28] Instead, it is symptomatic of a tendency to "understand" immigration in terms of a double danger: one external (some nonwhite "ethnic" other)[29] and another, possibly even more insidious, internal (misguided, impractical intellectuals).

The danger, moreover, is frequently decked out in the trappings of war.

Norman and Naomi Zucker, in a highly critical depiction of U.S. refugee policy after the crisis of communism, note that "the enemies now face off from north to south, and the threat is not annihilation, but invasion, invasion of the countries of the north by armies of migrants from the south."[30] The fear of persecution that characterizes the refugee in official discourse is reiterated, altered, and shifted into a generalized fear of invasion on the part of the sovereign state itself. The deliberately provocative, cavalier use of bellicose metaphors, as in "culture wars," must therefore be measured against a reality of police power and, in some instances, militarization.[31] It is, admittedly, a reality that is often rationalized and justified be appealing to a reality marked by crime, drug traffic, and terrorism. By thus relying on superficial but politically powerful clichés—undocumented immigrants take jobs away from citizens, burden public services, and are criminals in need of deportation—public officials, including the president, keep the tension high. So high, that disaster, for some, seems imminent: the invasion, destruction, and disappearance of the United States, according to this quite effective rhetoric, waver on the proverbial horizon. Such rhetoric is as effective as it is ubiquitous.

I want to turn now to some of the supposedly plain historical facts, inflected with a certain dosage of ethical sense, common or uncommon, so as to provide a different take on what I too might tentatively call America's immigration disaster. It is not, mind you, a disaster done, as Brimelow would have it, to some putatively white core but, rather, a disaster done all too often in the name of a *limited* diversity, a *controlled* multiculturalism. For the land of opportunity, the melting pot, the bastion of democracy, the leader of the free world, and the nation of immigrants, the stakes are high indeed.

History in the Making: (Homo)sexuality, Health, Race, and Politics

The United States admits more immigrants than any other nation.[32] According to Beverly Baker-Kelly, "During the 1980s the United States admitted an estimated 8.9 million immigrants, more than in any decade since 1900–

1910, the peak of U.S. immigration."[33] In the light of such facts, contemporary immigration to the United States acquires an inclusive, even magnani-
mous, quality: like so much else, entry to the United States can be celebrated
as generous and denigrated as all too generous: witness the apocalyptically
xenophobic "common sense" of Peter Brimelow. There are, then, any number of possible responses—from "common sense" to nonsense—to the "fact"
that immigration to the United States is so great: more than any other and
more than ever before. But facts themselves, and not just the responses they
elicit, are hardly free from ideology. For even as the United States admits
more immigrants than any other nation, it also just possibly excludes more
than any other nation. Then again, it is the world's only remaining "super-
power," not to mention the self-designated model of democracy, and as such
it cannot expect *not* to receive more immigrants. And so, depending on the
accent, facts too may sound different; their "doneness" is also "our" doing
(the word "fact" comes from the past participle of the verb *facere*, "to do").
This is not to say that reality simply disappears as rhetoric but, rather, that it
appears, comes to mean, inevitably in rhetoric.[34] Accordingly, the facts of immigration are themselves the sites of contention and contestation: to assume
neutrality is to assume a posture that denies its worldliness. As Renato Rosaldo has indicated, "we" are, whoever "we" are, "positioned subject[s], not a
blank slate."[35]

It is with an appreciation for subject positionalities, his own included,
that Robert Foss provides a different entry into the subject of immigration,
one that I want to follow further.[36] Foss focuses on the fate of homosexual
immigrants, places it in contact with that of other immigrants, and provides
in the process a compelling reading of the general history of immigration in
the United States. Despite Foss's guarded optimism (his paper is titled "The
Demise of the Homosexual Exclusion: New Possibilities for Gay and Lesbian
Immigration"), the history of immigration is largely one of incremental,
if modified, exclusions, beginning with the thirteen colonies' aversion to
"paupers and convicts" and continuing up to the present.[37] This is not to say
that things have not changed. The Immigration Act of 1990, permitting a

significant increase of immigrants and building on previous acts of amnesty (as in the Immigration Reform and Control Act of 1986 that legalized the status of considerable numbers of those already in the United States), *was* different from previous acts. Still, many things have not changed. At the risk of stating the obvious, U.S. immigration policy continues to be extremely charged politically. If refugee policy was expanded, so was the policy that grants millionaire entrepreneurs their own special, highly privileged, classification.[38] Refugee policy is, moreover, subject to all sorts of reconfigurations. For example, the Clinton administration's policy toward Haitians, like that of the previous administration, has involved perfunctory refusals of admission, interdiction at sea (by which the borders of the United States are effectively extended to the Haitian coast), and immediate deportation. The putative liberalization of immigration policy is relative, prone to all sorts of *ad hoc* manipulations, and indeed, as more recent immigration policies (1997) indicate, far from secure.[39]

The history of immigration is punctuated, clearly enough, by moments of national, or rather international, crisis. As Foss notes, "The first national regulation of aliens, the Alien and Sedition Act of 1798" comes in the wake of the French Revolution.[40] Other regulations arise with the Russian Revolution, World War I, World War II, and the Korean conflict, but also at times of economic depression and political fervor. And so, after the "paupers and convicts," along with them, one finds "criminals and prostitutes" in 1875; "insane persons, beggars . . . and anarchists" in 1903; "feeble-minded persons . . . persons afflicted with tuberculosis . . . [and those with] a mental or physical defect" in 1907; the illiterate in 1917; "ex-Nazis, war criminals, members of totalitarian parties and those who worked for collaborationist governments in Nazi-occupied areas" in 1948; communists and people with a "psychopathic personality, epilepsy or a mental defect," implicitly including homosexuals, in 1952;[41] people infected with HIV in 1990 and, more explicitly, in 1993.[42] A current application for naturalization asks whether the applicant has, among other things, "advocated or practiced polygamy," "been an illicit trafficker in narcotic drugs or marijuana," "been a prostitute or procured anyone for prostitution," or "been a habitual drunkard." The oddly outdated ring of the term *drunkard* (instead of *alcoholic*) ironically signals something current. For instance, although communist affiliation as a ground for exclusion was supposedly struck in the early nineties, the following question still tops the section titled "Additional Eligibility Factors": "Are you now, or have you ever been a member of, or in any way connected or associated with the Communist Party, or ever knowingly aided or supported the Communist Party directly, or indirectly, through another organization, group or person, or ever advocated, taught, believed in, or knowingly supported or furthered the interests of communism?" Anarchism, the first explicitly political category adduced as grounds for exclusion, may have faded as a threat to national sovereignty, but communism has apparently not.[43]

The specter of communism continues to haunt immigration policy: the wall may have toppled in Berlin, but it persists, almost melancholically, as a paper wall in the rhetoric of the INS. As Michael Teitelbaum and Myron Weiner remark, "The hallowed assumptions of more than four decades of cold war die hard" and continue to fleck current immigration policy.[44] This, as so much else, may seem to be the concern of a clearly delimited group (i.e., members and supporters of the Communist Party), one that hardly constitutes a viable constituency in American politics. But even if the number of bona fide Communists is now small in the United States, it is worth remembering what was once evoked in and along with such political designations. For in the dominant discourse of a good part of the late-nineteenth and twentieth centuries, Catholics and, more explicitly, Jews were seen by the dominant Protestant order as especially prone to anarchism and communism. Explicitly political exclusions could thus also be implicitly—and yet not always just implicitly—anti-Catholic and anti-Semitic.

Something similar holds for gays and lesbians. As Foss, Lee Edelman, and others remind us, communism and homosexuality have long been intertwined in the official and unofficial discourse of the American government.[45] Though all too easily forgotten, it is not a discourse so easily erased. It endures, fitfully, not just in old newspaper articles and congressional reports but also as a sort of political unconscious that can be activated, however trivially, in the epithet "commie pinko fag." If I recall this connection here, it is in order to signal the multifaceted screens of memories, the "chains of equivalents,"[46] that render problematic dreams of authenticity, purity, totality, exclusivity, and so on. These dreams of exclusivity are themselves not exclusive, for they inhabit a vast array of so-called social groups, both large and small, and affect the ways in which identities are constructed, replicated, solidified, and experienced. The dreams of exclusivity are not exclusive, I repeat, for the not so simple reason that, in the words of David A. Hollinger, "most individuals live in many circles simultaneously and . . . the actual living of any individual life entails a shifting division of labor between the several "we's" of which the individual is a part."[47] I would add only that living is not wholly conscious and, as such, individuals may live in circles, be understood to live in circles, of which they are not necessarily aware.

There may be, that is, more ties that bind "us" than "we" realize: ties not just of restriction but of other possibilities of movement. This is the spirit of Foss's self-positioned assertion that "the gains we have made as gays and lesbians ought to be defended and at the same time the queer community should more clearly express its solidarity with immigrants."[48] I will nuance Foss's statement by pointing out the obvious: the existence of gay, lesbian, and bisexual immigrants.[49] Foss, of course, knows this (it is, after all, the subject of his paper), but it is worth reasserting. It is also worth teasing out some other implications of immigration policy. For inasmuch as homosexuality has constituted grounds for exclusion, any homosexual, regardless of his or her national status, has historically been a suspect citizen. And inasmuch as seropositivity and AIDS currently constitute grounds for exclusion (although information is here, as with so much concerning current immigration policies and procedures, curiously murky), a similar sense of suspect citizenship attends anyone who is HIV-positive or has AIDS.[50] Suspect citizens, potentially subversive citizens, citizens who are, in a sense, not proper citizens and who threaten the health and welfare of the body politic: such are some of the ideological implications of immigration policy. As Foss notes, "Immigrants increasingly came to be perceived as politically subversive as well as a bio-logical threat."[51] But the perception of immigrants continuously folds back upon the perception of citizens. Other implications hold as well. For the his-tory of so-called sexual minorities in the United States, not to mention other countries, is bound up in the history of racial and ethnic minorities. For all their differences, indeed for all their internal divisions, they are troped as questionable citizens.

This said, I want to return to the roster of the *explicitly* excludable. For as Foss and others point out, beneath ahd behind the list of sick, criminal, de-viant, "social charges," entire national and "racial" groups were implicated: Irish and German Catholics in the 1830s; the Chinese and other Asians in the 1870s and '80s; Italians, Slavs, and Jews in the early 1900s; Haitians and, more subtly, Black Africans in the early 1990s.[52] Of these exclusions, few were more brutally forthright than the so-called Chinese Exclusion Act of 1882, an unashamedly racist piece of legislation that remained in effect until 1943.[53] Legislation aimed at excluding other Asians, including Japanese, Filipinos, Indians, and Indochinese, was also enacted. As was often the case, waves of immigrants willing to perform hard work for low wages in times of economic prosperity and expansion (the building of the transcontinental railroad, for example) were followed by waves of xenophobic protectionism once projects were completed and prosperity waned.

African Americans, whose history is less one of immigration than of en-slavement proper, are also implicated in immigration policy. Bill Ong Hing, for one, has examined how American immigration policy sends subtle, and not so subtle, messages of exclusion to African Americans. As a case in point, he refers to the internment of around 270 HIV-positive Haitians at the U.S. Naval Base at Guantánamo Bay in 1993.[54] Here fear of AIDS is wedded to fear of blackness. Creola Johnson, studying the same case, shows how the United States violates international law even as it maintains, internationally, the rhetoric of civil liberties and human rights. It does so, once more, by appeal-ing to science, by attempting to ground itself in supposedly objective, ra-tional, and verifiable health concerns. As Johnson notes, "Unlike the Jews [themselves denied entry at the height of Nazi persecution], the Haitians were the object of discriminatory treatment arguably because of their medical condition, not their ethnic and racial composition."⁵⁵ And yet, even the most cursory comparison between the treatment of Haitians and the treatment of Cubans in the same time period reveals to what degree medicine could be a devastating red herring: Haitians were rigorously screened for HIV-AIDS (when they were not simply returned); Cubans were subjected to, or rather benefited from, a considerably more arbitrary medical screening. And as with HIV-AIDS, mental health was also a concern.⁵⁶ Race, nationality, and wealth, not just physical and mental health, were the issue. A wealthier, lighter, presumably healthier Cuban community was pitted against—and in some ways pitted itself against—a poorer, darker, presumably sicker Haitian community. The chain of equivalents crucial to Laclau and Mouffe's radical democratic project was here resoundingly broken.

The insistent turns to science, particularly medical science, should give us pause: not merely when these turns are arbitrary, as seems to be the case with the application and enforcement of HIV-AIDS laws, but also when they are systematic, "fair" in their presumed blindness.⁵⁷ Science indeed has played an important role in immigration policy. It has provided the grounds, or reasons, for an ostensibly balanced policy beyond what many consider to be the bugbears of race, class, and gender. It is invoked as the realm of factual neutrality, where a certain common sense finds its finest home, and where studies, records, and examinations, not examiners, speak for themselves, as if beyond the pressures of time. And yet, though it is a fact all too often forgotten, science and its facts are historical as well; they change, even in some of their surest and most fundamental claims. One of these changes bears on homosexuality, where an ethical, moral, and religious discourse was hushed, and yet rearticulated and further legitimated, in scientific discourse.

I do not have time to enter into the twists and turns of the history of homosexual exclusion, but I will point out, through Foss, some of its most salient features. Homosexuality itself was never explicitly mentioned in the laws on immigration (only in congressional reports and so on).⁵⁸ "It was not

108

included under the 'moral exclusions' like prostitution, but rather among the medical exclusions" and was only shadowed forth in such concepts and categories as "constitutional psychopathic inferiority" (from the Immigration Act of 1917), "mental defect" (added by the INS in 1952), and "sexual deviation" (1965).[59] Little wonder, then, that the American Psychiatric Association's decision to drop homosexuality as a psychiatric disorder in 1973 was not without repercussions for the INS, for it effectively left it without scientific ground. And yet, without scientific ground, the INS did not change its position. In so doing it revealed a paradox: science, understood as objective reason, is both necessary and unnecessary to political policy. Which does not mean that politics is indifferent to science. After all, the neat coincidence of scientific and political positions can engender a comfortable faith in liberal democratic principles of fairness, equality, and reason that falters when the coincidence is not neat, when science does not serve as a compliant support to social policy. The refusal of the American psychiatric community to provide any longer a "rational" basis for the exclusion of homosexuals as pathological subjects did not leave the INS indifferent, even though its policies did not change in any dramatic or immediate way. Change did come, however, gradually, even subtly. For the loss of objective grounds can have, did have, some profoundly personal ramifications.

Without a rational object set by the medical community, the agents of the government thus ran the risk of an irrational subjectivity, one that threatened to expose the seamy side of American liberty (exclusion is kept no longer by appealing to, but by rejecting, scientific opinion) and that also threatened to bring homosexuality a little too close to home: after all, it was now up to the INS investigating agent, in his or her capacity as a solicitor of stories, to fish out the homos. As Foss puts it, "Absent some statement from the alien, no decision was possible. The examining INS official also had no objective non-medical criteria to follow, except the official's own 'feelings' or perception."[60] Foss's argument finds unexpected corroboration in a participant observation study by George Weissinger, a former criminal investigator (or special agent) for the INS. According to

Weissinger, "Agents develop a *feel* for the kinds of people they encounter in the field," a "feel" that is both cause and effect of "typification."[61] Whether out in the field or in the confines of the interview, a *feeling* is *typically* involved. Weissinger is not referring here to homosexuality, but he nonetheless acknowledges the slippery, and yet apparently quite entrenched, significance of subjectivity in official INS business. With respect to sexuality, the play of subjectivity could take some particularly "odd" turns: the examiner, bereft of scientific ground and medical backing and relying on personal perceptions and "feelings," ran the risk of implicating himself or herself. Throwing himself or herself into the mental position of the other, "getting into" the other's mind, the examiner thus ran the risk of staying "there" or, even more, of having already been "there." This risk could be summarized in common parlance: it took one to know one.

It is at this point, where knowledge, power, identity, and risk intersect so intensely, that I want to make one more observation before passing into the final lines of my paper. Homosexuality, even as an implicitly excludable category, was struck from the books in the 1990 Immigration Act (supposedly along with communism), prompting Foss to remark that "in this strange way, the exclusion of homosexuals, which had never been explicitly mentioned in the statute, was repealed, again without explicit recognition of what had transpired."[62] For Foss, this is a promising change of events. Also promising is the more recent inclusion of a "well-founded fear of persecution" based on sexual orientation among grounds for asylum. That homosexuality should pass from being grounds for exclusion to being grounds for asylum is indeed noteworthy. And yet, for me, struck by the play of visibility and invisibility, silence and articulation, around homosexuality, I remain somewhat more guarded. Asylum is here, after all, a function of legal precedent, not of congressional action. In fact, where homosexuality is concerned, congressional action takes the form of the so-called Defense of Marriage Act (1996), itself bound up in a military policy that effectively institutionalizes invisibility and silence ("don't ask, don't tell"), and in the persistence of sodomy laws in many states of the Union. As Deborah Anker notes, such

laws, upheld by the Supreme Court in the *Bowers v. Hardwick* case (1986), render the distinction between status and conduct (or act) at once critical and
complex.[63] For inasmuch as homosexual acts still constitute in some states a
punishable offense, the asylum claim must be based on "the immutable characteristic of [the applicant's] homosexual status" that is, furthermore, exten-
sible to an entire social group.[64]

In the movements of immigrants and immigration, the immutable individual is bound to the immutable group. The constructs of history appear to
be almost beside the point, and yet individuals and groups are nonetheless
constructed: constructed as at once natural and socially (re)cognizable. As Jin
S. Park puts it, "The biggest challenge in establishing the claim that gay men
and lesbians are persecuted as a social group is recognizing them as a 'social
group.'"[65] Recognition is double-edged, to say the least, because while it may
issue in inclusion it has also, and more commonly, issued in exclusion. In the
country from which the applicant is fleeing, recognition of this sort might
well issue in electric shock, "conversion therapies," sexual assault, police harassment, imprisonment, internment, torture, castration, and capital punishment.[66] In the country to which the applicant is fleeing, the United States,
recognition is also fraught with peril, for here too homophobia can have
devastating, even deadly consequences.[67] Be that as it may, the INS distinguishes, or has attempted to distinguish, between a "conduct-based group"
and a "social group,"[68] as if sexual activity, or "conduct," were inimical to social formation.[69] The INS evidently does not look favorably on claims based
on "volitional associations," by definition subject to change, and insists instead on characteristics that are "immutable" or "so fundamental to a person's identity [that] there should not be a requirement [. . .] to change."[70]
Homosexuality, caught between a rhetoric of will and necessity, mutability
and immutability, act and identity, perception and substance, is a category
whose juridical contours remain vexed.

The Board of Immigration Appeals (BIA)—an entity independent of the
INS—has rejected arguments by the INS that gay men and lesbians do *not*
constitute a social group and—with the case of Fidel Armando Toboso-

Alfonso (1990), a gay Cuban who fled to the United States in the so-called
Mariel Boatlift in 1980—has effectively opened the way for other claims for
asylum involving sexual orientation. Still, the argument for asylum is far
from easy and must contend, as already indicated, with the continued criminalization of homosexual activity in various states of the Union, by which
persecution might assume—as it does in a good number of other nations—
the form of prosecution.[71] So identity outweighs activity, but at a price: homosexuality is declared immutable, fixed, and immobile, in order, mind you,
for individual "homosexuals" to be admitted into the United States.[72] What
follows, as Kristen Walker asserts, is that "asylum-seekers must take on an
identity in order to fit within an appropriate legal category."[73] The assumption of an identity at once determined and debated by the U.S. legal system
can be quite arduous for an individual unfamiliar with that identity, with homosexual, gay, or lesbian "identity," but also with *individual* "identity" itself.
The notion of identity as performative gets into trouble here. For however
fluid the performance, the performer, negotiating national borders, comes up
against a prior and more powerful instance of power that rules that identity
is immutable and fundamental.[74] This does not spell the end of performativity but its constraint and complication. Performativity may thus entail the
performance of immutability, the performance of a performance that cannot
be otherwise, the performance of a performance that is—or rather that strives
to pass itself off as—not one.

The possibility of asylum on the basis of sexual orientation, though
complicated, does indeed constitute a significant development in the otherwise homophobic history of U.S. immigration. But Foss's and Goldberg's
optimism,[75] appealing as it may be, cannot but be guarded. For there is
more. As Brian McGoldrick observes, the dissent in the aforementioned
case argued that the "examinations" to which Toboso was subjected in
Cuba were "legitimate health and crime-related investigations that did not
amount to persecution."[76] The invocation of health is, in the light of recent changes in immigration policy, especially significant.[77] Call me suspicious, but as I see it there is something queer about the "fact" that even as

homosexuality, as an excludable category, "disappears," another category, that of HIV and AIDS, appears. I do not mean to say that one category merely replaces or substitutes the other, as if AIDS were a metaphor, and *only* a metaphor for (male) homosexuality. In fact, instead of metaphor, or rather along with metaphor, metonymy, as the figure of contiguity and displacement, attribute and association, is what I would here invoke. For if HIV-AIDS arguably replaces homosexuality in official discourse, it also displaces it, slipping it alongside blackness or brownness, "third-worldliness" or "underdevelopment," and such ostensibly moral issues as prostitution and drug use. The chain of signifiers is not "merely" rhetorical but is entangled in and as reality. It is also a chain of people, of people restricted, united, separated, shackled, and mobilized.

Passing Lines, Immigration Acts, and the Shibboleths of Identity

The final arbiter of fashion here is the border patrol.　　　　*—Debbie Nathan*

So far, I have concentrated on some of the larger historical and geopolitical issues involved in border crossings, but now, in closing, I want to shift my perspective, scatter it and concentrate it at the same time. For in the rhetoric and realities of immigration, in the play of the visible and the invisible, the spoken and the unspoken, there are any number of terribly *intimate*, yet terribly *alienating*, scenes. Among other things, I am thinking of the interview with the INS agent or agents that every would-be legal immigrant must undergo. It is a deceptive term, "interview," because the "viewing-between," the exchange of sights, that it implies is actually a viewing-of, a radically unbalanced act of interrogation, investigation, and identification, a skewed speculation in which some are subject to at times almost unbearably incisive insight. By this, I do not mean to imply that it is a relation, or nonrelation, of binarisms: the powerful on the one side and the powerless on the other, the seer and the knower over and against the seen and the known. I am far too touched by the work of Michel Foucault for that.[78] At the same time, it would be folly to pretend that things were evenhanded. I have already referred to the risk of the examiner, the risk of an all too intimate identification, of cognition as re-cognition, but the examined is, needless to say, at even greater risk. The tactics the INS uses, or has used, to "establish" identities, to draw out, or determine, "confessions" of identity, may be banal, or silly, or even sensible; they may even be performed with the purpose of helping, rather than simply hindering, admission;[79] but they may also assume some rather frightening forms: isolation, detention, surveillance, and so on. With respect to homosexuality, in some cases the examiners went so far as to identify and exclude homosexuals who were not even aware that they were homosexuals, as if the examining self held the other's truth.

I do not wish to discount the possibility that the self does hold an other's truth, but only if the self of the other, the other's self, is counted as well, and only if the relay between selves—and others—is understood as nonreciprocal and nonsynthetic. Truth, then, like reality itself, moves between and among subjects, is constantly possessed and dispossessed, appropriated and altered. And yet, amid so much movement, so much blockage, there are still so many stops. In the micro-arena of the INS interview, each one different and yet each one in some sense the same, the movements of truth, reality, knowledge, and power are such that the crossing of borders is also the passing of lines. By *passing lines* I mean, among other things, the discursive and bodily acts by which one person "relates" to another, though not necessarily as another: the acts, for instance, by which an examined "other" tries to pass himself or herself off as the same—or almost the same—as the examiner. What one says and does; how one says and does it; when, where, and to whom, are matters of concern. The lines one passes are not just topographical marks but also, as the dictionary indicates, calculated and glib ways of speaking, usually to obtain an undeclared end. The end may be entry into, or escape from, a country; admission into, or exclusion from, a social group; it may be privilege and power; peace of mind or just plain survival. It may be greater or lesser visibility, the star that stands out or the Zelig-like being that blends in, the spy or the fugitive or the undocumented worker. Passing lines are uttered and deployed across bodies, in and though bodies: black passing as white, Latino as Anglo, Puerto Rican as Cuban, Cuban as Italian, Jew as gentile, gay as straight (and married, to boot), but also white as black, Anglo as Latino, and so on. Passing lines also entail questions of gender or transgender, class, age, morality, political affiliation, and religion, to name but a few.

It is along these lines—the lines that one passes as well as the lines *by which* one passes—that I would give special notice to what those who desire to pass do not want one to notice: for example, accents, lisps, and, on a different register, symptoms of sickness. There is an inevitable irony, and risk, in such an endeavor, for it comes close to replicating the very tactics of detection that it would criticize. And yet, inattention to the dynamics of passing is hardly any better; indeed, I would argue, it is a great deal worse, and for at least two general reasons. First, to see passing is to see, or to attempt to see, how and what certain officials see, or at least look for, and may thus be a way of exposing official strategies, of bringing them to public notice, of breaking the confines of the interview, and perhaps, through political intervention, of wrecking their semisolitary game. Second, to see passing might not so much close passing down as open it up, give it over to dissemination, and in so doing disrupt the surety of dominance, or at least of dominant notions of identity as fixed, eternal, and incapable of entering—and I use this word deliberately—self-defined different fields, nations included. For though passing can be a strategy of domination, it more often than not involves the resistance to domination. Generated in and out of fear, insecurity, and a relative lack of power, passing lines, telling stories about one's self, and so on, are tactics of empowerment, weak and partial though they may be. At the same time, it is important to keep in mind that the lines of passing are recognized as such only when they falter and fail. Their successes tend to be either invisible or visible only retrospectively: after and away from danger, from the time and place of passing.

Passing lines are thus, so to speak, shibboleths of identity, shibboleths not just in the sense of slogans, catchwords, or turns of speech by which a member of one group is identified and excluded, or worse, by a member of another; but also shibboleths in the sense of distinctive markers, linguistic but also gestural and corporeal, that "give one away." These markers do not admit of easy control; they may come to the surface, erupt, and slip out: in a word, betray.[80] They require a sort of performative self-vigilance that often borders on the ascetic—think of the queen who tries to pass as the "regular guy"—and a sort of ritual self-stylization—think of the young Jewish boy in *Europa, Europa*, who "manufactures" a prepuce for his penis or, more currently, the gang member who conceals a tattoo, the person with AIDS who conceals a blotch of sarcoma, the dyke who dies her hair back to its "natural" color. This is not easy and is often made more difficult, if not impossible, by anything and everything from time, climate, and the body itself. One of the so-called Haitian boat people in Edwidge Danticat's short story "Children of the Sea," makes this poignantly clear. Noting how his companions in the boat "are showing their first charcoal layer of sunburn," he rather wistfully remarks, "'Now we will never be mistaken for Cubans,'" even though, as the narrator interjects, "some of the Cubans are black too."[81]

Passing is no easy task and tends to work, when it works, only by a certain amount of luck and deviousness: a deviousness often aimed, by the way, at following, or appearing to follow, the straight and narrow path. Inasmuch as this path typically leads to the institution of marriage, marriage fraud, as it is called, is an important concern of the INS, motivating detection and, once more, deviousness: that of the examiner but also, and perhaps more importantly, that of the examined.[82] And yet deviousness, even for the most devious of subjects, is itself subject to all sorts of giveaways: to coughs, sniffles, quiverings, and blotches of various and sundry sorts; to a trilled "r" or an "e" dropped ever so revealingly before an "x" or an "s"; to various forms of malapropism; to the all too stereotypical lisp.[83] Which brings me to another point, passing is rife with stereotypes, their making and unmaking, their suppression and their parodic assumption. If I were Judith Butler I might speak of a "parodic inhabiting of conformity,"[84] but where borderlines are concerned, where "inhabitancy" is itself at issue, parody must be more along the lines of passing—over and into and through and around—rather than inhabiting. The assumption of some signs, then, but also the suppression, or taming, of others, for instance, the lisp. If the lisp is a stereotypical homosexual sign, a not quite dead metaphor for homosexuality, the accent and the symptom are likewise signs of identity, figures of being, each one capable of any number of alternate figurations. The lisp, for example, might well be a gasp or a sigh or an unintended shriek, a phrase too shrill, a move too soft, a flip of the wrist, a snap of the fingers, a fluttering of the lashes. For both women and men, it may even be a penchant for denim, a tug at the crotch, a wandering eye, a crossing or spreading of the legs. It may be a less than delicate and demure demeanor, or a demeanor all too delicate. It may be, in short, anything that engages the stereotypes of identity, anything that engages previously mentioned "the Look" of legality and illegality.

Passing lines are, then, the stories, moves, and gestures that may be deployed in border crossings, borders that include what Gloria Anzaldúa calls a "1,950 mile-long open wound" between Mexico and the United States,[85] but that also include the waters of the Caribbean, the naval base at Guantánamo, Coast Guard boats, "international" airports, INS offices; borders that are even, maybe even especially, streets and parks and schools and stores, banks and clinics, courtrooms and emergency rooms; borders that are our minds and our bodies, our words and our deeds, our thoughts and our thinking. Borders that are "our" own and that provoke these lines, here and now. Coming full circle, I want to remind "us" that the circle is never really full, that the possibilities and pitfalls of passing lines and border crossings are not available for everyone, everywhere, always, equally. Some of "us," can simply not pass as something, or someone, else, cannot go wild in the storehouse of stereotypes, cannot be other than others already see "us," do not have a flair for theatrics. Some of "us" may not enjoy the "possibility for a counter-speech, a kind of talking back"[86] that would be effective, that would not detain "us" or send "us" packing. "We," whoever "we" are, might do well to remember that humanity, however constructed or deconstructed, however felt, imagined, or conceptualized, is subject to all sorts of cuts and constraints and that "our" coming together is bound by realities that resist, for

117

whatever reason, rhetorical replay. In playing with passing lines and border crossings, in thinking and performing them, "we" might remember that there are many who cannot move, write, speak, and perform so publicly; many who do not have the "proper" credentials, the "necessary" title, the "right" papers. "We" might remember this. Remember it and resist it.

Notes

1. This paper was first presented at "Crossing National and Sexual Borders: A Latin American and Latino/a Lesbian, Gay, Bisexual and Transgendered Conference," City University of New York, Graduate Center, October 3–6, 1996. Significantly altered versions were presented subsequently at the State University of New York at Stony Brook, the University of Pittsburgh, Stanford University, Washington University in Saint Louis, Harvard University, and the University of Connecticut, Storrs. A shorter version has been published in Spanish as "Actas y actos de inmigración," in *Nuevas perspectivas desde/sobre América Latina: El desafío de los estudios* culturales, ed. Mabel Moraña (Santiago, Chile: Editorial Cuarto Propio/Instituto Internacional de Literatura Iberoamericana, 2000): 261–272. I owe much to the comments, questions, and suggestions from colleagues, students, and others at each of these events. I owe even more, of course, to the people who have narrated, between 1995 and the 1999, their experiences, their stories, to me. My formation is not, as will be evident, sociological, nor are my protocols. I have nonetheless drawn extensively on sociological materials, and maintain a respectful, if critical, distance from the statistical imperatives and "methodological imperialism" of many studies on immigration and naturalization to the United States. (The term "methodological imperialism" is from P. A. Cowan et al., *Family, Self, and Society: Toward a New Agenda for Family Research* [Hillsdale, N.J.: Lawrence Erlbaum, 1993], cited in Carola Suárez-Orozco and Marcelo Suárez-Orozco, *Transformations: Immigration, Family Life, and Achievement Motivation among Latino Adolescents* [Stanford: Stanford UP, 1995], 185). My findings, no doubt conditioned by my formation as a Hispanist and hence as a scholar of language and literature, are at once speculative, narrative, and experiential; that is to say, they speculate on the narrated experiences of others. As such, they are not, nor do they pretend to be, "generalizable" in any firm and final sense. Generalizability is a concern of Philip Q. Yang ("Explaining Immigrant Naturalization," *International Migra-*

tion Review 28.3 [1994]: 449–477, 451) in his reading of work concentrating on Hispanic immigrants by A. Portes and R. Mozo ("Political Adaptation Process of Cubans and Other Ethnic Minorities in the United States: A Preliminary Analysis," *International Migration Review* 19 [1985]: 35–63).

The group from which I draw my ideas is concentrated and yet quite diverse: some forty to fifty immigrants, both "legal" and "illegal," naturalized and not, from Mexico, Central America, Cuba, Venezuela, the Dominican Republic, Haiti, and Puerto Rico (the last, holding U.S. passports, presented interesting twists on nationality, sovereignty, and citizenship) who have taken up residence, with varying degrees of (im)permanence, in or around Boston, New York, and San Francisco. Most of the conversations were conducted in Spanish and French (not, given my linguistic limitations, Creole). The group is concentrated yet diverse because I was particularly interested in the function of so-called nonnormative sexualities (homosexuality, bisexuality, transsexualism, etc.) in the (im)migration process. Accordingly, in a willful "inversion" of established percentages, more self-identified nonheterosexuals than self-identified heterosexuals were interviewed. To be sure, such self-identification is itself culturally marked, for the far from simple reason that many of the identities deployed in the United States (gay, lesbian, bisexual, etc.) are often deployed differently or, in fact, not at all in certain areas of Latin America (these identifying designations are more common in urban areas and along the border—i.e. in areas of greater contact with the United States—than in rural areas). As a result, the very notion of a truly *international* gay and lesbian *community* is fraught with problems, not least of which is the cultural hegemony of the United States and other Western nations.

The fact that the interviews, or conversations, dealt in one way or another with other, more official, interviews and conversations (typically with an agent or functionary of the INS) was also not without its ironies and difficulties: it signals what may well be an intractable problem of knowledge and power. My desire to know, and to know how sexuality figures alongside nationality, ethnicity, language, and so on, reflected, even as it refracted, more commanding modes of knowledge. In this, academic research, whatever its professed political positions, whatever its sympathies, dovetails official governmental research and must contend with a cloud of suspicion. It also must contend with silences, omissions, and resistances of various sorts. Many of the people interviewed contend, for their part, with a sort of double

119

silence: with respect to INS agents, other officials, "concerned" U.S. citizens, and possible employers, they must conceal either their "illegality" or factors that may jeopardize their "legality"; with respect to other immigrants, including at times their own friends and family members, they find themselves having to conceal their sexual desires and practices. HIV-AIDS complicates the situation, constituting yet another area of silence and concealment, even within the so-called gay community. A number of the people interviewed conceal their seropositivity even as they live more or less openly as gays. These silences, omissions, and resistances bear significantly on the discursive and performative aspects of *passing*, generating all sorts of stories, acts, and "lines." Although I focused on immigrants whose stories touched, in one way or another, on same-sex desire, I also interviewed a number of self-proclaimed heterosexuals, similarly constrained to tell stories, to "pass lines," to play, in short, a fairly limited range of roles: the happy, legally married couple; the hardworking citizen; the admirer of American values.

Finally, by focusing on (im)migrants and "aliens," I am clearly at odds with George Weissinger, who, in *Law Enforcement and the INS: A Participant Observation Study of Control Agents* (Lanham, Md.: University Press of America, 1996), asserts that "[f]ocusing on those who define the parameters of the illegal alien *problem* [i.e. INS agents] will provide more useful information than focusing on the illegal alien directly. As a corollary to this analysis, we may make certain inferences about the nature of the illegal alien population, the *raison d'être* of the INS control agent," 2 (emphasis original). My study, in contrast, makes certain inferences about the nature of the INS—inferences supported by published statistics, legal analyses, activist work, and so on—and questions the supposedly well-defined "parameters" of the "problem." Be that as it may, Weissinger's work is critical to an understanding of U.S. immigration, particularly its more discursive and performative aspects, and may serve as a counterpoint and, at times, corrective to my own. His distinction between service and control; his delineation of the various roles and duties of those involved in INS enforcement (special agents, border patrol officers, deportation officers, et al.); his description of the referral and processing apparatus; his examination of the rights of aliens; his presentation of problems of status and morale among agents, are among the things that recommend his agent-centered study.

2. Edna Acosta-Belén and Carlos E. Santiago, "Merging Borders: The Remapping of

America," in *The Latino Studies Reader*, ed. Antonia Darder and Rodolfo D. Torres (Oxford: Blackwell, 1998), 29.

3. Roger Rouse, "Mexican Migration and the Social Space of Postmodernism," *Diaspora: A Journal of Transcultural Studies* 1.1 (1991): 8–23, 9.

4. Oscar Montero, "The Signifying Queen: Critical Notes from a Latino Queer," in *Hispanisms and Homosexualities*, ed. Sylvia Molloy and Robert McKee Irwin (Durham: Duke University Press, 1998), 162.

5. Debbie Nathan, *Women and Other Aliens: Essays from the U.S.-Mexico Border* (El Paso: Cinco Puntos Press, 1991), 17–34.

6. Suárez-Orozco and Suárez-Orozco, xiv.

7. Alberto Sandoval Sánchez, "Puerto Rican Identity Up in the Air: Air Migration, Its Cultural Representations, and Me 'Cruzando el Charco'," in *Puerto Rican Jam: Essays on Culture and Politics*, ed. Frances Negrón-Muntaner and Ramón Grosfoguel (Minneapolis: University of Minnesota Press, 1997), 190.

8. The Immigration and Nationality Act (INA) of 1988, drawing from the Refugee Act of 1980 and the United Nations Protocol Relating to the Status of Refugees from 1967, lists "race, religion, nationality, membership in a particular social group, or political opinion" as determinative categories for refugee and asylum claims. The definition of "social group," through which sexual orientation is shadowed forth, remains, as we shall see, a subject of contention.

9. Cornel West, with Jorge Klor de Alva and Earl Shorris, "Our Next Race Question: The Uneasiness between Blacks and Latinos," in *The Latino Studies Reader: Culture, Economy, and Society*, ed. Antonia Darder and Rodolfo D. Torres (Oxford: Blackwell, 1998), 183. The uneasiness announced in the title is indeed borne out in this conversation, with Klor de Alva towing the constructivist line to such an extent that he says—with the evident satisfaction of polemic for polemic's sake—that "Blacks are more Anglo than most Anglos because, unlike most Anglos, they can't directly identify themselves with a nation-state outside the United States. They are trapped in America," 184. Klor de Alva may be the one who is trapped, if not in "America" at least in a specious constructivist logic that relies insistently on essentialist generalizations—for example, "Latinos are in a *totally different* situation" (emphasis mine)—and that holds fast to the category "Latino"—as well as to the centrality of *identification* with a *nation-state*—even as it purports to destabilize it.

10. Kristen Walker, in "The Importance of Being Out: Sexuality and Refugee Status," *Sydney Law Review* 18 (1996): 568–597, notes that "'[n]arrative legal scholarship' or 'storytelling' is a technique increasingly used in what might broadly be termed 'progressive' legal scholarship, although it is not without its critics," 568.

11. For more on the language requirement, see Susan Huss, "The Education Requirement of the U.S. Immigration Reform and Control Act of 1986: A Case Study of Ineffective Language Planning," *Language Problems and Language Planning* 14.2 (1990): 142–161. For an interesting analysis of the role of language in national identity, see Frances Negrón-Muntaner's "English Only Jamás but Spanish Only Cuidado: Language and Nationalism in Contemporary Puerto Rico," in *Puerto Rican Jam: Essays on Culture and Politics*, ed. Frances Negrón-Muntaner and Ramón Grosfoguel (Minneapolis: University of Minnesota Press, 1997), 257–285.

12. My sources in what follows are theoretical, legal, and historical studies; familiarity with and/or involvement in a variety of activist organizations, including the International Gay and Lesbian Human Rights Commission, Amnesty International, and the Lesbian and Gay Immigration Rights Task Force; and finally, and most important, interviews and conversations with recent immigrants, legal and illegal, themselves.

13. For more on the varieties of migration, see Wayne A. Cornelius and Philip L. Martin, "The Uncertain Connection: Free Trade and Rural Mexican Migration to the United States," *International Migration Review* 27.3 (1993): 484–512; Edward Funkhouser and Fernando A. Ramos, "The Choice of Migration Destination: Dominican and Cuban Immigrants to the Mainland United States and Puerto Rico," *International Migration Review* 27.3 (1993): 537–556; and Rogelio Sáenz and Alberto Davila, "Chicano Migration to the Southwest: An Integrated Human Capital Approach," *International Migration Review* 26.4 (1992): 1248–1266.

14. In a newsletter of the Lesbian and Gay Immigration Rights Task Force, *LGIRTF Status Report* (Fall 1999), the importance of personal narratives by immigrants (or would-be immigrants, and their friends and lovers) is made in connection with the highest governmental official. At an October 8, 1999, meeting of the Empire State Pride Agenda in New York City, President Clinton, after hearing the story of a binational gay couple who could not live in the same country, reportedly stated that immigration law should be changed, thereby "affirming once again the power of . . . stories to bring about change," 1.

15. Suárez-Orozco and Suárez-Orozco, 14.

16. See, for example, Norman L. Zucker and Naomi Flink Zucker, *Desperate Crossings: Seeking Refuge in America* (Armonk, N.Y.: M. E. Sharpe, 1996), 3–8.

17. Zucker and Zucker, 83.

18. Zucker and Zucker provide some telling statistics: "[F]rom June of 1983 to March of 1991, 2.8 percent of Salvadoran applicants were given asylum. In that same period, approval rates were 74.5 percent for Soviet Citizens, 69 percent for Chinese, and 61 percent for Iranians," 85.

19. Zucker and Zucker, 134.

20. Walker goes so far as to endorse "the notion of rights as a violent gift, as it is a Western version of identity [in this case homosexuality or gayness] that must be adopted in order to receive the gift of rights," 591.

21. If immigrants come to the U.S. in search of "economic opportunities," plenty of U.S. citizens benefit economically as well. The history of immigration is affected by the ebb and flow of the market: when the economy is strong and cheap, undocumented labor is in demand, local, state, and federal governments tend to turn a blind eye to irregular or illegal immigration, even "liberalizing" legal entries; when the economy is weak, when recessions arise, then the scapegoating of immigrants begins in earnest. For more on the economic question, including how immigrants contribute to the national economy, see Michael S. Teitelbaum and Myron Weiner, eds., *Threatened Peoples, Threatened Borders: World Migration and U.S. Policy* (New York: W. W. Norton, 1995), especially 24–25.

22. Loida Lewis, *How to Get a Green Card: Legal Ways to Stay in the U.S.A.* (Berkeley: Nolo Press, 1995).

23. This is certainly not to say that all crossings are the same, or that there is no qualitative difference in crossing by land, sea, or air. If airline controls are more condensed and rigorous, they are also, generally speaking, safer, the risk being repatriation rather than death. It is important to note, as Carola Suárez-Orozco and Marcelo Suárez-Orozco do, that "[a]nother strategy is to turn part of the 'policing' function over to the airline personnel; airlines that transport passengers without proper documentation are fined," 18. From a different perspective, as Teitelbaum and Weiner point out, "the most problematic migrations seem to be those taking place in boats—not because the numbers involved are higher than those crossing land borders (the reverse is true), but because of the greater

concentration, vulnerability, and 'tele-visibility' embodied in mass movements undertaken in small boats and homemade rafts," 22. The "televisibility" of migration, by which life-and-death passings are rendered *spectacular*, is indeed critical. Current policy stipulates that arriving to U.S.-controlled waters does not signify arrival to the United States; quite the contrary, it signifies that the United States can interdict and repatriate, by force, the passengers. Immigrants must literally *land* in the United States, touch its soil, a requirement that generates some dramatic, highly "televisible" scenes of immigrants jumping ship and desperately swimming for shore before being apprehended by the Coast Guard.

24. In the words of Debbie Nathan, immigration "affects all Americans, no matter what our ethnicity, our citizenship or residency status may be—and no matter how we act in the world through our speech, haircuts, lipstick shades, clothing, our bodily movement . . . in short, no matter how we choose to look," 34.

25. I take seriously the assertion made by Ernesto Laclau and Chantal Mouffe, in *Hegemony and Socialist Strategy: Towards a Radical Democratic Politics* (London: Verso, 1985), that "the task of the Left cannot be to renounce liberal-democratic ideology, but on the contrary, to deepen and expand it in the direction of a radical and plural democracy," 176.

26. Benedict Anderson, *Imagined Communities: Reflections on the Origin and Spread of Nationalism* (London: Verso, 1991).

27. Peter Brimelow, *Alien Nation: Common Sense about America's Immigration Disaster* (New York: Harper Collins, 1996), 10.

28. The rhetoric of common sense is frequently deployed in discussions about immigration. The Federation for American Immigration Reform has published advertisements in major national magazines such as *Newsweek* that urge support for "sensible immigration levels." These ads seem to be concerned with public well-being ("uncontrolled growth hurts everyone") and address both "native born and immigrant alike," but they also include not so veiled threats: "[F]or the preservation of the good life we all enjoy . . . reduce the numbers before it's too late."

29. Brimelow collapses race into ethnicity by qualifying a "specific ethnic core" as "white." The collapse is perhaps not entirely accidental: to state that the "American Nation has always had a specific *racial* core"—which is what Brimelow is indeed stating—would make *all too clear* an affinity with any number of more overtly racialist and racist positions.

30. Zucker and Zucker, 3.

31. Nathan, 34.

32. Sharon Stanton Russell, "Migration Patterns of U.S. Foreign Policy Interest," in *Threatened Peoples, Threatened Borders: World Migration and U.S. Policy,* ed. Michael S. Teitelbaum and Myron Weiner (New York: W. W. Norton, 1995), 41.

33. Beverly Baker-Kelly, "United States Immigration: A Wake Up Call!" *Howard Law Journal* 37.2 (1994): 283–304, 283–284.

34. As Hayden White declares, in *Tropics of Discourse: Essays in Cultural Criticism* (Baltimore: The Johns Hopkins UP, 1978), "[t]here is no value-neutral mode of emplotment, explanation, or even description of any field of events . . . the very use of language itself implies or entails a specific posture before the world which is ethical, ideological, or more generally political: not only all interpretation, but also all language is politically contaminated," 128. Even the metaphor of contamination is, I might add, politically contaminated: now, through AIDS, perhaps more than ever.

35. Renato Rosaldo, *Culture and Truth: The Remaking of Social Analysis* (Boston: Beacon Press, 1989), 207. Rosaldo is referring specifically to the social analyst, but his proposition extends, as he indicates, beyond that.

36. Robert J. Foss, "The Demise of the Homosexual Exclusion: New Possibilities for Gay and Lesbian Immigration," *Harvard Civil Rights–Civil Liberties Law Review* 29.2 (1994): 439–475.

37. Foss, 440.

38. Lewis, 175.

39. According to a 1991 study by Deborah Anker (*Determining Asylum Claims in the United States: An Empirical Case Study,* Final Report), "[T]he current adjudicatory system remains one of ad hoc rules and standards. Despite Congress' goals in creating statutory asylum procedures, factors rejected by Congress—including ideological preferences and unreasoned and uninvestigated political judgments—continue to influence the decision making process," cited in Zucker and Zucker, 99.

40. Foss, 440.

41. Foss, 444–448. Marian Nash Leich, in "Contemporary Practice of the United States Relating to International Law," *American Journal of International Law* 85.2 (1991): 334–335, refers to the Immigration and Naturalization Act of 1951 as excluding people on the grounds of Communist affiliation, 334.

42. Sarah N. Qureshi, "Global Ostracism of HIV-Positive Aliens: International

Restrictions Barring HIV-Positive Aliens," *Maryland Journal of International Law and Trade* 19.1 (1995): 81–120, 96.

43. Leich, 334, notes that the 1990 Immigration Act, signed by George Bush, revises the provisions for exclusion contained in the Immigration Act of 1951 [1952] and eliminates Communist affiliation as a motive of exclusion or ineligibility, but *only* for nonimmigrant visas.

44. Teitelbaum and Weiner, 22.

45. Lee Edelman, *Homographesis: Essays in Gay Literary and Cultural Theory* (New York: Routledge, 1994).

46. I take the term from Laclau and Mouffe, who stress the importance of "chains of equivalents between the different struggles against oppression," 176.

47. David A. Hollinger, *Postethnic America: Beyond Multiculturalism* (New York: HarperCollins, 1995), 106. Hollinger advocates a "postethnic perspective" that "recognizes the psychological value of bounded groups of affiliation" (107), but that resists the deceptively ample embrace of universalism as well as the troublingly tight embrace of ethnocentrism. Without embracing the term "postethnic," I agree with Hollinger's assessment of the "potentially overlapping character of various local communities" (108), even when the local community purports to be "global" or "international." Many others, for all their differences, seem to concur. Gianni Vattimo's notion of a "mixed reality" (*The End of Modernity*, trans. Jon R. Snyder [Baltimore: The Johns Hopkins University Press, 1988], 159) in which Otherness with a capital "o" is weakened; Edward Said's view that "imperialism consolidated the mixtures of cultures and identities on a global scale. But [that] its worst and most paradoxical gift was to allow people to believe that they were only, mainly, exclusively, white, or Black, or Western, or Oriental" (*Culture and Imperialism* [New York: Random House, 1993], 336); James Clifford's proposition that "we should attempt to think of cultures not as organically unified or traditionally continuous but rather as negotiated, present processes" (*The Predicament of Culture: Twentieth-Century Ethnography, Literature, and Art* [Cambridge: Harvard University Press, 1988], 273; Rey Chow's observation that "[p]ressing the claims of the local . . . does not mean essentializing one position; instead it means using that position as a parallel for allying with others" ("Postmodern Automatons," in *Feminists Theorize the Political*, ed. Judith Butler and Joan W. Scott [New York: Routledge, 1992], 114); Alberto Sandoval's assertion that in the "webs of action, transaction, and interaction, identity is multiple and heterogeneous" ("Staging AIDS: What's Latino Got to Do with It?" in *Negotiating Performance: Gender, Sexuality, and Theatricality in Latin/o America*, ed. Diana Taylor and Juan Villegas [Durham: Duke University Press, 1994], 53); and Gloria Anzaldúa's call for "a tolerance for contradictions . . . [and] ambiguity" (*Borderlands/La frontera: The New Mestiza* [San Francisco: Aunt Lute Books, 1987], 79), all point to the processes of the "we."

48. Foss, 475.

49. Divisions continue to exist, as Foss indicates, and for many gay Americans, as for many straight Americans, immigrants constitute a separate category. The fact remains, however, that the "gay community" is *also* a community of immigrants or, to put it somewhat more flatly, that among immigrants there are gays, lesbians, bisexuals, and transsexuals: problems of self-identification, classification, and nomenclature notwithstanding. Which is not to discount problems of identification. Consider, for example, the manipulations, from a variety of positions, of the much-publicized presence of homosexuals in the Mariel "exodus" (in 1980, some 125,000 people were granted permission by Castro's government to leave Cuba from the port of Mariel) or the concept of "sexilio"—"sexile"—by which a number of Hispanics qualify their move to the United States. For more on "sexilio," see Manuel Guzmán, "'Pa' La Escuelita con Mucho Cuida'o y por la Orillita': A Journey through the Contested Terrains of the Nation and Sexual Orientation," in *Puerto Rican Jam: Essays on Culture and Politics*. ed. Frances Negrón-Muntaner y Ramón Grosfoguel (Minneapolis: University of Minnesota Press, 1997), 227. Guzmán claims the term "sexilio" is his, which may well be the case, but it has been circulating among Spanish-speakers for years. See also Sandoval's "Puerto Rican Identity," in which homophobia and heterosexism in Puerto Rico are adduced as a motives for emigration. As a person with AIDS, Sandoval asks some wrenching, autobiographically inflected questions: "[S]hould I now go home sick when I have never been 'homesick'? Being gay with AIDS, and having death around the corner, does not convince me at all that I have to get an airline ticket to return *para bien o para mal* to a homophobic and chauvinist society," 204.

50. Sandoval may be right, in theory, when he states that "with AIDS, there are no borders" ("Puerto Rican Identity," 204), but a significant number of governments obviously disagree. With AIDS, there are in a sense even more borders. The confusion surrounding the issue of HIV-AIDS is considerable. The newsletter of the Lesbian and Gay Immigration Rights Task Force, *LGIRTF Status Report* (Summer 1999), states that "due to their unfamiliarity with preparing and representing lesbian, gay and HIV-positive asylum seekers [but not just asylum seekers], many legal assistance organizations have inadvertently contributed to the plight of those they are trying to help. It is typically very distressing for those detained to reveal their sexual orientation during 'credible fear interviews' to INS officers or at the initial screening procedures of such organizations," 3.

51. Foss, 444.

52. Creola Johnson, "Quarantining HIV-Infected Haitians: United States' Violations of International Law at Guantánamo Bay," *Howard Law Journal* 37.2 (1994): 305–331, 305.

53. For more on Chinese immigration and the western expansion, or "manifest destiny," of the United States, see Ronald Takaki, *A Different Mirror: A History of Multicultural America* (Boston: Back Bay Books, 1993), 191–221.

54. Bill Ong Hing, "Immigration Policies: Messages of Exclusion to African Americans," *Howard Law Journal* 37.2 (1994): 237–282.

55. Johnson, 328.

56. For a comparative statistical approach to the question of mental health, see William W. Eaton, "Mental Health in Mariel Cubans and Haitian Boat People," *International Migration Review* 26.4 (1992): 1395–1415.

57. See United States Immigration and Naturalization Service, *Codes, Operations Instructions, Regulations, and Interpretations*, "Interpretation 316.1" (Washington, D.C.: US GPO, 1988–present) 5246.10.

58. "The curious thing about the statutory exclusion of homosexuals," Foss writes, "is that the statute itself never actually mentioned homosexuality. This was undoubtedly another example of the *crimen innominatum* mentality," 445.

59. As Foss notes, "[T]he legislative history of the INS would explain that this language was broad enough to exclude, as a Senate Report from 1952 put it, 'homosexuals and sex perverts,'" 446. Jin S. Park, "Pink Asylum: Political Asylum Eligibility of Gay Men and Lesbians Under U.S. Immigration Policy," *UCLA Law Review* 1069 (1995): 1115–1156, refers to amendments to the Immigration and Nationality Act of 1965 (superseded in 1990) and remarks that "Congress further clarified its intent to exclude homosexuals by adding 'sexual deviation'" to the list of grounds for exclusion, 1118–1119.

60. Foss, 456. Foss writes that the Public Health Service (PHS) "did not want diagnostic responsibility, and the Senators did not want any mention of homosexuality," 452.

61. Weissinger, 14.

62. Foss, 462.

63. Deborah E. Anker, *Law of Asylum in the United States* (Boston: Refugee Law Center, 1999), 394–398. Other articles on sexual orientation and asylum include Suzanne B. Goldberg, "Give Me Liberty or Give Me Death: Political Asylum and the Global Persecution of Lesbians and Gay Men," *Cornell International Law Journal* 26 (1993): 605–623; Brian J. McGoldrick, "United States Immigration Policy and Sexual Orientation: Is Asylum for Homosexuals a Possibility?" *Georgetown Immigration Law Journal* 8 (1994): 201–226; Erik D. Ramanathan, "Queer Cases: A Comparative Analysis of Global Sexual Orientation-Based Asylum Jurisprudence," *Georgetown Immigration Law Journal* 11(1996): 1–44; Park; and Walker. "Under current U.S. law," writes Anker, "criminalization of homosexual *conduct* is not necessarily unconstitutional, whereas distinctions based on homosexual *orientation* may be," 396, n. 747 (emphasis original). Parallels with the religious distinction between the sin and the sinner are here unavoidable.

64. Anker, 396. As Park notes, bisexuals and bisexuality do not commonly figure in asylum claims (1116, n. 5).

65. Park, 1119.

66. Park, 1115–1116. Park specifies that "gay Romanian men have the option of being informants against other gays or being castrated, and must sometimes submit to both. Gay Iranian men are beheaded upon proof of committing [*sic*] homosexual acts; lesbian Iranians are stoned to death" (1116). Not surprisingly, such information is often sketchy and contested. See also Goldberg, 605–606.

67. Walker questions the assumption that "movement to the 'enlightened' west will solve the problems of oppression in the 'east,' in Asia, Africa or South America." Debatable as her use of "west" and "east" may be, Walker is right to acknowledge "an underlying ambivalence about the law" in herself and "in other feminist and queer writers," 568. In the United States, Justice Brennan stated that "[b]ecause of the immediate and severe opprobrium often manifested against homosexuals once so identified publicly, members of this group are particularly powerless to pursue their rights openly in the political arena," quoted in Goldberg, 619–620.

68. Anker, 396.

69. According to McGoldrick, in general, "American courts have tried to keep the doors shut to social group claims by narrowing the definition of a social group. However, the original intent [expressed in the United Nations Handbook on Procedures and Criteria for Determining Refugee Status] was to keep the social group criteria flexible and to narrow the number of claimants by making them show these special circumstances. The circumstances are simply the facts that give rise to a well-founded fear" (208).

70. McGoldrick, 214. Stuart Grider, in "Sexual Orientation as Grounds for Asylum in the United States—*In re Tenorio*, No. A72 093 558 (EOIR Immigration Court, July 26, 1993)," *Harvard International Law Journal* 35 (1994): 213–224, refines the distinction between the volitional and the immutable by presenting it as part of a larger question of (re)cognizability, of how a group is identified. Grider states that "the federal courts and the BIA [Board of Immigration Appeals] in the United States . . . have developed two seemingly mutually exclusive concepts of cognizability. Under its '*Acosta* test,' the BIA has recognized a particular social group where there exists an 'immutable characteristic' shared by the group members, while the Ninth Circuit, with its '*Sanchez-Trujillo* test,' has recognized a particular social group where there exists a 'voluntary association' among group members," 217–218. *Acosta* concerns a claim for asylum by a unionized taxi driver in El Salvador forced to transport armed guerrilla fighters; *Sanchez-Trujillo* concerns a young working-class male, also from El Salvador, who feared persecution for not having joined the armed forces. Both cases figure prominently in the small but growing legal literature on asylum and sexual orientation; see, for instance, Foss, 472.

71. McGoldrick, 219. McGoldrick makes the claim that "abuse of process. . . . constitutes persecution rather than prosecution" in reference to Cuba under Castro, but, as he makes clear, the *Bowers* decision effectively indicates that "homosexual activity [is] not so fundamental that it deserve[s] protection," 218. Undeserving of protection, it is, obviously, prone to prosecution.

72. Goldberg maintains that "[r]egardless of whether sexual orientation has a genetic origin, lesbian women and gay men cannot disassociate themselves from the basis of their persecution. To that extent, sexual orientation is indeed immutable," 614.

73. Walker, 593.

74. "Immutable" is not "innate," as the BIA made clear in *Acosta*; see Grider, 218. Grider persuasively notes that "each line of reasoning [*Acosta* and *Sanchez-Tru-jillo*] is . . . rooted in a notion of individual identity, the paradigm of an internal analysis," 219. According to Grider, external analysis, used by various European courts, holds that "if the persecutor or society at large views the group as existing, it exists," 217.

75. Goldberg is, it appears, even more optimistic than Foss. "Recent changes to United States immigration law," Goldberg asserts, "reflect a Congressional intent to end discrimination against lesbians and gay men in some areas of federal law," 619. The qualifier "some" is important: the fact remains that, as McGoldrick notes with respect to the *Toboso* case, "the dissent noted that prosecution under laws against homosexuality would not qualify one for asylum since our Supreme Court has recognized that governments may enact anti-sodomy laws," 217. Such a statement, based on reference to a specific court case, contrasts markedly with Goldberg's statement that "[t]he Supreme Court's ruling in *Bowers v. Hardwick* that the constitutional right to privacy does not encompass sexual relations between consenting lesbian and gay adults is largely irrelevant to the discussion of whether lesbians and gay men are eligible for asylum," 621.

76. McGoldrick, 218.

77. Ian Lumsden, in *Machos, Maricones, and Gays: Cuba and Homosexuality* (Philadelphia: Temple University Press, 1996), observes that the Cuban government's reaction to AIDS included, at least at first, a "policy of quarantining—that is, seemingly imprisoning—for life all people who had tested positive to HIV antibodies," 162. The relation between "health and crime-related investigations" was here tight indeed.

78. See especially, Foucault's *Surveiller et punir: Naissance de la prison* (Paris: Gallimard, 1975) and *La volonté de savoir*, vol. 1 of *Histoire de la sexualité* (Paris: Gallimard, 1976).

79. It is important to note that the agents of the INS cannot be reduced to the INS agent, however much a "proper role" (i.e. that of the INS agent) is figured out of rules and regulations. A number of the stories immigrants recounted included sympathetic portrayals of the INS official, or officials, who attended them. In some cases, officials reportedly turned a blind eye to infractions or even helped steer the interviewee away from potentially problematic issues. Within the constraints of the role "ideally" assigned to, and assumed, by the official, he or she can perform any number of revisions. That said, he or she can also be decidedly less than "sympathetic" to the plight of the immigrant (or "alien") and can even rationalize infractions on the part of those who enforce the law. Weissinger's work, distinguishing between the theoretical and the practical, provides important wrinkles in the presentation of INS officials. As a case in point, he notes the absence of warrants in the arrest of aliens: "INS agents are bound by the same guidelines [as FBI agents] but they rarely have the time to obtain an arrest warrant before the violator absconds. The majority of arrests made by INS agents are without a warrant simply because the likelihood of the illegal alien absconding is very high. As a result, agents develop a *feel* for the kinds of people they encounter in the field. A great deal of *typing* goes on in the field, especially regarding suspected law violators," 14 (emphasis original).

80. Given the importance of performance, speech, and (lack of) control in what I am formulating, Judith Butler's *Excitable Speech: A Politics of the Performative* (New York: Routledge, 1997) bears mentioning. Butler proceeds from the "presumption . . . that speech is always in some ways out of our control," that it is "excitable," 15. "In the law," Butler says, "'excitable' utterances are those made under duress, usually confessions that cannot be used in court because they do not reflect the balanced mental state of the utterer," 15. In INS interviews, and certainly on the border, however, such excitable utterances, and gestures, *are* used, and are used in ways, legal ways, that can impede or render impossible *access* to court: the noncitizen is "before the law" in a manner that is not reducible to that of the citizen before the law. But whose law? What law? It may be all well and good to say that speech is "always in some ways out of our control," but the very generalizability, or vague (re)citability, of said utterance is troubled by the existence of borders, languages, and laws, in the plural. Butler has a penchant for singular substantives such as speech, language, interpellation, and law, and largely takes for granted a legal and linguistic horizon that necessarily cuts the force of her argument. Unlike J. L. Austin's *How to Do Things with Words* (Cambridge: Harvard UP, 1975) from which Butler draws, *Excitable Speech* does not seem especially concerned about *qualifying* speech and language as English or about *qualifying* law as, say, American, or at least as pertaining to a constitutional democracy. Against so many unqualified, abstract, singular nouns, Butler's use of the plural pronoun "our"—as in "out of our control"

and, implicitly, "our day in court"—begs a crucial question, one that is at the center of the reality of immigration. For however (ex)citable speech may be, however much it may be, "in some ways," out of "our" control, in some very important ways it *is* in *someone's* control, circumstantial and contingent though that control may be. Butler obviously knows this—her study is, after all, concerned with hate speech, censorship, authority, and agency—but her own language lacks some far from insignificant nuances and differences. Then again, Butler preempts such criticism by stating, again in the plural, that "[w]e may think that an elaboration of the institutional conditions of utterance is necessary to identify the probability that certain kinds of words will wound under such circumstances. But the circumstances alone do not make the words wound," 13. In theory, this may be correct, but what Butler accomplishes by setting "us" straight about what "we may think" comes close to discounting circumstances almost altogether. Her examples—gays and lesbians in the [U.S.] military, rap music, etc.—assume a sort of national belonging, or citizenship, that simply *cannot* be assumed when borders are at issue, when the circumstances of speech and action are even partially specified as those of immigration. Circumstances—indeed maybe even circumstances alone—*can* make words wound. Butler does not deny that, but the well-placed use of "alone" can have the effect of blinding or deafening "us" to the circumstantiality of speech, the devastating circumstantiality of speech and, of course, of so much more. Later on, however, Butler raises interesting questions about "the performativity that is the linguistic condition of citizenship," 81. It is important, I believe, to set Butler's work alongside Weissinger's.

81. Edwidge Danticat, *Krik? Krak!* (New York: Random House, 1996), 8.

82. Attempts to alter this situation include legalizing marriage for same-sex couples and, perhaps more interestingly, introducing legislation that would "provide for same-sex couples all the privileges that currently accrue to legal spouses under federal law," including, of course, the right to sponsor a foreign partner to immigrate. On February 14, 2000, U.S. Representative Jerrold Nadler (D-NY), introduced just such legislation, the "Permanent Partners Immigration Act of 2000." Currently, some thirteen nations, mostly European, provide immigration rights to same-sex couples (LGIRTF Press Release, February 14, 2000). On a related front, Californians voted, in March 2000, to approve Proposition 22—sponsored by Republican state

133

senator Pete Knight—which declares that only unions between men and women are valid. The insistence with which public discussions of homosexuality are coupled with discussions, and defenses, of marriage is telling.

83. No one, of course, is excluded from the United States on the basis of accent; but accent, and linguistic "competence" in general, can be a concern for someone wishing to maintain or reassert "the Look" of legality: so much so that it might be possible to speak of "the Sound" of legality as well.

84. Judith Butler, *Bodies That Matter: On the Discursive Limits of "Sex"* (New York: Routledge, 1993), 122.

85. Anzaldúa, 2.

86. Butler, *Excitable Speech*, 15. Butler's attempt to uncouple "sovereignty" and "agency," to "'[open] up the possibility of agency,' where agency is not the restoration of a sovereign autonomy in speech, a replication of conventional notions of mastery" is admirable, but unclear. Whatever their place in academic theory, "sovereignty" and "agency" are also deployed with respect to immigration and border control (the sovereign state, the governmental agent) to such a degree that their redeployment and resignification are vexed indeed.

5 From Victorian Parlor to *Physique Pictorial*

The Male Nude and Homosexual Identity

Michael Bronski

While the public presentation of the male body as an erotic object has a long, complicated history, displaying the specifically *gay* male body as an object of beauty and eroticism is a fairly recent phenomenon. In this essay, I want to suggest that the eroticized gay male body has a very specific, modern genealogy that first blooms in Victorian England and, after half a century of various cultural transfigurations, finds its contemporary apotheosis in the early 1950s in U.S. culture.

In Western culture, the male body was, for the most part, not an object of desire but a subject of desiring. Yet there are significant exceptions. Classical Greek statuary, for instance, celebrated the male nude, and centuries later, during the Italian Renaissance, these classical forms were the primary influence on artists such as Michelangelo, Da Vinci, and Caravaggio, whose works glorified an eroticized male body. It was to both the Greeks and their Italian imitators that the Victorians turned when, in the 1880s and '90s, the male body once again became an acceptable object of aesthetic contemplation and sexual desire.[1] The Victorian male nude was praised as an emblem of both heterosexual normativity and racial purity by adherents of the physical culture movement; at the same time, it could function as a symbol of "Greek love" and homoerotic passion for nineteenth-century artists and aesthetes. One of the most important conditions for this paradoxical relationship was the emergence, in the 1880s, of a distinct and clearly visible homosexual identity and culture. I will argue that this paradox and the anxieties surrounding it—prompted by the same dynamic of a newly public homosexual culture—surface again in the 1950s, when once more we see an onslaught of representations of the glorified, exposed male body. As in the 1890s, the meaning of this body could pass between various significations, functioning as a sign of both normative, patriotic heterosexuality and sexual deviance.

The enormous popularity, for the Victorians, of the objectified male body is evident in the number of venues in which it could be found. Scholarly work about classical Greek and Renaissance art by J. A. Symonds and Walter Pater, and popular writings by Oscar Wilde (among others) promoted aesthetic theories of beauty that drew heavily upon idealized versions of the male body. These themes were also reflected in the photography of Wilhelm Von Gloeden and Guglielmo Pluschow, German photographers who, from the 1870s to the 1930s, took thousands of portraits of mostly male Sicilian youths in "classical" and religious poses. American photographers Thomas Eakins and F. Holland Day were the first photographic artists to exhibit male nudes in the United States. All of these artists were extremely influential; inexpensive reproductions of Gloeden and Pluschow's work were easily available, and both Eakins and Day exhibited widely and greatly shaped the future of what became known as "art photography." Because all of these men had (to varying degrees) erotic attachments to other men, Symonds, in *A Problem in Greek Ethics* (1883) and *A Problem in Modern Ethics* (1895), argued that there was a strong connection between homosexual desire and the development of this new male image.[2]

While Eugene Sandow, the first popularizer of the physical culture movement in Britain and the United States, was self-avowedly heterosexual, the movement broke cultural ground not only in uncovering and exhibiting the unclothed male body but in marketing it as well. The physical culture movement emphasized the fitness and health of the male body through scientific methods of exercising, marking the birth of what is now called "bodybuilding." From its beginnings, the movement was inextricably intertwined with commercialism and the production and sale of photographs of mostly naked physical culture practitioners and superstars, as well as how-to exercise books, equipment for exercising, and even gymnasiums. Eugene Sandow began as a circus strongman who moved his career onto the more respectable British music hall stages in the 1880s and eventually ended up as a headliner in Florenz Ziegfeld's turn-of-the-century, elaborately staged traveling revues. The allure of Sandow was not simply as a performer but also as a personality and a sexualized body. In a stroke of marketing genius, Ziegfeld broke the fourth wall and, after his star's stage performance, allowed both male and female audience members to go backstage and touch Sandow's body for an additional price (See figure 5.1).

During Sandow's theatrical career he promoted himself by merchandising his image. This was performed primarily through the sale of cabinet cards—6-x-4 1/2-inch photographs that were available at newsstands, theater concession stands, and through the mail. (In 1893 cabinet cards sold for thirty-five cents; larger formats could cost as much as five dollars.) In 1894 Sandow allowed Thomas Edison to make a Kinetoscope of him flexing his muscles, which was shown to great applause at Kinetoscope parlors. After Sandow's theatrical career ended, he pursued other commercial ventures: in 1897 he opened his Institute for Physical Culture, the first of several very upscale gymnasiums in a fashionable London neighborhood, and published his second (of five) books, *Strength and How to Obtain It*. A year later he commenced the publication of *Physical Culture*, a monthly magazine that quickly spawned the Half-Crown Postal Course—a mail-order business that for two shillings and six pence sent out monthly, personalized, exercise instructions. Other physical culture instructors followed suit, and within a few years the

FIGURE 5.1. Sandow in the pose of the *Farnese Hercules* from *Sandow's System of Physical Training,* 1894.

number of gyms, magazines, books, and mail-order courses burgeoned in both Britain and the United States.[3]

The male body as aesthetic object was now big business, but, more important, appreciation of the male body was an established, accepted, and valued cultural norm. As the physical culture movement thrived, however, it faced an enormous problem: its emphasis on the nearly naked, exposed male body—held up as a model for other men to emulate—appeared, to many, to be blatantly homoerotic. While the writings and art of Symonds, Wilde, von Gloeden, and Day were clearly fueled by homoerotic desire (at times so strong that their simple articulation of it placed them at great risk), the innate homoeroticism of the physical culture movement was far more covert, and by necessity, overtly denied. It was this ever-present suspicion of physical culture's homoeroticism and the movement's continual denial of it that forced it into a defensive position. As homosexuals and homosexuality became more public in the early part of the century, it became imperative that the physical culture movement define itself clearly and decisively as being about normative masculinity and heterosexuality. It marked this difference by positioning the well-developed male body as heterosexual and the underdeveloped body as homosexual. This medicalized model—the undeveloped male body as unfit, unhealthy, and diseased—drew a clear distinction between those who promoted the beautiful male body as simply an aesthetic object (Symonds, von Gloeden, et al.) and those who exhibited it as a model of sexual and racial purity, health, and morality.

These two categories of masculinity are clearly differentiated in the writings of the early physical culture promoters. In an editorial from the first issue of *Physical Culture,* for instance, Sandow, whose fervent belief in eugenics included killing the "weak and infirm,"[4] wrote that the ultimate aim of physical culture "is to raise the average standard of the race as a whole. That is, no doubt, a tremendous task, and one which it may take many lifetimes to accomplish."[5] Within two years, Sandow's magazine was running articles equating physical culture with Christianity itself:

Between Muscular Christianity and Physical Culture is, at farthest, a short step: the praise of one is praise of the other, the apostle of one is also the apostle of the other. . . . Muscular Christianity is Physical Culture from the point of view of the minister of religion.[6]

Other spokesmen for the physical culture movement drew more explicit lines between moral fitness and heterosexuality. Lionel Strongfort(the stage name of Max Unger), one of Sandow's most prominent challengers in the marketing of physical culture, clearly equated the fit, muscular male body with healthy and energetic heterosexuality. In his popular book *Do It With Muscle!* Strongfort argues that "it is a wise law of nature that woman shall ever be drawn to the strong and vital man," and then goes on to suggest that "yes, faint-hearted lover, you very likely have her if your body is fit or when you make it so. If she seems cold to your advances, a full length mirror will probably disclose the reason why."[7] Casting his net beyond the personal to the more broadly social, Strongfort's *Promotion and Conservation of Health, Strength, and Mental Energy* carried an introduction by the grandson of Lord Douglas, marquess of Queensberry, the man famously responsible for beginning the legal proceedings to put Oscar Wilde in prison:

Parents ought to have their sons take up the practice of Strongfort to develop that manliness, that courage, that moral fiber, that strength of purpose, that would lead them onward and upward and prevent the very existence of degenerative influences.

Queensberry's reputation would have secured in the popular imagination the idea that homosexuality and deviant male sexuality were the diametrical opposite of fitness, health, masculinity, and true physical culture. It was, indeed, a short step between sexual deviancy and criminality, as Oscar Wilde had so profoundly proved. Bernarr McFadden, an American physical culturalist who lived in London and whose magazine *Physical Development* appeared almost simultaneously with Sandow's *Physical Culture*, used as the pitch line for his rubber chest expander, "Weakness is a crime. Don't be a Criminal."[8]

While the Victorian aesthetes and physical culturalists at first appear to be diametrically opposed in their views on masculinity, sexuality, and social organization, they are also, of course, profoundly united in their appreciation of—even obsession with—the male body. I would argue that the cults of the beautiful male body as celebrated by both groups possess such a number of

intersections and shared aspects that it makes less sense to view them as contradictory forces than as aspects of the same cultural phenomenon. Take, for
instance, the way both the aesthetes and the physical culturalists discuss the
important influence of Greek art on their philosophy. In *Sandow's System of
Physical Training* (1894), we learn how Sandow's personal vision and career
began. In his teens, as a treat for being a diligent student, Sandow's father
takes him on a trip to Rome:

*Arriving at Rome, what the youthful scholar had imbibed of the classics led him to
take a keen interest in the art treasures of the Eternal City, particularly the statuary,
representing the gods and heros of antiquity. Under the local influence of the place, his
imagination repeopled the Corso and the Colosseum with the stalwart deities of
Roman mythology, and he seemed to see in a vision, the great pageant of a past day,
where mighty concourses of people applauded their laurel-crowned favorites in the
wrestler's arena. But, practically, he liked most to frequent the art-galleries, and there
to hang about and admire the finely-sculpted figures of heathen deities and the chis-
eled beauty of some Herculean athlete or wrestler in the throes of life or death struggle. With the inquiring mind of youth, he asked his father why our modern race had
nothing to show in physical development like those lusty men of the olden times. Had
the race deteriorated, or were the figures before him only the ideal creations of god-like
men? His father's reply was a disappointment to him, for he had to admit that the
race had suffered physical decline, and even in its choicest individual specimens had
fallen grievously from its once mighty estate. Later ages, with their ignoble ideals, and
the sordid habits and fashionable indulgences of the race, had wrought their due
havoc—a havoc which the father took occasion to impress on the youth's mind, and
the admonition was not lost. Eugene, contrasting his own slight figure with the mighty
thews and graceful forms of the statued heros about him, conceived the idea to train
his body to the utmost pitch of perfection, and so approach, if he did not attain, the
Ancient ideal of physical power and beauty.*[9]

Sandow's description—including the fretting about the decline of the race
—is close to the aesthetic writings on Greek art by Symonds and others. In
his *Memoirs*, Symonds charts the influence of Greek statuary on his artistic

and sexual imagination. After a recurrent dream of being kissed by a beautiful man young man with blond hair, blue eyes, and a halo, Symonds notes:

*This vision of ideal beauty under the form of a male genius symbolized spontaneous
yearnings deeply seated in my nature, and prepared me to receive many impressions
of art and literature. . . . A photograph of the Praxitelean Cupid taught me to feel the
secret of Greek sculpture. I used to pore for hours together over the divine loveliness,
while my father read poetry aloud to us in the evenings. He did not quite approve, and
asked me why I would not choose some other statue, a nymph or Hebe. Following the
impressions made on me by Shakespeare's Adonis and the Homoeric Hermes, blending with the dream I have described and harmonizing with the myth of Phoebus in the
sheep-cote, this photograph strengthened the ideal I was gradually forming of adoles-
cent beauty.*[10]

Even in his writings on art Symonds makes clear the implicit connections between male beauty, sexuality, and national identity:

*We need not embark on antiquarian or metaphysical, or historical discussions, in
order to understand the sense of Beauty which was inherent in the Greeks. Little hints
scattered along the wayside are far more helpful. . . . Of this sort are the two wrestling
boys at Florence, whose heads and faces form in outline the ellipse which is the basis
for all beauty, and whose strained muscles exhibit the chord of masculine vigour vi-
brating with tense vitality. If we in England seek some living echo of this melody of
curving lines, we must visit the fields where boys bathe in early morning, or on the
playgrounds of our public schools in the summer, or the banks of the Isis when the
eights are on the water, or the riding schools of young soldiers. We cannot reconstitute
the elements of Greek life: but here and there we may gain hints for adding breath and
pulse and movement to Greek sculpture.*[11]

Sandow and other physical culturalists quite consciously posed (both in
their exhibitions and for cabinet cards) in emulation of classical Greek or
Roman statues such as the *Farnese Hercules* and the *Dying Gaul*. Dusted with
white powder and standing on a plinth, the physical culturalist would become the object of beauty lauded and adored by the aesthete. These poses

would often translate into products as small, mass-produced molded replicas of the model were made available to an eager public. At the behest of the British Museum—for an exhibit on the races of the world—Sandow was immortalized in a life-size plaster cast that was meant to illustrate the Caucasian race. (Sandow's visions of himself immortalized next to the Elgin Marbles and the work of Phidias were dashed because—due to the extraordinary difficulty in creating a plaster mold of a living body—the replica lacked its original's proportion and symmetry, and was met with ridicule by the press and physical culturalists.)[12]

While it is not unimaginable to think that the statuettes of Sandow found their way into the homes of homosexual aesthetes—in much the same way that Michelangelo's *David* was a staple of "gay decor" in the homes of many homosexuals in the 1950s—we do know that Sandow's cabinet cards were circulated among gay men. But the role that these photographs played in these men's lives were not so much ambiguous as manifold. It is important to remember that photography, for the Victorians, was a new art, treated with respect and as a novelty. Photos of a near-naked Sandow and von Gloeden's "Socratic" poses of boys were as acceptable as subjects of contemplation as were family portraits and nature photography. It was not uncommon, for example, for John Addington Symonds to send his friends photographs of himself, his family, Venetian gondoliers, male models posed as classical Greek statuary, and even Sandow. It certainly was possible for the photographs of near-naked men to function differently in various social, emotional, and relational contexts. It may well have been impossible, however, for Symonds to separate his erotic feelings from his aesthetic appreciation when looking at a photo of Sandow or one by von Gloeden.

In 1889 critic and poet Edmund Gosse sent a newly released set of Sandow photographs to Symonds, who was in Switzerland recuperating from tuberculous. Symonds wrote back:

The Sandow photographs arrived. They are quite interesting, and the full length studies quite confirm my anticipations with regard to the wrists, ankles, hands, and feet.

143

The profile and half-trunk is a splendid study. I am very much obliged to you for getting them to me.[13]

A fine example of how these varying positions might intersect—and be wildly misinterpreted—can be seen in the much-noted anecdote of Gosse looking at "pornographic photos" (which he had received in the mail from Symonds earlier that day) during Robert Browning's funeral at Westminister Abby in 1889. In *Feasting with Panthers,* Rupert Croft-Cook uses the story to attack the poet's personal morality; David Chapman, in his critical biography of Sandow, notes that Gosse used the photographs (which he claims are of Sandow) to relieve the tedium of the very long service. Yet when we read Gosse's letter to Symonds recounting his day, the experience of looking at the photo becomes one of contemplating death and inspiration:[14]

[I have] only yet have been able to enjoy the beautiful photograph, which is full of poetry. As I sat in the Choir, with George Meredith at my side, I peeped at [the photograph] again and again, and at last, while waiting in the deep silence for the ceremonial to begin, with many thoughts of love and life and genius and decay, moving in my mind, this sextain formed itself—I hardly know how—and I send it to you as the onlie begetter of all that sehnsucht:

    Dark-stamed-flower, across thy beauty
    Sighing, I cast the veil.
    In Youth's high spring-tide Love's a duty
    And rose-crowned hopes prevail;
    But autumn comes, and brings I see
    Not rose, but rosemary for me.[15]

If Gosse and Symonds could have these complicated, multitudinous responses to male nude photography, it is easy to imagine that physical culturalists could have experienced them as well. It is clear that Sandow and other proponents of physical culture viewed the male body in a variety of ways: as an emblem of physical and mental health, a signifier of traditional heterosexual masculinity, a symbol of racial purity, a commercial commodity, an object of beauty, a marker of heterosexual eroticism. It is also possible that on some, probably unarticulated, level they also experienced it as an object of homoerotic eroticism as well. Thus, on a foundational level, the two positions were not antithetical, or even complementary, but diverse articulations of the same experience. This is not to say that there were not profound differences between the two groups. Many physical culture enthusiasts—the marquess of Queensberry is the metaphorically appropriate stand-in here—would consider the sexual implications behind Symonds's and von Gloeden's "appreciation" completely degenerate. Some aesthetes, conversely, would thoroughly disagree with the overtly heterosexually masculinist, racialist, or nationalist implications of the physical culturalists' views. These disagreements are not simply theoretical but had ramifications in the material world. Queensberry's endorsement of Strongfort is synchronous with his attacks on Oscar Wilde, just as Wilde's espousal of aesthetic theories, as well as his sexual activity with men, were determining factors in his prosecution and conviction.

But rather than contradicting or negating one another, these positions are locked in a mutually supportive relationship in which they come to define each other. The normative, heterosexual ideology of the physical culture movement is demarcated by the transgressive, homosexual philosophy of the aesthetes. This paradox makes itself manifest in the visible displays of the exposed male body that both aesthetes and physical culturalists embraced. Once the male body is displayed, it becomes open to multiple interpretations. While this was partially true of paintings and sculptures of male nudes, the invention of photography—which featured "real" male bodies—heightened the stakes of the ideological conflicts.

Even the language used to describe these activities reveal the tensions regarding male sexuality that they inevitably produced. To "pose" for an audience or a photograph is to promote oneself, much in the way that Sandow promoted his career by "posing." But to "pose" is also to offer a suggestion or an idea—as in "to pose a question." In this way Sandow was "posing" not only as a heterosexual but as a promoter of heterosexuality.

145

This is highlighted by what is perhaps the most famous, notorious, use of the word "posing" in Victorian literature and history—when the marquess of Queensberry left a note to Oscar Wilde accusing him of "posing as a somdomite [sic]." The implication here is not only that Wilde is publicly presenting himself as a "somdomite" but also that he is posing, or suggesting, homosexual or "sodomitical" behavior. Thus, the images of the exposed male body were, for physical culturalists, "posing" (and promoting) heterosexuality while the very same images were, for the aesthetes, "posing" (and promoting) homosexuality.

As the physical culture movement grew quickly and steadily over the next four decades, this paradigm was repeatedly reinforced. The most obvious, and pervasive, example of the shift was the advertisements for Charles Atlas's mail-order bodybuilding course from the twenties to the seventies. Appearing in physical culture publications, as well as comic books and periodicals aimed at boys and young men, Atlas's advertisements proclaimed:

> *Yes! I Turn Weaklings into He-Men!*
> *Let Me Make YOU a NEW MAN*
> *in Just 15 Minutes a Day*
> *Yes, Sir, that's my job! I "RE-BUILD" skinny, rundown weaklings—fellows so embarrassed by their second-rate physical condition that they always hang back, let others walk off with the best jobs, the prettiest girls, the most fun and popularity. I turn weaklings like these into HE-MEN—REAL SPECIMENS OF HANDSOME, MUSCULAR MANHOOD—overflowing with pep, power, vitality! I'll* PROVE *that, in only 15 minutes a day, I can make YOU a NEW MAN too!* [16]

Atlas's most durable pitch was the image—it spanned decades on the back pages of comic books—of the ninety-eight-pound weakling on the beach who gets sand kicked in his face as the He-Man gets the girl. In the easily understandable code of popular culture, the ninety-eight-pound weakling was the unfit and unhealthy homosexual (See figure 5.2). In comparison to the manly He-Man, the feminized weakling bore a striking resemblance to the well-established concept of the "invert"—the She-

FIGURE 5.2. This Charles Atlas advertisement, in various versions, appeared in fitness and health journals as well as boys' magazines and comics from the late 1920s to the 1970s.

Man—that flourished during the first half of this century. The strategy of continually heterosexualizing physical culture became increasingly necessary, I suggest, as discourses about homosexuality escalated in the public sphere. As early as the thirties, for instance, the promoters of physical culture magazines made it clear that they were concerned and "disturbed by the overtones of voyeurism surrounding the 'artistic' displays of physique photography." In this context, there is no doubt that Charles Atlas was effectively "posing" as heterosexual.[17]

The Second World War not only helped create recognizable gay communities but also radically altered how the individual male body was viewed and understood. Photographs in popular magazines such as *Look* and *Life* of shirtless sailors and GIs on battleships and in trenches exposed the image of the nearly naked male body to a wider viewership than ever before. Often the exposure of the men's flesh in these photographs was complemented by their obvious emotional vulnerability as they faced the possibility of death. Coinciding with this new exposure and vulnerability was the emergence of a new, more emotionally demonstrative masculinity on Broadway and in Hollywood as method actors such as James Dean, Marlon Brando, and Montgomery Clift broke out of the limited emotional range previously allowed to male performers. Uncovered male flesh was also more permissible on screen as actors in a whole range of genres bared their bodies as well as their souls (Brando in *A Streetcar Named Desire,* Victor Mature in *Samson and Delilah,* Charlton Heston and Yul Brenner in *The Ten Commandments,* William Holden in *Picnic).*

But the most obvious manifestation of the exposed male body during this period was in the world of physical culture magazines, publications that were primarily aimed at a gay male audience. These magazines, usually measuring 8 by 6 1/2 inches and containing between sixteen to thirty pages, sported names such as *Vim, Adonis, Tomorrow's Man,* and, most famously, *Physique Pictorial* (See figure 5.3). These magazines presented themselves as promoting physical culture, health, fitness, and an aesthetic appreciation of the male form. They also featured a quirky mix of political and erotic material: opinionated editorials on topics ranging from police harassment of gay men to the spiritual worth of the human body; drawings of near-naked men in "classical," "artistic," "historical," or humorous poses by artists such as Tom of Finland, Quaintance, and Art Bob; and ad-

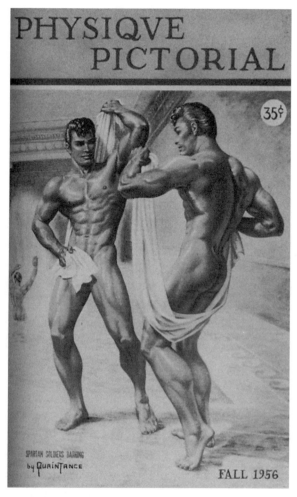

FIGURE 5.3. Cover of *Physique Pictorial,* Fall 1956. Art by Quaintance.

vertisements for posing straps and other "intimate" apparel. Most importantly, they featured photographs of "models," who ranged from professional bodybuilders to young men who hustled for a living and used the magazines for advertising and making connections.[18]

These gay-physique magazines were seen by both the established, mainstream muscle magazines and the postal authorities (the venue through which most censorship occurred) as specifically gay-oriented and thus deviant. They were, as it were, too obviously "posing" as homosexual: *Physique Pictorial* and its numerous imitators became the foremost venue for displaying the male homosexual body in the postwar years. As such, they were at the center of a volatile combination of cultural conflicts that had to be constantly negotiated. *Physique Pictorial*, for instance, went out of its way in editorials to assure its readers that they were not at risk of arrest for subscribing, and that the publication's motives were idealistic, if not downright spiritual:

Physique Pictorial *is dedicated to creating in all people a greater body-consciousness. Almost every religion teaches us that the body is a temple of the soul, and whereas we would never advocate that any person become so pre-occupied with the physical side of life that he neglect the intellectual or spiritual, we feel that the maintenance of a fine, healthy physique by those who are able to do so is to pay a great compliment to our creator who planned for the utmost perfection in our universe. If we believe God is perfect and that God created man in his own image, does it not also follow that the perfection of our bodies is of next importance to the perfection of our souls?* [19]

Such disclaimers might have been necessary in the fifties, but for the contemporary reader they verge on camp. Their emphasis on beauty, nature, and noble sentiments now reads as a naive, middle-brow parody of the language and sentiments of the Victorian aesthetes. This is not surprising, since in many salient ways, the social and political context in which *Physique Pictorial* existed was analogous to the position of Victorian aesthetes a scant fifty years earlier. Like the writings and photographs of the British aesthetes, fifties magazines such as *Physical Pictorial*, fearing serious legal and social reprisal, had to hide their homosexual concerns behind an explicitly stated ideology of beauty. Neither the aesthetes nor the physique magazines could bring male homosexuality, which was at their core, out of the closet of subtext. While the primary motivation for this closeting was to avoid legal conflict

FROM VICTORIAN PARLOR TO *PHYSIQUE PICTORIAL*

with censors, it also placed *Physical Pictorial* and other such magazines in a highly ambiguous, if advantageous, cultural position. For even while they were understood by many to be "posing" as explicitly homosexual publications, they also secured enough mainstream cultural space to present themselves as simply promoting a more general, socially acceptable aesthetic of the male body. They accomplished this by continuing to affiliate themselves with the more mainstream bodybuilding publications. In so doing, they were able to make the gay body simply one facet of a broader continuum of newly exposed and aesthetically celebrated male bodies.

But this alliance with the mainstream bodybuilding magazines was an increasingly uneasy one. When *Physique Pictorial* began publication in 1951, and garnered an increasingly large readership, the mainstream bodybuilding magazines began a sustained attack. This was undoubtedly fueled by the hard reality of declining sales: gay men, who had for years been relying on the established bodybuilding publications *Strength and Health* and *Iron Man* for images of the unclothed male body, began buying the new gay-oriented publications instead. Explicit attacks on the gay physique magazines surfaced in the editorials of the apparently "straight" bodybuilding publications and were met with a lively response by their gay counterparts. In the fall of 1956, for instance, *Physique Pictorial* ran an editorial demonstrating its "support" for the older, mainstream bodybuilding magazines, a strategy that allowed it to promote itself as a legitimate publication in the field *and* answer its attackers:

Support Urged for the "Hard Core" Muscle Magazines
While the public's support of such physique magazines as Vim, TM, Physique Pictorial, Adonis, BB, *etc., and other books which promote physical culture from an aesthetic point of view has steadily risen, many of the old school muscle books, such as* Strength and Health, Iron Man, Muscle Power *etc., have suffered an almost steady decline in sales. To be sure, part of this decline is attributable to unrealistic editorial policies, and of course some very offensive editorials and articles which tended to*

151

alienate the great bulk of their readership. But on the staffs of many of these books are some highly capable writers with many years of physical culture experience, and we cannot afford to lose them from the field. Encourage the editors of these books to recognize that body-building has left the cellar gymnasiums and is being accepted by the masses—who will not tolerate petty, prejudicial attitudes. Compliment them on their worthy articles. Editors always find time to read complimentary mail and a thoughtful, interesting letter may produce considerable effect![20]

This editorial is a minor masterpiece of spin control. It equates "publications that promote physical culture from an aesthetic point of view" with the more traditional bodybuilding magazines, thus negating any cultural or sexual difference between them. It also marginalizes the older, mainstream bodybuilding culture by implying not only that "the great bulk" of the older magazine's readership is gay but that a new, broad-based movement ("the masses") now accepts bodybuilding (and by extension, homosexuality) and will refuse to tolerate prejudice. By ending with the campily smug suggestion to write "thoughtful and complimentary" letters to produce change, the *Physique Pictorial* editorial adamantly refuses to place itself in a defensive position and explicitly states its determination to reframe and set the terms of the debate. The *coup de grace* of the editorial is in its designation of the traditional muscle magazines as "hard-core," a term that, in the midfifties, necessarily implied a connection to pornography.

The underlying, and very vital, issue in this ongoing aesthetic and political battle between the traditional muscle publications and the newly emergent gay physique magazines was, of course, the much larger cultural war over changing definitions of American masculinity. The advent of an increasingly public gay community and presence in the postwar U.S. brought this question of masculinity to the fore, and the tensions between these publications was a struggle over representation, for the older, mainstream magazines wanted sole control over how the male body was being posed and portrayed. While this specific confrontation was located in the world of physical culture, the ramifications were much broader, and the anxiety over the public emergence of homosexuals—represented, I argue, by the "new" image of the gay male body—was far more pervasive.

For decades mainstream heterosexual culture had acclimated itself to the idea and image of the invert, often a figure of ridicule, humor, or pathos. The threat of the invert was containable because he was visible and instantly identifiable. The visibility may, at times, have placed him in physical danger, but it also positioned him firmly in the public eye and imagination. The new image of the muscular and fit gay male body that emerged in the fifties, however, radically destabilized the notion that the homosexual could be easily recognized. Now the potential for same-sex desire and activity resided not only in the highly identifiable invert but in men who exhibited the trappings of "normal" masculinity as well. This apparent disappearance of physical cues caused enormous apprehension and fear in a culture that had, up until now, relied on clearly demarcated gender differences to contain its fear of sexual deviancy. The anxiety caused by this shift in how the gay male body is imagined is made manifest in much of the sociological and journalistic writings about male homosexuality in the fifties. Faced with a new gay body "type," their authors often engage in a desperate attempt to exactly describe and securely pinpoint the physiognomy, dress, demeanor, and affect of the homosexual.

These attempts often end in disarray and confusion. In *Society and the Sex Variant* (1955), for instance, a large-scale survey of gay men and lesbians, George W. Henry exhibits a deeply rooted cultural schizophrenia in his descriptions of the salient physical, sartorial, and behavioral signifiers of male homosexuals. In a chart labeled "Sex Variant Characteristics," Henry paints a picture of what looks like the typical "invert":

[Hair is] [L]ong, soft silken, waves, well-kept, sometimes dyed or bleached. Scanty on face and body. Eyelashes long. Eyebrows plucked.

[Voice is] [S]oft, high-pitched, petulant and mealy mouthed; sometimes deep in marked contrast to other feminine characteristics. Much hissing and other accessory sounds in speech.

153

[Talk is] [E]xcessive, chatty, gossipy, mincing; many sexual innuendos; extravagant use of superlatives.

[Extremities are] [D]elicate, small slender hands. Long, tapering fingers. Well manicured nails. Highly flexible wrists. Feminine carrying angle of arms.

[Gait is] [U]ncertain, prim, mincing. Tendency to display by rocking and rotary movements of hips ("swish").

Yet as Henry outlines the feminine attributes of the typical homosexual, he argues that "even the masculine-looking homosexual dresses in a fashion to accentuate his masculinity!" and notes that many homosexuals wear dungarees, T-shirts, and uniforms. And while "one can almost say with certainty that any male who bleaches his hair is a homosexual," it also seems that "many homosexuals conform to the heterosexual male's taste for the close or 'crew' cut and 'clean neck' styles." Henry also admits to the existence of "hoodlum homosexuals"—usually trade or hustlers—who are "virile in appearance" and "verbally aggressive and brawling."[21]

Henry is so determinedly obsessed with pinpointing *exactly* what a homosexual looks like that his classifications become meaningless, as when he notes that the typical homosexual body form is "athletic with broad shoulders and narrow hips; sometimes narrow shoulders and broad hips" or describes scenarios that are so curiously odd as to be baffling: "Homosexuals who wear glasses frequently remove them in the company of other homosexuals. Many wear the heavy frames which were originally worn exclusively by homosexual men and women." But while Henry cannot come up with a coherent profile of a homosexual, he is clear in his belief that all homosexuals are obsessed with how they look and their ability to attract attention: "Homosexuals possess a keen awareness of the value of clothes in creating impressions. Whether they spend a great deal on their wardrobes or whether they must limit their clothing purchases, they dress with a purpose." For Henry, getting attention, especially sexual attention, is at the root of almost all homosexual fashion: "Much attention is paid to slacks, dungarees, shorts, or swimming trunks, or to trousers whether they are parts of suits or uniforms. Care is taken to accent the contours of the buttocks and the genitals!" Yet even here Henry realizes that he is on shaky methodological ground, and his thesis is fraught with contradiction:

Many readers will object that any of the above characteristics can be found in well-adjusted persons, that a heterosexual man often wishes to be well dressed, to have his handkerchief neatly arranged in his pocket. This is true, especially on formal occasions and when there is a need of making the most favorable impression. It is equally true that the homosexual is fastidious about his appearance when he wishes to make a good impression on another homosexual. The average man wishes to be neatly dressed, but beyond that he does not want to bother. (27)

As if this were not enough, Henry qualifies his theory once again:

In brief, the dress of the homosexual, to a much greater degree than the heterosexual male, serves to attract attention to the wearer. Even when the homosexual claims that he dresses in an inconspicuous fashion, one notices that there are elements of the dress that attract attention because of their distinctive quality. Many of his heterosexual brothers exhibit this absorption in dress, but this clothes-consciousness, along with other characteristics, indicates homosexuality. (27)

Henry's panicked desire to distinguish between the dress, deportment, and social affect of homosexual and heterosexual men ultimately fails because he cannot prove his simple postulation that there are concrete, observable differences. What we do see here, however, is the invention of the homosexual narcissist that is specific to post–World War II American culture. The term "narcissism," in a strict clinical sense, had been linked to male homosexuality since the earliest psychoanalytic writings. Here, in its simplest formulation, men turned to other men, seeking (like Narcissus) a similar vision of themselves. But in the fifties the use of this term, in common parlance, had become corrupted, and "narcissism" and "homosexuality" were linked in a more vulgar sense. Homosexuals, in this conception, still turned sexually from women to men because their "narcissism" compelled them to

155

choose a sexual object that replicated themselves, but they were also portrayed as preening, self-obsessed neurotics whose inability to care for no one but themselves verged on megalomania, who needed to bolster their fragile egos by attracting attention to their own bodies, and who were unable to sustain any committed emotional relationships because they could not reach outside themselves.

Commonly accepted "proof" of this narcissism was found in how homosexual men dressed and deported themselves. But as the quotations from *Society and the Sex Variant* show, this proof was often tenuous: clothes, it seemed, could make many types of men. The situation became further complicated when the burden of proof for "narcissism" shifted onto the physical bodies of homosexual men. The demise of the invert—and the subsequent invention of the butch homosexual—brought about the need to create a category, personality type, or behavior by which the homosexual could be easily identified. This became the obviously narcissistic personality, which would be manifested in the narcissistic body.

In his popular expose *The Sixth Man: A Startling Investigation of the Spread of Homosexuality in America*, Jess Stern attempts to describe and culturally locate the narcissistic gay male body:

> The gyms of New York are paradises for homosexuals. Here they come to posture, flex muscles, and establish an intimacy among themselves in apparently conventional surroundings. Not all gymnasiums welcome or want them. In fact, many take steps to discourage their trade. Some arbitrarily bar the most obvious. Others are put through such vigorous routines that they are only too glad to look elsewhere for their exercise and fun. . . . In some gyms on Manhattan's more effete East Side, there are so many homosexual muscle men that the ordinary male interested in keeping fit gets the feeling of being surrounded.[22]

Even the gym, previously the province of heterosexuality, becomes easily readable and recognized as a site of homosexual "posing" and activity. Once again, as in the nineteenth century, the sculpted male body passes as a signifier for both conventional masculinities and deviant ones. As the visual signification between the gay male body and the heterosexual body becomes less discernible, the cultural anxiety produced by this lack of difference dramatically escalates. It is the threat—and reality—of the gay male body and the heterosexual male body becoming one, indistinguishable and equally desirable, that emblematizes, in visual terms, the fear of male-male sexual contact and the possibility of love.

Notes

1. Scholarship detailing the shifting meanings ascribed to the male body has grown over the years. Kenneth R. Dutton's *The Perfectible Body: The Western Ideal of Male Physical Development* (New York: Continuum, 1995) and Margaret Walters's *The Nude Male: A New Perspective* (New York: Paddington Press, 1978) are comprehensive and intelligent studies. I use much of this material to place the male body within the historical and social context of gay male culture in *The Pleasure Principle: Sex, Backlash, and the Struggle for Gay Freedom* (New York: St. Martin's Press, 1998). David Chapman's introduction to *Adonis: The Male Physique Pin-Up, 1870–1940* (London: Gay Men's Press, 1989) contains many enlightening facts about the history of male-physique photos. Michael Hatt's "Physical Culture: The Male Nude and Sculpture in late Victorian Britain" in Elizabeth Pettijohn, ed. *After the Pre-Raphaelites: Art and Aestheticism in Victorian England* (New Brunswick: Rutgers University Press, 1999), 240–56, is an original and important addition to the discussion of the role of the male nude in both aesthetic and physical culture.

2. Although the works of the artists mentioned here have been highly instrumental in shaping conceptions of the nude male form in contemporary culture, little has been written about the artists themselves. Often, decent reproductions of their work are difficult to obtain. Baron Wilhelm von Gloeden's *Photographs of the Classic Male Nude* (New York: Camer/Graphic Press, 1975), is now out of print, but Peter Weiermair's *Wilhelm von Gloeden: Erotic Photographs* (Cologne: Taschen, 1994) and *Guglielmo Pluschow: Erotic Photographs* (Cologne: Taschen, 1994) are well-produced collections of their photographs. Susan Danly and Cheryl Leibold's *Eakins and the Photograph: Works by Thomas Eakins and His Circle in the Collection of the Pennsylvania Academy of the Fine Arts* (Washington, D.C.: Smithsonian Institution Press, 1994) is indispensable in understanding the painter and photographer, as is Estelle Jussim's

Slave to Beauty: The Eccentric Life and Controversial Career of F. Holland Day (Boston: David R. Godine, 1981), the only full-length study of this important American artist. *The Memoirs of John Addington Symonds*, ed. Phyllis Grosskurth (New York: Random House, 1984), published ninety-one years after Symonds's death, is essential to an understanding of the construction of a male homosexual Victorian identity. Symonds's *Male Love: A Problem in Greek Ethics and Other Writings*, ed. John Lauritsen (New York: Pagan Press, 1983), is also fundamental in discerning how the Victorian idealization of Greek culture influenced a nascent homosexual identity. While it is riddled with crankiness and flashes of homophobia, Rupert Croft-Cooke's *Feasting with Panthers: A New Consideration of Some Late Victorian Writers* (New York: Holt, Rinehart and Winston, 1967) brings together a wealth of material that is sometimes illuminating on the interrelationships of many of these writers and artists.

3. Eugene Sandow's importance as a cultural figure is not reflected in recent scholarship on the male body. David L. Chapman's *Sandow the Magnificent: Eugene Sandow and the Beginnings of Bodybuilding* (Urbana: University of Illinois Press, 1994) gives an intelligent overview of his life but contains little theoretical analysis. Sandow published five books in his lifetime, as well as numerous pamphlets and magazine articles. Although the books had large press runs, and in some cases several editions, they are now difficult to locate. The quotations in this essay come from the second edition of the first and most influential of the books, *Sandow on Physical Training*, ed. G. Mercer Adams (London: J. Selwin Tait and Sons, 1894). Linda Mizejewski's *Ziegfeld Girl: Image and Icon in Culture and Cinema* (Durham: Duke University Press, 1999) not only details Sandow's role in the *Ziegfeld Follies* but also provides detailed information on the making and marketing of theatrical spectacle, a determining factor in Sandow's career.

4. Hatt, 247.
5. Chapman, *Sandow the Magnificent*, 109.
6. Ibid., 113.
7. Ibid., 75.
8. Walker, 293.
9. Adam, 24–5.
10. Symonds, *Memoirs*, 77–8.
11. Symonds, "Studies in Greek Poets" in *Male Love*, 128–30.

12. Hatt, 245.

13. Chapman, *Sandow the Magnificent*, 34.

14. Croft-Cook, 141.

15. Ann Thwaite, *Edmund Gosse: A Literary Landscape, 1849–1928* (Chicago: University of Chicago Press, 1984), 323.

16. Dutton, 230.

17. Ibid., 139.

18. Any work on the physique magazines of the fifties must rely on *The Complete Reprint of Physique Pictorial* (Cologne: Taschen, 1997). There has been little scholarly work on these publications, but F. Valentine Hooven III's *Beefcake: The Muscle Magazines of America, 1950–1970* (Cologne: Taschen, 1995) is a brief but decent overview. John D. Fair's *Muscletown USA: Bob Hoffman and the Manly Culture of York Barbell* (University Park: Pennsylvania State University Press, 1999) is an examination of the economics, social world, and politics of serious bodybuilding through the lens of the most noted physical culture companies. Terry D. Morgan's "Pages of Whiteness: Race, Physique Magazines, and the Emergence of a Public Gay Culture," in Brett Beemyn and Mickey Eliason, eds. *Queer Studies: A Lesbian, Gay, Bisexual, and Transgender Anthology* (New York: New York University Press, 1996), 280–97, is an important contribution to the discussions of race, nationalism, and ethnic identity in gay culture and politics. Micha Ramakers's *Dirty Pictures: Tom of Finland, Masculinity, and Homosexuality* (New York: St. Martin's Press, 1999) deals with the complex issues of race, nationalism, and misogyny that the artist's work raises. These volumes give an overview of the work of the most noted artists of the physique magazines: *The Art of George Quaintance* (Berlin: Janssen-Verlag, 1989); *Lon of New York, American Photography of the Male Nude 1940–1970, vols. 1 and 2* (Berlin: Janssen-Verlag, 1996); *Bruce of Los Angeles*, ed. Jim Dolinsky (Berlin: Bruno Gmunder, 1990).

19. *Physique Pictorial* (4:4) Winter 1954–55, 2.

20. *Physique Pictorial* (6:3) Fall 1956, 2.

21. George W. Henry, M.D., *Society and the Sex Variant* (New York: Collier, 1965), 22–27.

22. Jess Stern, *The Sixth Man* (New York: Doubleday, 1961), 117–18.

6 Slumming

Peter Hitchcock

[The] curse of class-difference confronts you like a wall of stone. Or rather it is not so much a stone wall as the plate glass pane of an aquarium; it is so easy to pretend that it isn't there, and so impossible to get through it. Unfortunately, it is nowadays the fashion to pretend that the glass is penetrable.   —GEORGE ORWELL

For as long as there have been classes, there has been slumming. While this makes the phenomenon immediately of interest to materialist critique, slumming has had a shadowy existence in class analysis. There are several important reasons for this tendency. First, it has been seen simply as a pastime or cultural signifier rather than as a more scientific economic marker of socialization. Second, it has been hidden from history both because hegemony ineluctably suppresses the narratives that identify its structure in dominance, and because those whose theoretical work is dedicated to the revelation of such structures often mimic the narrative of desire and disavowal that constitutes their own forms of identification.

The matter is at once both simple and complex. On the one hand, no one seriously interested in the history of class formation and antagonism should be surprised that the privileges of class also include the privilege of identification with those whose servitude provides a ruling class with a logical integrity (and thus, "we desire to know the nature of our superiority" and, furthermore, "we want to be loved for it"). On the other hand, the fantasy of

slumming invokes the somewhat thorny question of desire itself in class critique, one that troubles the certitude of a science of class to the extent that
it never fully disengages its complicity with the social relations that ground
the object of its analysis in the first place. That this marks a space for gendered readings of class is not coincidental and, while a subtext in the present
critique, it remains the challenge in understanding the displaced "objects" of
class. This is true whether one pinpoints the otherwise innocuous practices
of sociology or anthropology in the study of the lower orders, or whether one
attends to the cultural relations of I/Other imbricated with the imagination
in creative expression. If class as a subject of analysis, however, has waned in
direct proportion to the slow expiration of the Age of Reason, then slumming, paradoxically, increasingly betrays what is living and dead in class relations, situated as it is in the liminal worlds of identity and difference. Indeed, precisely because of its ambivalent role in discourses of desire, slumming emerges as a key integer of that which desire would otherwise seek to
subtend, the Real of class itself.[1]

From the time that Nero undertook nocturnal excursions to experience a
street life he had never known, to modern-day obsessions with classing down
in dress, dining, and a myriad of other forms of cultural masquerade, slumming has been a *sine qua non* of class identification and subsumption. But
what in ancient Rome might have seemed an anarchic and reckless deroga-
tion of imperial decorum and dignity has now become one more facet of cultural capital to ruling classes that believe in their rule but not their class. The
modern phenomenon of slumming is class passing as quotidian class activity while it simultaneously registers an immense incredulity with narratives
of class themselves.[2] Indeed, slumming has become an integral cultural logic
of modernity wherein the wonder of the social induces a vertiginous mix of
artistic investigation and assimilation in parallel with the explosion and col-
onization of the popular in the twentieth century. Whether one cites social
satirists like George Orwell, documentarians like Ansel Adams, high moderns
like Henry Miller or Henry Green, or postmodern *flaneurs* like Irvine Welsh,
slumming is a key characteristic of modernity's reinscription of class as the

161

contestable, negotiable, and unnameable border zone of social integration and hierarchization. The social history of slumming, whatever else it is, is a story of how class formation gets represented. It is the found object of dominant desire, the locus of that which one must otherwise deny, the process through which one explores economic inequity only to return to that place and space that guarantees it.

Obviously, that social history is too broad to engage in this context; what I will do instead is track specific literary strands of the constitutive logic of slumming, particularly that which invokes passing as its modus operandi. If passing is not only about identities and their boundaries but also about specularity and the culturally observed, then we should not be surprised that slumming encompasses and comments on many of passing's salient features. Indeed, if slumming is read not just as classing down but as specific attempts at redefinition or reclassification in the social, then it can be applied to more traditional discourses of passing (although not without controversy). Here, I am especially interested in modernity's increasing production of slumming as a quotidian discourse of class negotiation and in the articulation of the other in slumming's narratological sweep. But I want to begin with the history of the word itself, whose own ambivalence and contestatory nature is apposite with the class liminality to which slumming refers.

Slums are coterminous with the industrial revolution: they emerged as an urban blight as cities grew exponentially and value extraction by capital intensified with labor as its object. (Infrastructural requirements could not keep pace with macroeconomic expansion.) Slums were and are not just the accidental by-products of industrialization and modernization; they are intrinsic to their daily operations.[3] The word, of course, like its cognate in German (*schlamm*), invokes slime or general detritus of a distasteful variety. Slumming is closely related to this definition, in that slums were and are a place where slumming might proceed. But slums and slumming are much more than this.

The slum is a mark of deprivation that yet signals a demonstrable excess. A slum is a place unfit for habitation but must, indeed, be lived in for it to be a slum. A slum is, in this sense, alive with deprivation—the living matter of its lack is what constitutes it as an object. When a slum is abandoned, it becomes a ghost town or a vacant lot. But while inhabited, it seethes with the lack that is its paradoxical presence. This hiding in visual space is common to urban development. It is also characteristic of passing, if one thinks of the latter as a presence that signifies a loss, a crossing to and from an absence that stitches identity.[4] (The fact that in societies of assumed white supremacy "black" is associated with "the ghetto" is not out of step with the economy of the slum and slumming.)

One of the other meanings of "slum" is to do work hurriedly and carelessly, and this, ironically, seems to be in accord with the irrational manifestation of a slum in urban "development." But it is among the slang or vernacular variations of "slum" that some of its more interesting meanings are to be found. In the middle of the nineteenth century, for instance, "to slum" could mean to cheat or to do something on the sly. "To slum," by this account, was something conspiratorial and included both hiding and passing (as in "relaying"). At the beginning of Victoria's reign "slumming" already meant to pass bad money, but before long it came to denote secreting in general. It is at this moment that slum as place and slum as practice become demonstrably enmeshed. Note that I am commenting here on the practice of slumming when referred to in that name and not the emergence of slumming-like activity, which, as I have already argued, is as old as class in the social imaginary. In Victorian England, at least, it is fascinating that the meanings of "slum" and "slumming" become highly contested as a newly conscious public sphere struggles over whether bourgeois and petty-bourgeois excursions into the slums are merely fashionable or genuinely philanthropic. In response, the popular press of the day begin to demarcate several forms of slumming. The press rarely got around to examining the economic production of the slum (and its work is therefore to be distinguished from "social problem" writing), but it did attempt to understand the social conditions by which the slum came to be an urban exhibition.

Schematically, social-conscience slumming was ordinarily associated with church work and the more pure of soul (a phenomenon with its own complexity, as evinced in Samuel Butler's *The Way of All Flesh*). Bad-conscience slumming owed its emergence to a nagging suspicion on the part of wealthier urban dwellers that all was not well in other parts of the city and, as a thousand documents such as Matthew Arnold's *Culture and Anarchy* made clear, even poorly intended alms were better than social upheaval. Oblivious slumming included those who might have had a conscience but were more deeply attracted by the fashionable statement than the social conditions that gave rise to it. This last practice gave to slumming its association with an excursion or an expedition into the nether worlds of the poor and destitute. Slumming parties were sometimes put together as a form of entertainment or pastime "out of curiosity." It is also at this time that professional or vocational slumming came of age. This seems to have combined elements of all the other forms, in which the participant accepts "temporarily or voluntarily, a standard [of living] lower than that to which one is accustomed; to mix with one's inferiors" (as the *Oxford English Dictionary*, second edition, delightfully puts it). In vocational slumming, the pleasures of slumming are combined with the hardships it nevertheless represents and bespeak a level of class masochism that lives on, vicariously, in the everyday consumption of misery.

There are other ways, of course, that slumming may be interpreted. There is, for instance, a situational or dialogic slumming that need not take place in a slum at all but instead occurs at those moments when a tactical classing down may further another agenda (affecting supposedly working-class accents or mannerisms is typical of this approach—again, there is a clear correlation with a tactical deployment of racial identity on this point). Intellectual slumming has its own tortuous history, and has taken on a particularly controversial valence in postcolonial, "Third World," or subaltern and subcultural analysis.[5] And there is also a more general economy of slumming that is ardently relativist and that applies itself to almost any instance of downward mobility. While slumming is almost omnipresent, to be caught or to be accused of slumming retains much of the pejorative sense of slumming. It is the "don't ask, don't tell" of class relations.

Not all slumming is masquerade. A good deal of slumming takes place with class positions clearly demarcated. The working class and poor are not dupes and can tell readily when a person's economic condition is based on imperatives or options. Middle- class students, for instance, often accept a lower standard of living in lieu of the cultural capital that their degree will eventually confer. Similarly, artists, actors, writers, and the like regularly find themselves proletarianized by the difficulties of actually living off their professions. Naturally, this does not exclude working-class people, but bohemia has its own version of the reality principle, one that does not necessarily accord with the specific relationship between labor, labor power, and capital. Nevertheless, it would be both fatuous and inaccurate to label as "slumming" every instance of optional classing down, not the least because it tends to obfuscate the concrete conditions in which it is precipitate. An artist's proletarianization has much more to do with her relationship to the state, or society's evaluation of art than it has to do with the artist's intimacy with working-class communities (except, of course, when the working class becomes a subject of the art itself). The reason class passing adds critical weight to slumming is that it usually involves the status of class knowledge at any one moment of history and an attempt to voice the unspeakable of the unrepresentable: the relation behind or within the thing observed.

The Ur-Slummer, who is at once the slummer par excellence and the abyss of slumming studies is Nero Claudius Caesar Drusus Germanicus: the emperor of slumming, Nero. While there is no space here to consider Nero's contribution to the discourse of slumming, it is important to note that his nocturnal expeditions and carnivalizing identifications provided Petronius, the Arbiter of Elegance, with an aesthetic inspiration for Satyrica (Satyricon), which may well be slumming's first novel. One of the lessons of Petronius's work is that slumming often emerges precisely at moments of excess, when a class in dominance seeks to understand the logic of its excessive existence

and identity by foraging among its minions. There is a distinct transformation in the process of such identification in the nineteenth century, when
slumming as passing bad money (and bad faith) becomes slumming as class
investigations of various kinds and gives us the word as it is currently understood. In modern industrialization, slumming became the ward chiefly of
a newly extravagant bourgeoisie, cognizant not only of its dubious heritage
(leading to the purchase of said status from the declining aristocracy) but also
of the ground of its social position, the mass that gave to its constituency
both integrity and fear.

Slumming, then, becomes the social force produced in the grinding of two
tectonic plates of modern society, labor and capital. But it is not class war
pure and simple even as it signifies the sociocultural conditions of class difference. (To push the analogy a little further, it may provide those mini-
quakes that ease the stress in class relations.) Whereas Petronius described
slumming as one more facet of a decadent geist, slumming in modernity is
uniquely the emergence of bourgeois social contradictions, of an identity
snared between an offspring generally abhorred, workers, and a consciousness of a leading role despite the barbarism that seems to attend it.

Slumming, for instance, from the Victorian age on (and coterminous with
the rise of sociology and anthropology) enables social protest and critique.
This is the positive valence to identification in class difference, although historically many of those who pursue this avenue have emerged from a "slum
existence" themselves. This is not true of Friedrich Engels, and it is worth
considering his contribution to the sociological phenomenon within modernity that I am attempting to elucidate. Engels goes to England in 1842 at the
request of his father to investigate the business practices and factory system
of the cotton spinning industry. The difference between the father's interest
in the profit motive and the son's desire to criticize the same is very much
part of the Janus-faced nature of sociological slumming. Instead of empowering the German bourgeoisie with his analysis, Engels produced *The Condition of the English Working Class in 1844*,[6] a text very much alive to the new

social movements of its time, particularly Chartism, and with a keen eye to the very contradictions that precipitate the European crises of 1848. While Disraeli, Gaskell, and Dickens came up with a similar foreboding, Engels opted for a more engaged, early version of participant observation, partly based on an idealistic yet dialogic sense of an otherwise absent English working-class readership (the English translation did not appear until forty years after the German, in 1886).

The second-person plural in Engels's dedication is particularly provocative: "To you I dedicate a work in which I have tried to lay before my German countrymen a faithful picture of your condition, of your sufferings and struggles, of your hopes and prospects" (27). One is tempted to say that Engels is addressing ghosts, for the working "men" he invokes in the opening passage would have been long gone before the text reached them in a recognizable form (the dedication was, in fact, written in English but was unavailable to its addressees). This is not to belittle Engels's solidarity but, rather, to underline that the objective conditions of the slum dwellers are often rendered in the presence of an absent and silent interlocutor. Furthermore, it is unclear just how much significant contact Engels had with the workers he describes in great detail, even though the dedication insists on a sustained familiarity forged through a temporary sacrifice in the lifestyle to which he was accustomed:

I wanted more than a mere abstract knowledge of my subject, I wanted to see you in your own homes, to observe you in your everyday life, to chat with you on your condition and grievances, to witness your struggles against the social and political power of your oppressors. I have done so: I forsook the company and the dinner parties, the port-wine and champagne of the middle classes, and devoted my leisure-hours almost exclusively to the intercourse with plain working men; I am both glad and proud of having done so. (27)

This is classic slumming in what Engels himself calls a "classic slum." The addressee here is not, in fact, the infamous "working man" but precisely those educated and bourgeois souls who indulge in a dinner party or two during their leisure hours. Does Engels really believe that forsaking champagne would impress the English working class?

The dedication positions Engels between the English workers and their oppressors, and Engels fervently hopes that he will be a "foreigner" to the latter rather than the former. But while Engels never passed in clothes or speech in the slums of Manchester, the idea that he has rendered the condition of the English working class in "plain English" (and German!) is redolent with that narrative of passing as displacement for knowing that crops up all over the literary and sociological maps of class relations. Victor Kiernan suggests that Engels must have had a guide in his explorations of the underworld; Mary Burns is the most likely candidate. It seems clear that Engels would not have come as close as he did without some form of working-class mediation. Burns, of course, was a longtime lover of Engels and hailed from the Irish working class. Engels does not reveal how much help he got in his fieldwork, but it is not unreasonable to surmise that Burns could have been his "native informant." The point, however, is not to belittle the sincerity or veracity of Engels's efforts. The aim is to come to terms with the logic of engagement or class contact it implies, a logic that wants so much to overcome the abstract in the apprehension of the worker as subject that the observer may suppress the degree to which that abstraction is preserved by the social consciousness of class itself. The achievement of Engels's *The Condition of the English Working Class in 1844* is that it provides an immense intervention in class analysis while fending off the real foundations of class relations of its time that gird the distance Engels strenuously attempts to bridge.

Engels is spurred by the belief that proletarian conditions exist "in their classical form, in their perfection" (29) in the British Isles of the 1840s because of Britain's level of industrial expansion. What is curious is that the working class does not testify to this existence in Engels's text. Time after time, in addition to his own observations, Engels deploys references to other investigators of the working class, or even hostile commentators, in elaborating "conditions" of various kinds. While this clearly gives one an expanded sense of the complex components of proletarian life (the foul living quarters, the tainted food, the poor clothing, the work-related diseases and deformities of every description, the short life spans, and, importantly, the forms of resistance pursued by significant numbers of the class), one wonders why Engels did not include reports of his conversations with those to whom his tome is dedicated?

Rhetorically, he involves the reader in his explorations ("let us investigate some of the slums in their order" [71]) and records the horrible conditions he sees with the same disgust as his implied reader—the German bourgeois or intellectual. (Interestingly, in contemporary critical discussions of Engels's book, the most revered section is "The Great Towns," which contains both the highest proportion of his direct observations and a concomitant intensity of repugnance that could not help but impress his similarly class-positioned readers, sympathetic or otherwise.) Are those odors, which Engels records with vigor in "The Great Towns," any less objectionable to those who have to live with them? By not supplying any reaction to such conditions on the part of the working-class denizens of the slums, Engels tends to objectify the working class by feeding a common stereotype that this dirt and destitution is a natural disposition, as natural as the pigs that share their public spaces.

Even if Engels does elucidate how such squalor is produced by the machinations of capital, it is easy to see how the shock for a middle-class reader can be quickly followed by the idea that these conditions are not the effects of socioeconomic hierarchization but the very reasons *for* such differentiation: "Everywhere heaps of debris, refuse, and offal; standing pools for gutters, and a stench which alone would make it impossible for a human being in any degree civilized to live in such a district" (91). Capital debases the worker, dehumanizes him and her to an extent scarcely rivaled in human history, but too often in Engels's text his eyes glaze over when it comes to observing what remains human and civilized in working-class communities. The point would not be to concede some kind of satisfaction or acceptance of the dire conditions described but to acknowledge, if only for a second, that the working class, and not a visiting parson or condescending Carlyle, are every bit as aware of the meaning of slums.

The rhetoric of slumming is passing whenever it purports to represent an acquaintance or an experience as if it were self-identical with the subject position so described. Engels raises the stakes in the study of slums (which was already a practiced narrative of the time) by detailing the horrors of everyday working-class existence in its own name and by suggesting that his study was somehow textured by "chats" or direct contact with workers themselves (and therefore not "abstract," to use his own terminology). Significantly, when it comes to the bourgeoisie or factory owners, Engels ascribes class positions in the form of direct speech: "The bourgeoisie says: 'If we do not employ the children in the mills, they are only left under conditions unfavorable to their development'" (172). In effect, he characterizes them through speech; he personifies them, which, while also a metonymic displacement in its own way, at least implies that the bourgeoisie has speeches to make, can indeed make speech. It is rare in Engels's book that the workers are characterized through direct or indirect speech, but these moments are worth noting.

First, working-class members of the community are quoted by means of the reports that Engels cites (this material makes up the bulk of the book, for which the exploration of the "great towns" serves as a stunning contrast). To underline the almost complete lack of education available to the slum dwellers, Engels excerpts a Children's Employment Commission's Report where, in response to a question regarding simple arithmetic, a seventeen-year-old replies that he "was ne judge o' nothin'" (141). It is appropriate that the boy's double negative serves as speech within the text, since as a working-class subject he occupies a position of negation that historically provides one for negation; that is, the historical transcendence called revolution which is very much the spirit in Engels's forecasts. Later, Engels quotes from the *Morning Chronicle,* which had printed some letters of a stocking weaver from Hinckley. Again, the substance of the weaver's comments speak louder than the space provided: "No eye has seen, no ear heard, and no heart felt the half of the sufferings that these people endure" (204). This, of course, is answered by Engels's own narrative, which strives in the throes of youthful indignation to represent not just that which is unrepresented but also—and this remains the paradox of slumming—that which is unrepresentable. Even if the text were structured through working-class testimonial, this would not be the Real of class existence (which is a relation, not a voice, not an inflection).

The theoretical knot remains, in the same way that Engels knows that the social praxis requisite to end the conditions he describes cannot come to rest on the effect of his narrative, which may or may not make socialists of a few German bourgeois intellectuals. The lack of extant working-class voice is not just a determinate absence but a sign of a greater challenge to class consciousness. As we have noted above, the intimation of an uncivil essence in working-class existence flies in the face of nineteenth-century bourgeois beliefs in progress and benevolence. The English working class is a vital source of value in economic production and yet, as Engels painfully discovers, workers live as waste, they live in waste, and they are wasting away from the invisible hand of value extraction:

I found a man, apparently about sixty years old, living in a cow-stable. He had constructed a sort of chimney for his square pen, which had neither windows, floor, nor ceiling, [and] had obtained a bedstead and lived there, though the rain dripped through his rotten roof. This man was too old and weak for regular work, and supported himself by removing manure with a hand-cart; the dung-heaps lay next door to his palace! (100)

Engels does not expose the deep structure of class society but, in such portraits, provokes a revelation in reader response—that her or his difference from this old man is based on an economic bond. To some extent, Engels does want to inspire guilt (particularly his father's), but the tension in such descriptions is riven by Engels's own class position, for his research at this time was either directly supported by his work in the cotton factory or was indirectly provided for by funds from his father.

Engels certainly did not live in the Manchester slums, but he did stay close enough to the factories to provide easy access and constant reinforcement of his fundamental horror at industrial life. His slumming is designed to combat the very class difference he perceives. While I cannot do justice to the extraordinary range of social criticism Engels produces, I do want to underline the question of passing in class relations his text identifies and to some extent typifies. Steven Marcus has suggested that there is a fair degree of philistinism in Engels's existence, something that Engels often acknowledges, but something too that he characteristically represses. (Marcus, for all the tenacity of his reading, gently squeezes Engels into a conventional Freudian framework and, while the Oedipal trajectory is relevant to discourses of desire, the capital relation is something else again.)[7] The pathos in Engels's carping on his own situation ("it is too horrible to remain not only a bourgeois, but a manufacturer to boot, a bourgeois actively engaged in opposing the working classes" [117–118]) is undeniable, and the irony that some of the greatest works of socialist thought (including, most notably, *Capital*) were subsidized by a German textile capitalist are symptoms of a persistent dilemma in the class identification necessitated by class relations themselves.

Engels is a bad philistine to the extent that he, like many social activists in the nineteenth century, became a class traitor and exposed the ignorance and indifference of the industrial bourgeoisie at every turn. He "played" the bourgeois much more than he passed as a proletarian (if indeed he did the latter at all), but the truth of Marcus's criticism is that the ambivalence of class crossing never allows for class prejudice to be completely expunged. (Marcus underlines this by reference to what little is extant regarding the relationship of Engels and Burns.) My point would be that slumming is always a means to an end, but precisely because it is about a process of identification, the subject cannot possibly adjudicate all of the terms of that transgression. What makes it interesting aesthetically is also what recommends it as a phenomenon socially.

Engels is interested in the "passing" of the Victorian bourgeoisie—the way it strenuously masks the conditions of exploitation that secure its place in civilization. This is also the place where slumming as fabrication or forgery meets passing as disguise. One of the most provocative sections of Engels's study is when he describes how Manchester is organized spatially, not only to separate the classes but also to hide the existence of the working class from the city's other inhabitants. While Engels does not show the theoretical sophistication of David Harvey's reading of nineteenth-century Paris or Walter Benjamin's highly nuanced reading of the same, he nevertheless conveys a sense of how class consciousness unconsciously constructs its cityscapes.[8] Just as Benjamin's phantasmagoria is the vicarious display of the commodity relation, Engels relates how capital writes class location into its urban topography. Indeed, Engels's description complements Benjamin's Arcades Project by intimating what lies on the other side of commodity display:

[T]he finest part of the arrangements is this, that the members of this money aristocracy can take the shortest road through the middle of all the laboring districts to their places of business, without ever seeing that they are in the midst of the grimy misery that lurks to the right and the left. For the thoroughfares leading from the Exchange in all directions out of the city are lined, on both sides, with an almost unbroken series of shops, and are so kept in the hands of the middle and lower bourgeoisie, which, out of self-interest, cares for a decent and cleanly external appearance and can care for it. True, these shops bear some relation to the districts which lie behind them, and are more elegant in the commercial and residential quarters than when they hide grimy working-men's dwellings; but they suffice to conceal from the eyes of the wealthy men and women of strong stomachs and weak nerves the misery and grime which form the complement to their wealth. (86)

The longer Engels stays in Manchester, the more he comes to understand the cultural logic of separation. Just by walking these streets over and over he realizes that, planned or not, Manchester conceals the have-nots from the haves, even though the latter know just as much as the former that they are there. At this level, Marcus is not wrong to invoke a psychological framework in capitalist organization, for the city that Engels sees follows an almost-classic logic of objectification and disavowal. Without the means to survey the city from above, it is hard to imagine that Engels could have developed this aspect of his critique without sustained and up-close observation. The problem remains whether sociological slumming sustains the disavowal that it might otherwise oppose.

The greatest weakness in Engels's approach is not the mode of critique (combining official reports with personal observation) but that the condition of the working class that he records appears to have no room for culture. Rhetorically, this might be explained by Engels's broader arguments (that is, that the "social murder" he sees in the treatment of the working class includes a kind of cultural murder, whereby the capital process itself renders the workers and their communities mentally dead). Yet Engels will also argue that proletarians take to education at every opportunity, so the capacity for culture is obviously there. This is, I think, where an observation of the slums can obviate a more deeply engaged experience of the slums. Rather than spend so many pages explaining heavy alcohol consumption and sexual licentiousness, Engels might have devoted time to the complexity and depth of working-class cultural pursuits that, even amid the dire conditions, occupy a key role in everyday worker existence (culture, for instance, is very much a part of the "making" in E. P. Thompson's *Making of the English Working Class*). As such, statistical horror (life expectancy, health, and so on) can mask the ways in which cultural practices (music, games, writing, cooking, dress codes, and the like) contribute to an identity much greater than the animal existence that Engels often portrays.

Whatever Engels's political intent, his *Condition of the English Working Class in 1844* remains a crucial work in preparing the ground for slumming in modernity. Never in danger of being proletarianized himself, Engels brings forth the horrors of the slums for middle-class consumption—for righteous probity, or for vicarious pleasure in the unfortunate lives of a nearby Other. Just as industrialization guaranteed the production of slum life, so sociological investigation primed the pump of bourgeois desire. Similarly, the social problem novelists like Dickens and Disraeli exposed the scandals of progress only to find that the consumption of horror was a pleasure in its own right: hard times were better than soft for the leisure class. The danger (as Engels, to his credit, also outlines) was that the slum bred dissent and social unrest and that the proximity that oiled slumming could also facilitate insurrection on the owners' side of town. This difficulty in the allotment of class and space in the city has formed the not-so-hidden history of urban redevelopment.

By the end of the nineteenth century, sociological and cultural slumming mature and merge while, spatially, the urban classes divide as transportation affords commuting and compartmentalization. Politically, the condition of slum dwellers remains a key concern, but for the factory owners, obliviousness to working-class drudgery is honed by increasing distance rather than by strategically developed shop "fronts." Sociological slumming did not die out (indeed, it remains today as "third-worlding at home") but, rather, found itself displaced to a degree by more creative engagements with slum existence. It is this writerly engagement that I have termed "vocational slumming." In brief, it is that artistic space where social conscience must pass into the very texture of slum living; where, in order to mark protest as authentic, the process of identification must become more and more "like" rather than "to" or "with" the slum dwellers depicted. It is as if the greater intensities of class consciousness (redolent in a variety of social movements) require more subtle models than scientific formulae or abstraction in order to garner substance. Nero wore wigs not to know slum dwellers but simply to experience them. The vocational slummer can never quite escape this desire (to do so would change the very nature of subject and object), but he or she hopes nevertheless that creative reportage will unhinge the normalizing tendencies of capitalist logic: that poverty and slums are inevitable.

While Robert Roberts's *The Classic Slum* is an important correction and extension of Engels's somewhat detached verisimilitude, the advent of vocational slumming forever changed the components of slum identification. Two examples may suffice here. Robert Baltrop has suggested that Jack London's slumming (referred to as a "masquerade") that became *The People of the Abyss* was successful because London had retained a sensitivity for the poor from his own years of poverty.[9] Of course, what everyone remembers about

Jack London is not the authentic acumen he brought to his depiction of working-class communities but, rather, the idealized and romantic conclusions he draws from his experiences (that ultimately pitch socialism into a volatile mix of hero-worship and individualism). Nevertheless, London's class position affords him more ease in the task of double-voicing slum life (one voice of the poor, another about it).

London approaches his six months in the East End of London with the attitude of an "explorer," and to that extent preserves the logic of exhibition that is built into slumming.[10] Like Engels wanting to "see" the workers in their own homes, London wants "to see things for myself. I wish to know how these people are living there, and why they are living there, and what they are living for. In short, I am going to live there myself" (7). Engels, of course, much better schooled in the science of economics, knew why "they are living there," just as he knew that the old man he describes did not choose to live among manure. Despite London's own life of poverty, his professional ardor refuses the knowledge that this provides. And this is why, unlike Engels, the vocational slummer must invoke the realm of the mimetic: London must be "like" the slum dwellers, he must engage in masquerade.

Hilariously (to the modern reader), London seeks travel aid with Thomas Cook's, the famous agency. But, whereas the travel agent has no problem in recommending a route to "Darkest Africa," a trip to the East End is discouraged: "It is so—ahem—unusual" (8). A highly unlikely encounter, it is used nevertheless as a stylistic embellishment that is in step with the function of the slum in the bourgeois imagination—an exotic world of penury, but so close to home! In the modern economy of slumming, the beggar occupies the sign for this persistent, if unfortunate, symbolic. Do you look beyond his destitute condition, do you avert your gaze, or do you marvel in the same instant at its proximity: could that which provides such luxury also produce this "unaccommodated man?" We should grant London the right to irony, and there is humor in his send- up of Edwardian prudery, but he remains a fool of his perceived egalitarianism. From the beginning, his spirit of adventure is fired by the same systemic racism that indeed got Cook to organize

African expeditions: "the region my hansom was now penetrating was one unending slum. The streets were filled with a new and different race of people, short of stature, and of wretched or beer-sodden appearance" (9-10). On this day, London is after only his outfit, a suit for slumming as it were. Again, that this is a masquerade is underlined by the contrast of necessity and choice. London manages to buy well-worn trousers, a frayed jacket with one button, and dirty shoes and cap. He insists, however, that although his underwear and socks are new and warm, even a "waif, down in his luck" would have been able to buy them. The mask preserves the purity of his soul! And, in case that is not enough, he sews a gold sovereign into the armpit of his jacket.

The emphasis on dress code is important in the history of slumming as passing. The cognitive confusion that marks the appearance of the subject in passing is conditioned by perception, the idea that the passer looks the part. London's tactics are intriguing in that they so brazenly embody the categorical fissures between the counterfeit and the authentic that is the discursive genealogy of passing. Thus, London "proceeded to array myself in the clothes of the other and unimaginable men" as if indeed that other and the unimaginable are revealed precisely through the process of masking. For London, if not for theory, this transformation is nothing less than magic:

No sooner was I out on the streets than I was impressed by the difference in status effected by my clothes. All servility vanished from the demeanor of the common people with whom I came in contact. Presto! In the twinkling of an eye, so to say, I had become one of them. My frayed and out-at-elbows jacket was the badge and advertisement of my class, which was their class. It made me of like kind, and in place of the fawning and too-respectful attention I had hitherto received, I now shared with them a comradeship. (12–13)

Perhaps this is only to say that slumming depends upon a shared delusion. But it is more than this: in the course of London's "descent" among the "people of the abyss" we come to understand those frail ideological sutures that make class difference hold together, that persuade us that even in crossing such tenuous borders the otherness they mark must be preserved or the game will be up, the conventions themselves will be at stake as well as the social apparatus that produces them.

Many of the sociological details London provides are not very different from those found in Engels's analysis of Manchester almost sixty years earlier: the conditions of want, poor diet, poor housing, and high mortality rates reveal a continuing reproduction of human detritus for the want of finery. The difference is not so much in the dire life portrayed but in the interactions that London seeks to confirm it. *The People of the Abyss* is full of recorded conversations (complete with phonetic approximations of Cockney dialect) that give London's expedition a greater expressive veracity even as his political intentions remain muddled or simply specious. The effect is particularly noticeable in the stark contrast between his exchanges with the people of the East End and his second-person address to the "soft people, full of meat and blood," those of the middle classes who (as with Engels) are his implied readers.

Each of London's chapters is headed by an epigraph (including a couple from Carlyle, another connection with Engels, perhaps) whose truth is measured by the reality that London confronts. In chapter eight, London accompanies two unemployed old fellows who are identified by the work they do not have as "the Carter and the Carpenter." London is deeply affected by their poverty, and in one italicized paragraph he records in detail how they pick up and consume waste food from the "slimy sidewalk." The three together try to find shelter in a poorhouse but, turned away, London then decides to reveal himself to them and produces his emergency fund, the gold sovereign:

Of course, I had to explain to them that I was merely an investigator, a social student, seeking to find out how the other half lived. And at once they shut up like clams. I was not of their kind; my speech had changed, the tones of voice were different, in short, I was a superior, and they were superbly class conscious. (52)

Their reaction is not surprising, and neither is London's assumption, redolent from the start, that whatever the level of abjection, the working-class subject will give up her or his meanings as long as disguise allays the suspicion that comes with class consciousness.

Once the mask has been dropped, London must buy back the old fellows' confidence with a slap-up meal, and sure enough, from meek responses both the Carter and the Carpenter are stoked into narration. True, London appreciates the hardships they have suffered and the political insight they display about how the world works. In general, however, the encounter reminds us that slumming in part depends upon a rhetoric of control, that any intensity in revelation is itself framed by the investigating subject's cognitive grasp on the conditions of interaction. Whether actually sewn into the armpit of a jacket or not, there is always the gold coin, always the quick exit without which the identification would border on forms of psychosis. Just to extend this analogy into the present, recently Gucci marketed denim jeans and skirts that were hand-embroidered at a mere $3,000 or so apiece. Slummer idols of the mass-market machine bought in profusion. Couture is a natural for slumming: its commodity aesthetic has always been primed by the ability to keep secret (in true fetishistic disavowal) the gold coin of class transaction.

Despite London's extreme example of a fiercely isolated individualist driven to a contradictory position of heroic socialism (a paradox in London's politics, it must be said, wantonly embraced in the next generation by the Soviets—especially if collected works are used as a measure), he is an important archetype in slumming. *The People of the Abyss* is based on an appreciable disgust with the ravages of capital but finds in the end that these excesses have occurred only because of the distractions of a disintegrating empire. The problem is not so much the logic of want produced, but that the society London sees requires a good deal of managerial fine tuning. For my purposes, the act of slumming in London's project is symptomatic of an impasse in class to which his work offers an enduring lesson. If class consciousness is the fruition of a desire to think and act in class ways, an identity reasserted by the Carter and the Carpenter at the moment of London's unveiling, then the task for the lords of inequity is to smother the basis for such differentiation, to provide the mask for the masquerade, or to declare it nonexistent by ideological fiat. This is, perhaps, as reductionist as London's spirit of identification, yet slumming confirms the persistence of this dilemma even as class distinctions themselves appear to have devolved into ever more fleeting and complex associations. In this sense, vocational slumming is always the mark of a negotiated class affect, a class-inflected reflex or duty to understand something of the logic of social hierarchization upon which the excursion itself is based.

Like London, George Orwell wants to pass for working class on the basis of a political and moral commitment. But nobody can mistake the difference in their class backgrounds. Here is Orwell, clothing himself appropriately to enter the slums of London:

It gives one a very strange feeling to be wearing such clothes. I had worn bad enough things before, but nothingat all like these; they were not merely dirty and shapeless, they had—how is one to express it?—a gracelessness, a patina of antique filth, quite different from mere shabbiness.[11] *(128)*

London may have acknowledged an awkwardness in his dirty disposition, but a "patina of antique filth"? This was middle-class Englishness of a high order. Nevertheless, Orwell, like London, notices an immediate change in response based on the nature of his clothing. A hawker calls him "mate," and Orwell goes on to note that "clothes are powerful things" (129).

Orwell's class affiliations are as complex as London's, but his period of slumming emerges from a quite distinct desire in identification. In *The Road to Wigan Pier,* Orwell is adamant that his petty-bourgeois upbringing brought out the worst in snobbishness and arrogance when it came to consideration of the poor and working classes.[12] Naturally, the very wealthy, and particularly the newly wealthy, were also to be despised for floating above the imperious "middle." Orwell explains, "The correct and elegant thing, I felt, was to be of gentle birth but to have no money. This is part of the *credo* of the lower-upper middle class. It has a romantic, Jacobite-in-exile feeling about it which is very comforting" (138). This level of class self-consciousness is particularly prevalent around the First World War, not just because of the concrete conditions of class struggle at the time (the intensities of which would be felt through the General Strike and into the Great Depression of the thirties) but because the relationship of writers in general to the social was also under transformation, as vocation and as a component of culture. The slummer could be the mildly curious but was more often precisely this "Jacobite-in-exile," one for whom the terms of class codes and control were demonstrably alienating.

Like another Eton contemporary, Henry Green, Orwell introjects the ideology of the outsider so that, even when despising the working-class people for their "accents . . . and habitual rudeness" he goes in search of the worker (140). It is a masochism born at once of a recognition of the tyranny of class as a social category, and as an initiation rite into the more noble ranks of those who combat oppression. Orwell saw no lasting value in such identification ("failure to me seemed the only virtue" [148]) but felt that it would purge him of his snobbery. He wanted desperately "to find some way of getting out of the respectable world altogether" (149). Even when he, like London before him, headed into the East End, he remained racked by class ambivalence: "I was still half afraid of the working class. I wanted to get in touch with them, I even wanted to become one of them, but I still thought of them as alien and dangerous" (151). This remains the hallmark of slumming: a temporary identification marked by an edgy thrill in the confrontation with the Other.

Of course, the psychic aura of class can also be explained in Orwell's case by his relationship to his parents (although that primal scene is not just a metonym for class), but let me focus for a moment on the specific process of his identification with the poor. In addition to his moral conviction that he must learn from the experience of poverty, Orwell clearly sought to broaden the base of his writing skills. The study of the languages of class was for him a means to infuse his writing with the living texture of the social as he saw it. In the last part of *Down and Out in Paris and London*, for instance, Orwell notes some of the peculiarities of Cockney dialect, as if the language of the Other were itself the key to creative veracity. His commentary does not bear too much scrutiny (the observation that rhyming slang is "almost extinct" has not stood the test of time), but nevertheless Orwell displays a professional interest in learning from his experience. Apart from dressing the part (slumming remains predominantly cross-dressing as class), Orwell works hard to immerse himself in the culture of poverty and homelessness—it being understood that one of the horrors of working-class existence was to be cast off (like the Carter and the Carpenter) into the destitute ranks of the unemployed. Just as Engels came to define the slum in terms of its olfactory attributes, so Orwell slums his way into a world of obnoxious smells and putrefying pastimes. Noting that less than half the tramps he knew bathed even when they had a chance, Orwell goes on to recount his horror at the smell of the toe-rags they wore. But Orwell's continual disgust at the conditions he experiences is mitigated by the knowledge that he can quickly remove himself from the spike, the flophouse, at any time. It is only in Paris that Orwell is temporarily cut off from financial life support (interestingly, at about the time when he becomes a *plongeur*, a dishwasher—that is, when he works for a living). Yet what does he learn? Whether suffering in a spike, or later "slumming" in the houses of coal miners (I believe this is the only time that Orwell uses the word), Orwell finds that his guilt has not been assuaged but accentuated.

Orwell appreciates the poor and sympathizes with them, workers and unemployed alike, but there is very little sense in his conclusions that reform or revolution will change a thing. This is remarkably in step with the cultural logic of slumming, which discovers a constitutive ambivalence in class relations only to confirm that class difference is a constant. As my epigraph attests, one can see through class (it conforms to a fairly basic scopic economy, especially in terms of *schaulust*), but that glass pane is also a division, and a shatter-proof one at that. As Orwell subsequently attests, "to abolish class distinctions means abolishing a part of yourself" (*Road*, 161), and even for the ardent social critic this is a prospect far more traumatic than the slumming that provides this realization. Indeed, most forms of slumming are a class negotiation in lieu of transformation. This is both a mark of its persistence and its passing.

I began by suggesting that slumming is now much more widespread, that it has become part of the quotidian discourse of class knowledge at a time when class consciousness itself appears in hasty retreat. This is not a coincidence of course, but from the class experiences noted above it is clear that slumming is not a simple or ready barometer of class struggle. Rather, slumming indicates a displaced discourse or counterdiscourse of class that clings, albeit ambiguously, to a logic of class division highly resistant to a shift in Being greater than a change of clothes, a relocation, a slip in accent, or an attitude adjustment. Perhaps the pervasiveness of slumming as class passing in the present is a greater, thoroughgoing popular expression of the affect in class being more ably negotiated than its real foundations in economic hierarchy and injustice. Yet it is more than that: it is the realization that in a thoroughly commodified socius even class as a relation can be represented as a thing, as an attribute, as a style, as a mode of living irrespective of the heady world of value extraction and exchange. From this standpoint, class is openly a consumer product: as a superceded concept (to borrow from Marx's reading of Hegel) it becomes yet one more commodity for consumption. Yet this is no more the rational kernel of class than dress is the essence of the human. What, then, is the value of a genealogy of slumming?

In part, the effort is to draw renewed attention to the mutations of class through the more ethereal aspects of class interaction. Slumming is always a contact zone in which class gets rearticulated or disarticulated in surprising ways. The task today would be to examine how entrenched this border crossing is in contemporary culture. It seems to me that Irvine Welsh's novel *Trainspotting* enacts precisely the logic of the commodity form in this regard.[13] Certainly this is not Welsh's intention, despite the fact that so many critics were and are obsessed with his depiction of drug culture and the wasted youth of Scotland. Yet, in writing a stunning portrait of conditions of deracination within a subculture, and doing it through language that, in its

183

very form, decolonizes English (one of the paradoxes of the postmodern is that it passes for nationalism), Welsh offers up a kind of working-class fragmentation in postindustrial society that is eminently objectifiable. Readers in that chimera, the international public sphere, indulged in the abjection of the main characters and made what is essentially a social protest novel a cultural event—to be categorized, consumed, and then allowed to provide a bridge back to the plodding world that it rejects (or as the film version adds, provocatively, "choose life"). On the one hand, this is merely to remark that an avant-garde or protest literature in the high modern vein is impossible, but on the other hand, the proliferation of cultural objects for consumption *as a class negotiation* loves social protest without consequences.

Slumming is now primarily an interpellation of the working class (or the infamous lower orders) as an object for consumption without, as in our earlier examples, direct authorial desire for objectification. This is why when Fellini makes his *Satyricon* as a critique of contemporary Italian politics and culture, it is taken up as one more spectacle, albeit a dangerous one, that disturbs its audience only to the extent that the audience derives pleasure from the diversion. The pessimist might say that this merely confirms the triumph of commodification and that slumming offers no exit strategy. I would say, however, that slumming demonstrates the logic in the impasse and asserts the persistence of class contradiction ever at the edge of normative and stultifying definitions.

What seems effortless in classing down today does not underline the eclipse of class but accentuates instead that the nature of class transaction requires new readings of the fear and loathing in class passing. At the very least, slumming is an ideologeme of class discourse and is never far removed from the social foundations of hierarchy. Its paradox may be that it insists on the mimetic faculty in cultures that have lost any meaning for such identification. Yet slumming continues to demonstrate the political unconscious of a class structured in dominance: there is always something else in what the slummer needs to know, as if the acknowledgment by the Other is itself the *jouissance* of class control. The slummer also fantasizes what the culture must otherwise hide, the ways in which the porous conditions of class augur the concrete possibilities of change. What can be crossed, can be abolished.

Notes

1. The Real of class, like the Real in Lacan, is unrepresentable (the capitalization itself departs from the real of the everyday). It is a relation that is always distilled into an object, but that object itself, *qua* class, is an effulgence of class in history, not its essence.

2. I have developed this approach in relation to the work of Henry Green, particularly his novel *Living*. See Peter Hitchcock, "Passing: Henry Green and Working-Class Identity," *Modern Fiction Studies* 40.1 (Spring, 1994): 1–32.

3. For a social history of the "classic slum" (in Engels's words), see Robert Roberts, *The Classic Slum* (Manchester: University of Manchester Press, 1971).

4. For literary criticism that draws on this insight, see Elaine K. Ginsberg, ed., *Passing and the Fictions of Identity* (Durham: Duke University Press, 1996).

5. Obviously, there is much work to be done on the class inflections in postcoloniality, although some attention has already been drawn to the function of social elites in the emergence of postcolonial theory—a subject that would require more space than is available on this occasion.

6. Here I am using the following edition: Friedrich Engels, *The Condition of the Working Class in England*, ed. Victor Kiernan (London: Penguin, 1987). The loss of the year 1844 in the title is in part a function of the number of years that elapsed between its German publication and the volume that appeared in English in 1886. But, as Engels asserts several times, the relevance of the original date remains crucial.

7. See Steven Marcus, *Engels, Manchester, and the Working Class* (New York: Norton, 1974). There is much to appreciate in Marcus's book, despite my misgivings. For one, he attempts to come to terms with the literary processes of narrating modernity that Engels's text inspires without naming.

8. Harvey's critique of Parisian space has been developed on several occasions. Of particular note is the way he analyzes it in terms of modernity (and postmodernity). See David Harvey, *The Condition of Postmodernity* (Oxford: Blackwell, 1989). See also Walter Benjamin, *The Arcades Project/Walter Benjamin*, trans. Howard Eiland and Kevin McLaughlin (Cambridge: Harvard University Press, 1999).

9. See Robert Baltrop, Introduction to *Revolution,* by Jack London (London: Journeyman Press, 1979).

10. See *The People of the Abyss,* in Jack London, *Novels and Other Writings* (New York: Library of America, 1982).

11. George Orwell, *Down and Out in Paris and London* (London: Secker and Warburg, 1933).

12. George Orwell, *The Road to Wigan Pier* (New York: Harvest, 1958).

13. Irvine Welsh, *Trainspotting* (New York: Norton, 1996).

7 The "Self-Made Man"

Male Impersonation and the New Woman

Sharon Ullman

On a warm September night in 1911, the magically named Biscauex took the vaudeville stage in New York City and dazzled the audience. Appearing first as a woman, the performer then put on "a man's evening dress for a male impersonation, thereby becoming a female impersonator attempting a male impersonation," according to reports. Critics were enthralled. "If this has been done before, it is not within memory," raved *Variety*. Without irony, the review noted that Biscauex "took the male impersonation best of all." In the end, however,

[t]he disclosure by removing the wig after the male impersonation did not at all convince the audience he was a man. It left them in doubt, and this perplexed condition seemed to be for his advantage in applause.[1]

While this audience apparently appreciated Biscauex's deceptive prowess, for many such confusion over what "made" a man produced infinitely more distress and significantly less pleasure. In the opening decades of the twentieth century, such questions haunted popular entertainment and cast a serious pall on the lighthearted tomfoolery of a supposedly innocent age.

Biscauex belonged to cadre of performers in early-twentieth-century America who traveled the country on vaudeville circuits impersonating members of the opposite sex to the bewildered fascination of national audiences. Although female impersonation has survived in popular imagination, male impersonation seems to have disappeared from our collective cultural memory. Yet it too had a heyday in late-nineteenth- and early-twentieth-century vaudeville. Although never quite as successful as their female impersonator counterparts, numerous male impersonators did develop extensive reputations and followings. Women such as the British icon Vesta Tilley (against whom all American-born male impersonators compared themselves), and American-born favorites Bessie Bonehill, Hetty King, Grace Leonard, and the beloved Kitty Donner all found fame in the years from 1900 until World War I dressing up as "swells."

This essay looks at this highly popular early-twentieth-century entertainment form and demonstrates the ways in which the discourse surrounding such onstage activity was deployed to negotiate the gender difficulties created by the call for women's political equality *offstage*. Women dressing like men for entertainment value provided fertile ground for those concerned with the possibility that women might "look like" men in terms of political privilege as well. While discussions of male impersonation included the perhaps anticipated critique that such entertainers had abandoned their femininity, many comments were more subtle and reframed the question of male impersonation—and its parallel political cousin, women's suffrage—in ways that reconstituted hierarchies within masculinity. Commentators inscribed a vision of masculinity onto the bodies of women who "pretended" to be men. I shall argue that this "double passing"—in which men re-created images of themselves through women who looked like or "became" men—provided a powerful tool for containing the subversive quality of feminist political critiques, while simultaneously revealing the depth of cultural anxiety over gender instability.

My discussion of male impersonation is, of course, influenced by the groundbreaking work of Judith Butler, who has contributed heavily to the theoretical reconceptualization of gender in various disciplines.[2] Butler introduced the now standard phrase "performative gender" to our theoretical vocabulary. In the more specific context of drag, she argues that "in imitating gender, drag implicitly reveals the imitative structure of gender itself."[3] While male impersonators in early-twentieth-century vaudeville cannot be strictly characterized as "drag performers," there are clearly comparable undertones. Such impersonation provides the opportunity, as Butler reminds us, to "see sex and gender denaturalized by means of a performance which avows their distinctness and dramatizes the cultural mechanism of their fabricated unity." In other words, the notion of performance does for gender what Toto did for the Wizard of Oz—it unveils the "man behind the curtain" (so to speak)—the public discourses that construct the artificial coherency of gender. Male impersonation on the vaudeville stage provides a sparkling view of these operations in a time of heightened gender anxiety.

The period was particularly marked by strife between men and women as they struggled to define their roles within the home and society. From the amount of angst that surfaces in any period over this subject, one might suspect that gender is *always* in crisis to some degree. Yet the public sabre rattling in the early part of this century has really been matched only by the gnashing of teeth in the past thirty years. It is no accident that we have designated the two periods as feminism's first and second waves. If we are often the reluctant inheritors of the second wave, male impersonators in the early twentieth century would no doubt have been equally reluctant to be characterized as part of the first. Indeed, as we shall see, several well-known performers strongly rejected any connection to activities promoting the "New Woman." Yet despite this refusal, male impersonators inevitably became embroiled in the gender contests of their era.

I

It is, of course, *not* male impersonators who first leap to mind when considering first-wave feminism's contentious history. Instead, we recall the

189

political and educational activity of white middle-class women's groups. Indeed, the remarkable expansion in women's educational opportunities in the late nineteenth century, the dominating presence of women in social reform activities (particularly in the Progressive Era prior to World War I), and, of course, the well-documented struggle for female suffrage culminating in the ratification of the Nineteenth Amendment in 1920 did create a national reevaluation of the possibilities available to white middle-class women. As we also know, many people strongly resisted this reconsideration of gender roles.

Although aggressive female political activity clearly problematized the question of women in public space, the counterassault, both then and now (demonstrating once again the staying power of particular imagery), focused extensively on the home and the private world occupied by men and women. We are familiar with the critique that women who left the home for the public arena deserted their natural function to the detriment of all. Some contemporary feminists, bowing to such concerns, fashioned an entire justification for their public activities that emphasized their roles as "social housekeepers." In this fin-de-siècle vision, the community became home and women's "natural" superiority in the private arena gave them a special insight into the social problems faced by children and the poor.

Such justifications carried their own internal (and self-limiting) contradictions and never fully appeased critics.[4] Yet the critical jeering also demonstrated a different, more subtle concern over the impact women's political equality might have on private life. Commentators unwittingly revealed fears of a lurking gender confusion located inside the home itself that could result from female absence. These attacks, often framed as sharp mockery, exposed a decided subtext of male uncertainty: the imagined potency of "masculinity" seemed remarkably fragile in the face of a desertion by "femininity." Many historians have noted the so-called crisis in white middle-class masculinity that dominated the public philosophizing of figures such as Teddy Roosevelt at the turn of the century. Pundits offered explanations ranging from the "closing of the West" to the absence of military struggle in order to explain the apparent "softness" that had overcome the American male. Those encouraging women to enter the political arena, a site of traditional male authority, received their fair share of blame as well.[5] As historian Gail Bederman has noted, "men objected so strenuously to woman's suffrage precisely because male power and male identity were both so central to nineteenth-century electoral politics."[6]

This problem of male power and male identity recurs repeatedly in early-twentieth-century popular imagery. One quick example—the henpecked husband—helps us readily see the insecurities surrounding gender identity in this period. The comedically tormented male spouse of a large, overbearing woman may have been a hackneyed image even in 1900, but it took on a special power and poignancy during tirades about feminism. Such women stood in for "real" women who "took up" public space. Early filmmakers often portrayed aggressive women as sexless old maids—a figure I have elsewhere characterized as producing social boundaries for acceptable objects of sexual desire[7]—but more often they appeared as married women who held their husbands both in check and in contempt.

The husband's political and social emasculation was represented, not surprisingly, by what we might call "forced gender impersonation." Comedians and filmmakers uniformly placed such men in female attire and tasked them with domestic chores. Always frocked in an apron with feather duster in hand, the husband sheepishly performed female tasks and cowered before his looming and physically abusive wife. Some henpecked husbands were linked to specific activist women. For example, in "Why Mr. Nation Wants a Divorce" (1901),[8] temperance activist Carrie Nation is satirized through the plot of a miserable husband left to baby-sit while Nation heads off to another meeting. Nation returns to find him drunk, an even more pointed satire on her temperance and hatchet-wielding activities: she famously chopped up saloons both in public relations stunts and on the vaudeville stage. (She then turns him over her knee and spanks him.)

Either slight in build or short, bald, and overweight, the henpecked husband represented more than just a reversal in gender roles. These men symbolized impotence—both metaphoric and actual. The henpecked husband not only lost his community power by being relegated to the domestic sphere but was stripped of masculinity at its sexual core. He was neither attractive to the audience nor did he attempt to elicit desire from his wife. To reinforce the point, it is precisely through futile attempts at sexual conquest that the henpecked husband is seen vainly trying to reassert himself. The flirtatious husband is presented as a buffoon whose attempts to charm conventionally attractive single women are firmly, and often cruelly, rejected.

The henpecked husband remains, even in our own day, a permanent sexual joke that ably demonstrates the connection between role reversal and masculine sexual power.[9] His longevity as a cultural laughingstock is evidence of the degree to which this figure correctly encapsulates concerns about male sexuality present in conversations about gender and masculinity. His continuous appearance in popular renditions of feminist activity at the turn of the century links him firmly to the larger question of public political authority and private masculine definition.

The henpecked husband is, however, only one of numerous images that reinforced a vision of problematic masculinity in the early twentieth century. The women who engaged in male impersonation on the vaudeville stage—a completely voluntary and quite lucrative career decision—provoked even more complex reactions. These responses attempted to fashion an immutable, uncontested masculine identity.[10] They failed, but not for lack of trying. Those commenting on male impersonation focused on private sexual practice as a way to ascertain what it meant to be a man in a modern world. But the questions of sexual practice raised by those watching male impersonators did little to relieve the anxiety provoked by the vision of women standing as men in those modern spaces.

Although the image of the turn-of-the-century feminist activist is entwined with "bloomers" in a mocking historical memory, in point of fact the women working for female suffrage did find themselves part of an extensive assault rooted in the language of gender impersonation. On this public plane, the conversation revolved around the image of women wearing men's clothing. This imagery is reflected not only in the fascinated attention given to women who "passed" as men in terms of employment and personal relations[11] but also in the insistent use of such representations to depict feminists in a derogatory light. Women dressing as men or women "acting" as men appeared as the primary characterization of suffrage and the "woman question." Many such film representations remained focused on the home; some twinned with the henpecked husband. The ones not so paired were usually matched with a dominant mate who "tamed" his suffragist partner. Several popular contemporary comedies, such as *In 1999* and *The Woman of Tomorrow*, dealt satirically with the theme of a world where women ruled society.[12]

One particularly sharp example of such wit appears in the 1909 film *The Newest Woman*.[13] The phrase "the New Woman" appeared everywhere in the early twentieth century and directly referred to the image of women as actors on the public stage—whether they fought for women's suffrage, opposed the use of alcohol, or simply asserted their right to be present in a public universe. *The Newest Woman* openly satirized this trend. The film portrayed what appears to be a relatively prosperous white middle-class household. After a pleasant meal, a wife shows off a new outfit to her husband—bloomers, the pants-like fashion craze sweeping the country and strongly associated with the suffrage movement. He becomes outraged and orders her to remove them, sending her into hysterical sobs. In the face of this despair, he exits the scene but returns moments later wearing pants rolled up to the knees to resemble bloomers and laced with ruffly cuffs. Looking silly, he dances around the room in an effeminate fashion and turns her tears to laughter. Having demonstrated the absurdity of the situation, he persuades her to throw out the bloomers; when the wife dons a dress at the end, the husband points and nods approvingly. The implication of *The Newest Woman* is, of course, that the "new woman" is no woman at all. Indeed, as the wife attempts to join the sorority of "new women" by virtue of wearing bloomers, the newest woman yet emerges. In the film's vision, the ultimate "new woman" is, in fact, a man.

While it takes no special historical insight to identify the problematic being presented in these images—that is, women demanding male preroga-tives in the public sphere and taking on "male" characteristics in the pri-vate—it is too easy to dismiss them with one simplistic explanation. The con-text in which these conversations take place and the clear anxiety present on various levels of male-female relations make the obvious somewhat less so. The public discussion concerning proper gender roles occurred in numerous forums: the more traditional avenues, such as newspaper editorials or politi-cal rallies, contributed staid commentary and the popular culture renditions lent a more raucous tone. The overall effect of this endless nattering, osten-sibly a social debate on female roles, was to reinforce a wider national dis-cussion among men about the nature of masculinity in a time when defini-tions of the masculine were no longer clear. It is only within the context of this wider discussion that the concerns underlying the confused reaction to male impersonators begin to emerge.

II

The commentary surrounding popular male impersonators in the first few years of the twentieth century provides valuable insights into the male fears that governed all forms of "passing" women. Reviewers swung wildly be-tween laudatory affection and open ridicule as they commented upon this strange novelty act in which women pretended to be men. Both those who performed on stage and those using the popular culture to castigate suffrage proponents employed similar mechanisms for identifying what constituted male and female behaviors. Definitions that appeared in assessments of a male impersonator's stage performance could be redeployed to discredit suf-frage activists. The assault was a particularly creative, vicious form of wit and could be found on stage, on screen, and in common jokes.

The most famous male impersonator of the era was the British star Vesta Tilley. Tilley provided the benchmark for excellence for all subsequent per-formers. She made periodic forays across the Atlantic to ply her wares in the

United States and was met with enthusiastic audiences during the first few years of the new century. During a 1906 tour, reviewers called attention to her "expression, feeling, and that indefinable something termed personality," noting particularly that she was "the one male impersonator on the stage today who really looks like a boy; her costumes are exact and she wears a wig that might well be her own hair, so exactly does it fit."[14] A return visit in 1909 found that "packed houses at the Colonial Theater all of the week demonstrated her drawing powers far better than any eulogism." Whether wearing "evening clothes of the very latest cut, with a single breasted black top coat and a silk hat" or "cream colored flannel trousers and a Panama hat of rakish shape," Vesta Tilley could be counted on to replicate male attire, reflecting "her own perfection of detail in her art."[15] Tilley's art brought her international fame and made her a star for many years.

Numerous other women also tried their hand at male impersonation. Some achieved a measure of fame, although most, like their female impersonating colleagues, worked in small-time vaudeville, roaming the country as the middle act on an equally undistinguished bill. Known only as "Wheeler and Harcourt," two performers did a fifteen-minute "song and talk" act in 1911 that did "well on 'small time.'" One was "a rather clever eccentric comedienne and proved it in a stump speech on Woman's Suffrage." The other sang "fairly well" and made a "pleasing appearance as a boy."[16] Just as "Love and Haight" hoped their nomenclatorial cleverness would propel them forward the following year, so too did a performer called "Juliet?" attempt to make her theatrical impersonation fortune with an evocative question mark. Juliet? did not limit her "character studies" to men, but certainly the gender challenge present in her name leaves little doubt as to her emphasis. According to one critic, a duly impressed 1912 audience "appreciated her artistic studies so spontaneously it made her take several demonstrative curtain acknowledgments." Juliet?'s primary claim to fame lay in her imitations of famous contemporary celebrities, both male and female, from Harry Lauder to Ethel Barrymore. In Vesta Tilley style, she also mocked "a swagger, dapper, foppishly attired English Johnnie." Yet, claimed the impressed

195

reviewer, "Juliet? got more applause on her imitation of the Scotch boy with the thumping, jumping toothache, the hot water bag, and bottled liquids as first aid to the suffering. This character, distinctly new and decidedly original, was splendidly worked out."[17]

Much better known American favorites like the "matchless impersonator of male roles"[18] Bessie Bonehill and Kathleen Clifford (who was often compared favorably to Vesta Tilley) succeeded in the cutthroat world of big-time vaudeville. Bonehill performed in the late nineteenth century and died in 1902 before most of her counterparts became famous.[19] Clifford, Emma Don, Hetty King, and Grace Leonard were all successful contemporaries competing for public affection in the years 1910 to 1915. Although few, if any, still remember most of these women, many familiar with entertainment history do know the name of Kitty Donner. Claimed to be the greatest American male impersonator, Donner became a Broadway star in 1914 when she played a man opposite Al Jolson in the hit *Dancing Around*. By 1916, even in Toledo, it could be said of Kitty Donner that "this young woman . . . is known . . . as 'a mirror of men's fashions' . . . Kitty has evolved a series of masculine attires that have real 'Johnnies' gasping."[20] Donner made her career out of portraying male characters in musical theater and eventually did turn to vaudeville. Donner, like the famed female impersonator Julian Eltinge, was perceived as an artist whose impersonation skills well matched her performing talents. Although never as popular as Eltinge (who had a Broadway theater named for him), Donner achieved extraordinary success and received a large measure of public affection.[21]

Most of these women performed vaudeville routines in which they impersonated a series of "male characters" while singing or dancing. Virtually none, however, actually played male parts in any formal theatrical stagings. Kitty Donner represented the notable exception to this rule when she played such parts in Broadway musicals. Some women played male roles in the nineteenth- and early twentieth-century theater—Maude Adams's 1905 Peter Pan and Sarah Bernhardt's famed 1899 Hamlet come immediately to mind, but relatively few actually played men on stage in a formal sense.[22] Women's forays into masculine presentation on stage were, by and large, purely for humorous effect.

This comic function immediately and importantly differentiated male impersonation from female impersonation. Female impersonators were judged on the *accuracy* of their portrayal. They received accolades if they could fool the audience and fully "capture" the essence of femininity.[23] For male impersonators, however, the requirements were very different: they were judged on the degree to which "real men" could *differentiate* themselves from them. That differentiation helped mark critical signs of masculinity in an increasingly public war over the ownership of male political and social privileges. Thus, despite the expressions of charmed delight that usually accompanied these performances, the most important attribute of a successful male impersonator, in fact, was that she not be *too* realistic. Male impersonators were not supposed to demonstrate what a real man was like. Instead they were, as commentators made evident, to show "the boy." This is a crucial distinction: female impersonators' skills lay specifically in representing *women* as opposed to young girls. Successful female impersonators had to prove that they could replicate adult femininity. Those offering schoolgirl images—even in jest—often found themselves reviled. That the reverse is true for male impersonators provides us with an important clue to the anxieties present in these commentaries. The male impersonator supplied an image that set men apart from both women and younger versions of themselves. In this way male impersonation helped create benchmarks of identification for men, as something they were *not* (or at least were no longer), rather than as something they might hope to be.

This emphasis on "the boy" received endless rehearsals in critical discussions of male impersonator performances. In 1906, *Variety* commented that Vesta Tilley was "the one male impersonator on the stage today who really looks like a boy."[24] "[H]er young swells are the real thing in dash and swagger," one critic wrote of Bessie Bonehill in 1899.[25] Kathleen Clifford told a reporter in 1908, "I'm just a lad for the moment," clarifying her other career options.[26] In 1914, *Town and Country* described Kitty Donner in this manner:

"[In]cluded among her accomplishments are eccentric dances in boy's clothes."[27] (This is one of Donner's least glowing reviews, it must be noted.) A more kind 1914 remark referred to Donner as "one of the best little 'boys' in the business."[28] Grace Leonard, according to a Minneapolis paper in 1912, impersonated "the ideal American boy."[29] Such comments are typical of virtually any contemporary article discussing male impersonation.

Such characterizations partially reflected the fact that some of the most popular male impersonators were physically diminutive women. Kathleen Clifford was variously referred to (somewhat scathingly given the context) as a "pretty little girl"[30] or, somewhat more kindly as "a charming atom" and a "midget impersonator."[31] The *New York Telegraph* found rival Kitty Donner to be "so small that even such 'half portion comediennes' as . . . Kathleen Clifford would outweigh her,"[32] and the *New York Times* specifically sized Donner at 4'4" in a 1914 review.[33]

It was precisely this quality of daintiness that most appealed to those who celebrated the male impersonators. When the *Toledo Blade* described Donner as a "mirror of men's fashion," it did so only after carefully informing readers that "this young woman is as demure and dainty in her own personality as one might wish."[34] The *New York Telegraph*'s assessment of Donner noted that "her size, or lack of it, is an asset, and not a handicap . . . from her slickly brushed hair to her tiny polished boots, she does the pocket edition man about town to the life."[35] Five years earlier, in 1910, the *Telegraph* had offered a similar analysis of Kathleen Clifford's charm: "One strikingly remarkable feature of Miss C's 'boys' is that while they look and behave real and genuine, Miss C does not in the least sacrifice her dainty feminine charm."[36] Obviously, such a feat required a certain degree of careful cultural navigation between some very sharply defined gender boundaries.

These remarks also reflected a confusion over the nature of masculinity itself. Perhaps the most telling comment on both Clifford and the entire phenomenon can be found in this assertion: "Among the many there is none whose brilliance outshines this fair masculine—yet most unmasculine—midget impersonator. This tender fragile idealist of unideal youth."[37]

Precisely what was being idealized remains the real question. The commentator approaches not only Clifford as an impersonator but also the project of impersonation with more than a little ambiguity. Was Clifford masculine or "unmasculine?" Could masculine be "fair?" Could a "midget" be masculine? The characterization of Clifford as a "tender, fragile idealist" sounds almost as if the writer is offering his own wistful recollection of a lost, younger, masculine self, yet he also insists that such youth remain inherently "unideal." Clifford's stage antics provided more than one commentator with the opportunity to hauntingly muse over what it meant to be a man—or a boy.

Yet this musing was not always so benign: the fluttering praise over "daintiness" was but one step away from a more ominous conversation about the ways in which male impersonators did or did not pass for men in other contexts. For example, one admiring review from 1907 noted that impersonator Hetty King defied expectations:

Popular opinion holds that women who occupy men's positions are mannish women, masculine in appearance, coarse, and bluff in manner. . . . While this graceful, pretty, clever young woman spends most of her time in trousers, there isn't anything mannish about her personality. When she's onstage impersonating a man, she's a man all over. But when she leaves the stage and her mannish clothes, there isn't a daintier, more gracious, refined, and graceful, womanly woman.[38]

Comments about what it means to be mannish and how male impersonators resisted such horrors reappear often. Critics characterized the offstage Bessie Bonehill as "a cheery, wholesome, domestic little woman."[39] Kitty Donner found herself the object of dueling public images when a 1914 *New York Times* article quoted her as saying, "I have never worn boys' clothes before and I hope I'll never have to wear them again" while a disturbing article a few months later in the *Detroit News* asserted that

since Miss Donner has been doing boy parts she has practically lived in men's clothing. So infatuated with masculine garments is Kitty Donner that she spends her spare time . . . gazing longingly into haberdashers' windows. In fact she spends more money on her mannish attire than on gowns and articles of apparel so dear to the feminine heart.[40]

Green Book repeated this characterization of Donner in 1916: "People ask why Kitty Donner is always cast for boy parts. The answer is simple enough: she prefers them. 'If the police weren't so sharpsighted,' said Kitty Donner, 'I'd abandon skirts altogether, even for the street, and wear boys' duds.'"[41] However, a *Los Angeles Examiner* feature appeared to settle the question in 1917 when it pointed out that Donner,

who struts about the Mason stage in the most ultramannish clothes, doesn't ignore any of the feminine attributes. While she knows all about bats and first bases, she is also on terms of utmost intimacy with the rolling pin. She can perform stage acrobatics of the most impish sort and then wield the egg beater in the production of the perfect souffle.[42]

This obsession with determining the presence or absence of "mannish" qualities in male impersonators certainly parallels the accusations of effeminacy, degeneracy, and homosexuality that trailed female impersonators.[43] In 1914, any discussion of mannish qualities carried with it an almost inevitable subtext of lesbianism.[44] Although fears of homosexual practice were much more pronounced in the discussions that governed female impersonators, the above comments indicate that male impersonators also needed to produce evidence of appropriately gendered behavior that could serve to "clear" them of any sexual stigma.

We now seem to be a far cry from the highly touted "charming renditions" of stage-door Johnnies so dear to earlier male impersonation audiences. Male impersonation raised complicated anxieties over definitions of masculinity, incorporating many meanings of "manhood" that required careful delineation. "Ultramannish clothes" (an interesting idea implying unacceptable excess), "bats and first bases," and "stage acrobatics," apparently provided clear markers denoting appropriate masculinity in the descriptions we have read of Kitty Donner. Connecting this concern for "mannish" practice with the review of Hetty King—which compares her, positively, to women who engaged in masculine pursuits—reveals a direct link between the discourses working to decipher male impersonators and those that attempted to contain women's political action.

But it is not necessary to speculate wildly or excavate too deeply in order to uncover the connections that existed between male impersonation and women's rights in the minds of contemporaries. Many articles discussing male impersonators made a point of raising the star's attitudes toward women's rights as a way of clarifying the impersonator's "properly" gendered opinions. Grace Leonard was quoted in 1912 as contemptuously dismissing a recent story of a couple who signed a prenuptial agreement designating that each could maintain her or his own property and that the marriage would terminate upon the wishes of either: "'Bah!' exclaimed Miss Leonard. 'That isn't love. It's a copartnership without any head of the firm. I don't believe a woman will live long with a man who will sign such an agreement. She wants to be bossed. If she doesn't want to be bossed, she really doesn't want to get married.'"[45] (The paper did not clarify why it thought its readers would be interested in the opinion of a minor male impersonator on this particular subject.) An 1896 interview with Bessie Bonehill reported her emphatically declaring "I am not a New Woman . . . but I do love male characters."[46] In 1907, the *Pittsburgh Leader* commented that "Hetty King spends most of her time in trousers but is a refined womanly woman and makes more than the President of the United States."[47] (Presumably, the Pittsburgh paper was encouraging an alternative employment goal rather than such high political office.) Kathleen Clifford's political opinions were the focus of particular attention. One 1914 article asserted that Clifford "thinks there are too many women in the world now, and the suffrage movement and other schemes to give women independence are due to oversupply."[48] According to another paper, Clifford was "not at all interested in suffrage—she is far too busy selecting clothes for the 'smartest chap in town' . . . to bother about such things as ballots, especially when you can't wear 'em and they can't add anything to the effective garbing of the most correctly dressed young fellow on this side of the pond."⁴⁹

Male impersonators may have tried, probably with some degree of futility, to separate their interest in wearing men's clothing from any concern over political questions, but others insisted that the two were inextricably linked. Billy Gould, a comic actor and regular contributor to *Variety*, presented an entire column on this subject in 1911. Gould offered "a few original hints for Suffragettes" on how to express their masculinity: "B.V.D.s are stylish, especially in the summertime. To be worn out of sight, of course," he sagely advises and then continues: "GILLETTE Razors are fine for shaving—corns—and sharpening lead pencils." Making sure that the ladies would not be misled, he added that they were "also very nifty for removing basting threads." Concerned that the women might be incapable of proper public behavior, Gould insisted that "AS A MATCH might tear the seat of your bloomers it is best to use one of those self-igniting devices until you learn the art of striking a match properly," and noted that "CIGARS should be carried in the left upper hand pocket of your waistcoat." Suffragists yearning to "talk like a man" should "join the Shubert chorus." Finally Gould unleashed his ultimate scathing assault: "AFTER 'graduating,' find some nice womanly woman. Listen to her and find out what a fool you have made of yourself— you self-made man."⁵⁰

Such remarks from an entertainment columnist bring together the arenas of gender impersonation on stage and female political activity in the streets. Gould's comment helps cement our understanding that a fragile masculinity was just as much at stake in these debates as was the overt resistance to civil rights for women. His attack was witty and on target as he detailed the masculine pretensions charged to women's suffrage supporters. Viciously exaggerating the political goals of the "Trouser Movement"⁵¹ (as he and others called suffrage activists) he intentionally collapsed the lines between political rights reserved to men and public behavior associated with them. Certain elements of "maleness" could be codified and used as a weapon against women. While votes for women may have been the official issue, the content of the response indicates that codes of masculinity remained the real concern.

Punning on the notion of men who rise by their bootstraps, Gould's reference to "self-made men" called into question all attempts at female self-fashioning that permitted access to male privilege. What it is that "makes a man" had obviously become a subject of some debate. Could a man truly be "self-made" by anyone—even a woman? To the Billy Goulds of the world, the answer was a resounding no. That they felt the need to state as much tells us more about their fears than their certainties.

In the end, when Billy Gould raised the specter of the "self-made man" he forced the question of who got to "make" masculinity real in the society at large. In the first twenty years of the twentieth century, many different actors performed masculinity on the public stage, as well as the theatrical one. Some women marched in the streets and demanded male privilege; others dressed as men to amuse the crowds. All such performances were viewed with a caustic eye by men who found their own performances of masculinity under equal surveillance and similar judgment. One common joke of the time captured the tenuous status of masculinity in the age of suffrage. A woman argues to a male companion, "We women should be allowed to vote." His response: "Do you think the vote would make women masculine?" Her reply? "Why no. It hasn't had that effect on you."[52]

How masculinity could be performed by *anyone* constituted the fundamental problem facing those fascinated by male impersonators and horrified by suffrage advocates. In marking male impersonators as boys, not men; dainty, not robust; pint sized, not fully grown; familiar with rolling pins, not bats and first bases, men sought to see themselves and their own representation of masculinity as competitive performances that demonstrated male mastery over masculinity—a mastery that could be replicated in the community contests over political power. Men looked to male impersonators *not* to depict a recognizable masculinity but instead to offer a conceptual mannequin upon which they could drape their own increasingly fraught gender ideologies. Commentators ripped open the facade presented by women who "seemed" to be men—whether on stage or in the streets—in order to pick apart the details that might prove their case. However, in that search for detail, the question that really seemed paramount was whether, in an age of gender uncertainty, anyone—female *or* male—could pass for a man anymore.

Notes

1. *Variety*, September 9, 1911 (24)1, 17.

2. See Judith Butler, *Gender Trouble: Feminism and the Subversion of Identity* (New York: Routledge, 1990) and *Bodies That Matter: On The Discursive Limits of "Sex"* (New York: Routledge, 1993). See also Judith Halberstam on the modern drag king phenomenon in *Female Masculinity* (Durham: Duke University Press, 1998). I think the evidence shows that "masculinity" was no more firmly located on male bodies in 1910 than it is in 1999.

3. Butler, *Gender Trouble*, 137–138.

4. Among many others, see Paula C. Baker, *The Moral Frameworks of Public Life: Gender, Politics, and the State in Rural New York, 1870–1930* (New York: Oxford University Press, 1991); Linda Gordon, *Heroes of Their Own Lives: The Politics and History of Family Violence: Boston, 1880–1960* (New York: Viking, 1988); Mary P. Ryan, *Womanhood in America: From Colonial Times to the Present*, 3d ed. (New York: F. Watts, 1983); Barbara Epstein, *The Politics of Domesticity: Women, Evangelism, and Temperance in Nineteenth-Century America* (Middletown: Wesleyan University Press, 1981).

5. See Kristin L. Hoganson, *Fighting for American Manhood: How Gender Politics Provoked the Spanish-American and Philippine-American Wars* (New Haven: Yale University Press, 1998); Michael S. Kimmel, *Manhood in America: A Cultural History* (New York: Free Press, 1996); Gail Bederman, *Manliness and Civilization: A Cultural History of Gender and Race in the United States, 1880–1917* (Chicago: University of Chicago Press, 1995); Anthony E. Rotundo, *American Manhood: Transformations in Masculinity from the Revolution to the Modern Era* (New York: Basic Books, 1993).

6. Bederman, *Manliness and Civilization*, 13.

7. Sharon Ullman, *Sex Seen: The Emergence of Modern Sexuality in America* (Berkeley: University of California Press, 1998), 20–23.

8. Edison, 8H1495, March 1, 1910, FLA4951, Paper Print Collection, Library of Congress.

9. See for example, "The Henpecked Husband," AmandB, 8H70259, December 19, 1905, FLA5235; "Appointment By Telephone," Edison, 8H17675, May 15, 1902, FLA4474; "Four Beautiful Pairs," AmandB 8H42043, and "After The Ball," Biograph, 8J150107, January 3, 1911, FLA3817. Paper Print Collection, Library of Congress.

10. Ullman, *Sex Seen*, chap. 3.

11. See Estelle Freedman and John D'Emilio, *Intimate Matters: A History of Sexuality in America* (New York: Harper and Row, 1988),124–125; Lisa Duggan,"The Trials of Alice Mitchell: Sensationalism, Sexology, and the Lesbian Subject in Turn of the Century America," *Signs:* 18 (4): 791–814.

12. See William C. DeMille, *In 1999* and *The Woman of Tomorrow*, performed by Iza Hampton Co., *Variety*, June 28, 1912, 16.

13. Lubin Manufacturing Co., 8J132444, FLA5116, Paper Print Collection, Library of Congress.

14. Anthony Slide, *Selected Vaudeville Criticisms* (Metuchen: Scarecrow Press, 1988), 184.

15. *Ibid.*

16. *Variety*, January 14, 1911, 19.

17. *Variety*, November 8, 1912, 21.

18. Caption, loose photo, Bessie Bonehill Clipping File, New York Public Library (cited hereafter as NYPL).

19. Vern Bullough and Bonnie Bullough, *Crossdressing, Sex, and Gender* (Philadelphia: University of Pennsylvania Press, 1992), 228.

20. *Toledo Blade*, November 2, 1916, found in Robinson Locke Collection, Ser. 2, v. 128, NYPL.

21. Almost all gender impersonation—both male and female—disappeared from mainstream entertainment after World War I. This partly reflects the demise of vaudeville itself in the face of competition from the movie industry. However, it also demonstrates a tightening of gender conventions. There were repeated crackdowns on homosexuality in this period, and female impersonators, in particular, came to be the object of persecution. Many municipalities specifically outlawed wearing apparel of the opposite sex. Despite its reputation as a time of social and sexual liberalism, therefore, the 1920s saw a rigidification of gender categories. Male impersonation was but one casualty of the "roaring twenties."

22. For a more extensive discussion of this phenomenon, see Robert A. Schanke and

Kim Marra, eds., *Passing Performances: Queer Readings of Leading Players in American Theater History* (Ann Arbor: University of Michigan Press, 1998); Lesley Ferris, ed., *Crossing the Stage: Controversies on Cross-Dressing* (New York: Routledge, 1993); and Marjorie Garber, *Vested Interests: Cross-Dressing and Cultural Anxiety* (New York: Routledge, 1992).

23. Ullman, *Sex Seen*, chap. 3.

24. Slide, *Selected Vaudeville Criticisms*, 184.

25. Loose clipping marked May 5, 1899 (paper unidentified), Bessie Bonehill Clipping File, NYPL.

26. *Broadway*, March 3, 1908, Robinson Locke Collection, Ser. 3, v. 335, 14, NYPL.

27. *Town and Country*, October 17, 1914, Robinson Locke Collection, Ser. 2, v. 128, 52, NYPL.

28. Photo caption, December, 1914, Robinson Locke Collection, Ser. 2, v. 128, 55, NYPL.

29. *Minneapolis Journal,* September 18, 1912, Robinson Locke Collection, Envelope 1158, NYPL.

30. *Indianapolis News* (undated), Robinson Locke Collection, Ser. 3, v. 335, 5, NYPL.

31. Unmarked clipping, Robinson Locke Collection, Ser. 3, v. 335, 5, NYPL.

32. *New York Telegraph*, February 16, 1915, Robinson Locke Collection, Ser. 2, v. 128, 59, NYPL.

33. *New York Times*, October 18, 1914, Robinson Locke Collection, Ser. 2, v. 128, 47, NYPL.

34. *Toledo Blade*, November 2, 1916, Robinson Locke Collection, Ser. 2, v. 128, 47, NYPL.

35. *New York Telegraph*, February 16, 1915, Robinson Locke Collection, Ser. 2, v. 128, 59, NYPL.

36. *New York Telegraph*, May 19, 1910, Robinson Locke Collection, Ser. 3, v. 335, 26, NYPL.

37. Unmarked clipping, Robinson Locke Collection, Ser. 3, v. 335, 5, NYPL.

38. Unmarked clipping, Robinson Locke Collection, Ser. 2, v. 265, 166, NYPL.

39. Loose clipping marked May 5, 1899 (paper unidentified), Bessie Bonehill Clipping File, NYPL.

40. *New York Times*, October 18, 1914; *Detroit News*, April 10, 1915, Robinson Locke Collection, Ser. 2, v. 128, 47, NYPL.

41. *Green Book,* September, 1, 1916, Robinson Locke Collection, Ser. 2, v. 128, 47, NYPL.

42. *Los Angeles Examiner,* 1917 [day unmarked], Robinson Locke Collection, Ser. 2, v. 128, 47, NYPL.

43. Ullman, *Sex Seen,* chap. 3.

44. See Duggan, "The Trials of Alice Mitchell"; Carroll Smith-Rosenberg, "Discourses of Sexuality and Subjectivity: The New Woman, 1870–1936," in *Hidden from History: Reclaiming the Lesbian and Gay Past,* ed. Duberman et al. (New York: New American Library, 1989), 264–280; Esther Newton, "The Mythic Mannish Lesbian: Radclyffe Hall and the New Woman," *Signs* 9 (4): 557–575.

45. *Minneapolis Journal,* September 18, 1912, Locke Envelope 1158, NYPL.

46. *New York Telegraph* Clipping File, February 1896, Bessie Bonehill Clipping File, NYPL.

47. *Pittsburgh Leader,* December 22, 1907, Robinson Locke Collection Ser. 2, v. 265, 163, NYPL.

48. Unidentified clipping, March 29, 1914, Robinson Locke Collection Ser. 3, v. 335, 42, NYPL.

49. Unidentified clipping, Robinson Locke Collection, Ser. 3, v. 335, 4, NYPL.

50. *Variety,* May 20, 1911, 19.

51. Ibid., 6.

52. *McNalley's Bulletin: A Book of Comedy for Vaudeville and Dramatic Entertainment Containing Monologues, Sketches, Acts, Parodies, Farces, Minstrels, First Parts, Afterpieces, and Numerous Other Stage Material, No. 4,* 116, circa 1917, NYPL.

8 Mimesis in the Face of Fear

Femme Queens, Butch Queens, and Gender Play in the Houses of Greater Newark

Karen McCarthy Brown

> The effect of mimicry is camouflage. . . . It is not a question of harmonizing with the background, but against a mottled background, of becoming mottled—exactly like the technique of camouflage in human warfare. —JACQUES LACAN[1]

Jennie Livingston's 1987 documentary film *Paris Is Burning* brought the fictive families known as "Houses" to the attention of the larger American public, yet she gave her viewers little sense of the multiple roles the Houses play or of the day-to-day activities of the people who belong to them. Viewers were left with an image of gay people of color continually getting ready for, participating in, or recovering from transvestite spectacles which the press, perhaps taking the clue from a song by Madonna, dubbed "Voguing Balls." That term is actually a misnomer. Voguing, a dance-like performance originally based on high-fashion poses, is only one Ballroom event among many. Participants in Newark, New Jersey, the focus in this paper, refer to the entire phenomenon as "The Ballroom Scene."

Balls consist of a potentially limitless series of competitive runway events. For example, Livingston's film featured, among other events, runway com-

This chapter was originally prepared for the Park Ridge Center project "Religion, Sexuality, and Public Policy" given on March 5–6, 1998, and funded by The Ford Foundation.

petitions calling for representations of traditional social personae such as "executive," "soldier," or "student." Balls held ten years later in Newark do not have these categories, perhaps because vocation is much less central to identity among poor people. In Newark the great majority of Ballroom categories focus directly on gender types: "Women's Best Dressed . . . Properly Accessorized," "Butch Queen face with a satin pillow as prop," and "Femme Queen foot and eye wear—Fall '97 pumps, please." There are many runway events, but by no means all, that involve cross-dressing and, since the Ballroom Scene has always been primarily an arena for gay men, the male-to-female variety dominates.

Balls evolved from La Cage aux Folles–type clubs, where transvestites wearing glamorous evening gowns lip-synched the hottest songs of popular female singers. In time, fashion show runways appeared in the clubs and runway activity soon expanded to include performative events such as Voguing. "Voguing—the old way" is based on high fashion poses of the sort found in *Vogue* magazine. In this type, each pose is held for only a fraction of a second. There is a staccato quality to the movements, gestures that condense into one body the erotically charged interaction between a model and the rapidly clicking camera of a fashion photographer. By contrast, "Voguing—the new way" is highly acrobatic and involves a much greater range of movement. "New-way" Voguing resembles break dancing and appears to be related to ritualized martial arts like Brazilian Capoeira. Both styles started as competitive street dances among young people in black and Hispanic neighborhoods. Both styles of Voguing are currently competitive, so there are always at least two dancers on the runway. As one of the characters in *Paris Is Burning* put it: "Voguing is like a safe form of throwing shade,"[2] that is "getting over" on someone, getting the best of someone through verbal insults that both draw blood from the target (figuratively speaking) and praise from the audience. Voguing might be thought of as performative anger. Whatever else the Balls are—and they are *many* things—they are also ways of strengthening and protecting a vulnerable community by ritualizing, and thereby containing and redirecting, a range of potentially negative energies such as anger, fear, frustration, competition, and conflict.

The Goals of the Essay

My point here is not to think about the Balls in a vacuum—there has been enough of that—but to understand them in the context of the Houses that stage them and also to acknowledge the contemporary urban location of those Houses. I want to consider the "mothers" and "fathers" of the Houses, as well as the "kids," and the roles they all play within the complicated push and pull of contemporary Newark. A more specific goal is deciphering the relation between the Houses and the interactive assaults of homophobia and AIDS currently experienced in Newark. In terms of theory, I am particularly interested in the mimetic dimensions of the Ballroom Scene and in the way this type of ritualizing interacts with phantom desires (in the sense of phantom pain in an amputated limb) for religious and familial belonging.

The Ballroom Scene

The Balls are hyperbolic events, but it is important to realize that their context is always the quotidian experience of being gay in Newark. More to the point, it is "The Life," that is, the gay life, that is being explored and transformed on the runways. The anchoring family-like structure of the Houses which stage the Balls exists in tension with the violence, racism, and homophobia of the larger city. House mothers and fathers (both positions are filled by men) seek to provide parental guidance for young black and Hispanic gay men who have often been rejected by their blood families, the religious institutions of their childhood, and society at large.

Mirroring gender arrangements in many biological families in Newark, mothers of the Houses often find themselves in the role of single parents and, even when that is not the case, the mother is always the more active and more involved parental figure. Angel Vizcaya, Mother of the House of Vizcaya, once acknowledged that "like every other mother" he sometimes feels abused.[3] The mothers of the Houses are the main role models for their kids. They act as mentors for young men who, given the social conservatism of many of Newark's ethnic communities, may be deeply confused about what it means to live as a gay man in the city. Mothers and fathers teach them how to live "The Life" and the Ballroom is a very effective classroom.

While members of the Houses do not usually reside in the same house or apartment, they self-consciously configure themselves as family, and their group activities are traditional family ones. In Newark most Houses gather to celebrate Christmas, Thanksgiving, and the Fourth of July, and they may take vacations together—a bus trip to the Poconos, a caravan of cars to Miami.

The Houses and Race Dynamics

Eighty-two percent of Newark's population is black and/or Hispanic.[4] Thus it is no surprise that virtually all members of the Houses of Greater Newark are people of color. Bernie Jourdan, mother of the House of Jourdan, did not mince words while discussing white presence in the Ballroom Scene. There's no white gay people . . . on the Ballroom Scene," he said. "There's one or two . . . but there's none. Know what I'm sayin'? We value white people and look up to them, especially on the Ballroom Scene. But we don't want them in there. You know?"[5] In the Ballroom, as in other venues in Newark, Hispanics count as blacks. Whites on the runway may make a "good impression," some people involved in the Ball may "look up to them," but things get distorted when whites look back. The gaze whose absence is constitutive of the event is the normative white gaze.

Mimetic Practices

I was not reared to sophisticated mimetic practice, yet I have had some experiences of it that inform my thinking. One story will suffice. As small children, my older sister and I used to play a game with our mother. We would line up behind her in descending order of height and proceed to mimic her every gesture and word. She found it especially embarrassing in crowded public spaces. "Stop it!" she would say in a stage whisper, while performing the quarter turn necessary to swat at the air behind her. Before she could connect with one of us, my sister and I had rotated around her like the arm of a windmill, while mouthing "Stop it," and swatting at the air behind us. We called this "Playing Ducks."

This little story actually reveals quite a bit about the complex magic of mimesis. "Mimesis," as I am using the term in this essay, is, at a basic level, the art of appropriating power by imitating it. "Playing Ducks" discloses the potential of mimesis to assist in the comprehension of an Other's world (my mother's adult world) while simultaneously realigning power in that world. (By imitating her precisely, my sister and I became swatters like our mother and escaped being swatted.) "Playing Ducks" also reveals the ambivalence at the root of mimicry. My sister and I both wanted to be like our mother *and* to make fun of her. From a child's perspective, the disempowered point of view, her world was both compelling and repelling. By not giving ourselves over entirely to our longing to be her, by exaggerating our gestures enough to create parody, my sister and I preserved our solidarity. This ambivalence, this longing for something, for some way of being in the world, while simultaneously holding it in disdain, is palpable in the Ballroom Scene. Michael Taussig flags the importance of mimesis in configuring identity when he remarks that "in an older language, this is 'sympathetic magic,' and I believe it is as necessary to the very process of knowing as it is to the construction and subsequent naturalization of identities."[6]

Gender and the Ballroom Scene

On the premise that the Ballroom is an arena in which people play with social roles, exaggerating and diminishing them, turning them inside out and upside down, it should be instructive to look at the categories for a particular Ball in terms of how they relate to one another. At the 1997 Fire Ball, Newark's major HIV/AIDS fund-raiser, the lion's share of the runway events (twenty-eight) were grouped under five rubrics according to the gender type of the persons competing in them.[7]

There were some competitions for "Women," that is, for biological women who present themselves to the world as women. Another group of runway events was solely for "Butches," those biological women who present themselves to the world as men. (In the age of AIDS the number of biological women in the Houses has increased.) A third group of events was for "Butch Queens," that is, for homosexual men who live as men. This last grouping had three times as many runway competitions as any other on the program. There was even a special section on the program for a subset of the Butch Queen category, "Butch Queens in Drag." Angel Vizcaya made it clear to me that Butch Queens in drag are not at all the same thing as Femme Queens. Angel is a Butch Queen and said, when he walked in drag, it was just "something I did for that event. . . . It was a deception, but not a deception . . . to fool people that I was real woman."[8]

On the 1997 Fire Ball program, there was a small grouping of runway events for Femme Queens, men who routinely present themselves to the world as women. Angel explained that fewer Femme Queens are in "The Scene" because they are not as comfortable there as Butch Queens. The latter can come to the Balls to be themselves, but Femme Queens are always in drag, even in their everyday lives. What further complicates the matter is that currently, many Femme Queens take body-changing hormones, and for them the disguise is now the "reality." It cannot be taken off. Coming to the Balls is harder for Femme Queens, Angel said, because "they are more exposed."[9]

There is no question that Butch Queens are the normative category on the Ballroom Scene. Others are defined in relation to them. Butch Queens have more freedom and power in the Ballroom because they can master all disguises. Yet this phenomenon is too complex to be explained by simple male

213

dominance. While, in the end, the masculine does dominate, it does so only as what Peter Savastano calls "feminized machismo."[10] Even the aggressive martial arts movements that underlie "Voguing—the new way" have been softened to such an extent that they resonate with those of fashion models, that is to say with "Voguing—the old way." Nevertheless, the dominance of Butch(Queen)ness does manage to keep Femme-ness at bay, in Angel's explanations and in the larger Ballroom Scene. Thus, in the last analysis, the Ball mirrors the gender structure of the larger society: men over women, butch over femme.

"Women," "Butches," "Butch Queens," "Butch Queens in Drag," and "Femme Queens"—it would appear that the categories that order the Newark Balls are determined by self-identified gender niches, rather than by biological sex. That impression is not wrong, but it is not entirely right either. I became aware of this paradox during the 1997 Fire Ball when Nicole, from the House of Infinity, walked "Women's Face." The last contestant to walk, willowy Nicole was striking in a simple black dress, her thick black hair in a fashionably short blunt cut. There was little doubt in anyone's mind that Nicole was the most attractive woman on the runway, yet she was not even halfway down its length when the arguing began. Months after the Fire Ball, people were still debating whether the judges were right to disqualify Nicole because she is a postoperative transsexual. Armand, father of the House of Genesis, thought the judges had been wrong:

She finished the operation. She's a woman now, but people felt since she was a Femme Queen she shouldn't be walking a women's category . . . which isn't fair to her. . . . It's horrible for them to slam doors in her face knowing that she comes from their community, and knowing all along what she was going through to get where she is. And she worked hard to do it! I assume she would feel very hurt.[11]

By contrast, Angel Vizcaya took the majority position:

AV: *Even though she looked like a woman, she is not really a true woman. Even with the sex change and all, she is still not biologically a true woman . . . because they*

didn't take out two rib[s]. . . . They didn't raise up her lungs. . . . They didn't give her
a uterus. All her inside organs are still manly . . . except her you-know-what.
KB: *So her personality is "manly" too?*
AV: *Well, no. Her personality becomes quite feminine,*
and someone who's in her aura for such a long time can tell. . . .
KB: *Does that means that no matter how hard she tries, no*
matter what she does . . . she can't get where she's trying to go?
AV: *She can . . . exteriorly. Yes. But interiorly, no.*[12]

Some contemporary theorists view parodic gender bending, of the sort that goes on in the Ballroom, as a form of social resistance,[13] but the level of abstraction from which the Ballroom Scene is typically analyzed has tended to prevent a fuller picture from emerging. Actually, what goes on with gender categories at the Newark Balls is genuinely liberating and simultaneously constricting to the point of enforcing gender essentialism. In Angel's words: "The Ballroom is very contradictive," and that is just the point.[14] The energy of the Ballroom comes from playing with the rules and regulations of society. The rules have to be in play, there, on the runway, in order for the game to work.

Ballroom categories reflect the mores of the socially conservative racial/ethnic communities that have historically made up Newark's working-class majority. Several forms of religious conservatism exist among Newark's ethnic groups, and their gender binarism has played a role in reinscribing traditional gender hierarchies in "The Life" itself. To be a gay male is to be forced to choose between being womanly or manly within that gayness, to be either a Femme Queen or a Butch Queen. In Newark, there is no such thing as a homosexual man who is both or neither. (Bisexuality is irrelevant since Ball categories are about gender identity, not sexual practice.) A gay man on the runway is either Butch or Femme, categories as rigid and as diametrically opposed as many assume "male" and "female" to be—those essentialist labels that caused Nicole to get "chopped" from the "Women's Face" competition.[15]

Ballroom Morality

Because of Newark's homophobia, both Butch Queens and Femme Queens, in their everyday lives, are to some extent always in disguise. The Balls provide relief, rare opportunities to let go of the vigilance required to maintain a social mask. Angel Vizcaya says the Balls provide him with "a place where I can be myself and not be criticized."[16] Angel can anticipate this sort of reception because the Newark Ballroom crowd is like a big family. Everyone knows everyone else.

In a way, the moral standards of the Ballroom are higher than those of the outside world. Although the Ballroom reproduces the social map, there are some rules specific to the Balls that could not be made to stick in the outside world. The lesson drawn from Nicole is ironic: in the Ballroom, you have to be yourself, and you have to be honest about who you are. This ethic makes it safe for everyone there, including spectators, to be who they are. It is, however, that very same mandate that guarantees failure for transsexuals, amounts to a Catch-22 for Femme Queens, and, as will soon be demonstrated in relation to the "Realness" category, mandates a convoluted, coded truth-telling in the midst of a similarly mandated deception.

Slippage in Reality and in the Ballroom Scene

In the topsy-turvy world of the Ballroom, "Realness" means deception. In the runway events that go by that name, House members practice at passing undetected in the "real" world, the world they see as filled with hypocrisy and deception; the world where, in contrast to the Ballroom, almost everyone is unaware of the games they play and the disguises they wear.

Nicole would no doubt have taken the trophy if she had walked "Women's Face, Realness" rather than simply "Women's Face." Then deception would have been her intention. In that case, the audience would not have been deceived because everybody would have been in on the act, and they would have applauded her for playing the deception game so well. From the perspective of the audience, a Femme Queen walking "Women's Real-ness" is simply exhibiting "her" act for the admiration of her peers. It is the larger public that would be deceived if they were to see her on the runway—but, of course, they will not.

To walk "Woman's Face, Realness" a person must, first of all, be a biologi-cal male. In order to win, "she" must be very convincing at imitating a woman, and yet, not too convincing. Femme Queens who want to be really good at walking Realness must know how to perform the *almost* undetectable gesture with hip, hand, or eyebrow that betrays the masquerade, at least to the cognoscenti, thus reminding the in-group of the secret they already know about the person doing the walking. The real value of Realness is that it makes community by provoking endless reiterations of the superiority of in-group knowledge. The ability to detect the game in the in-between spaces creates an in-group and makes a community out of previously marginalized persons.

Bruce N. Lancaster discusses the failed transvestite performance as one in which "the act is all too convincing, because "not enough space lies between the actor and the acted." Lancaster suggests that in such a case someone wit-nessing the performance might simply conclude, "this is the way you *are*." By contrast, he observes that successful "performative performances can never simply *imitate* or *mimic* . . . they're always in *excess* of their target."[17] On the runways of Newark, the space opened up by the lack of fit between actor and act, no matter how small, makes room for polymorphous, contra-dictory gender play, which in turn allows for the juggling of anger, resistance, humor, and desire.

Homi Bhabha makes a point about the "conflictual economy of colonial discourse" similar to Lancaster's insight about successful transvestite per-formances. Bhabha suggests that "colonial mimicry is the desire for a re-formed, recognizable Other, *as a subject of difference that is almost the same, but not quite.* He further explains that "the discourse of mimicry is con-structed around an *ambivalence*; in order to be effective, mimicry must con-tinually produce its slippage, its excess, its difference."[18] Colonial officials sought to change the world of the colonized to make it resemble the "superior" world from which the official came. At the same time, they virtually demanded to see "slippage" in the imitative efforts of the colonized. The colonized also needed slippage in order to gain leverage. Too perfect a reproduction would not only obviate the need for empire; it would also turn the colonized into simple mirrors. It is in the area of slippage that the colonized found space for resistance. Where there is slippage, there also exist possibilities for irony, satire, and other forms of social leveraging.

In a general way, it is the same sort of slippage, excess, and difference that enable the participants in Newark Balls to articulate both "The Life" they live and the "real" life of the larger society. For example, it is precisely the excess of color, makeup, and clothing that stands for femininity in the Ballroom Scene that makes it possible for any type of woman on the runway to be an object of desire and simultaneously an object of satire. The quick flick of an eyebrow, hip, or hand that gives away the game for those who walk Realness is another form of programmed slippage, but one that has been condensed to a small gesture in order to signal the power of the masquerader over the mask. As Angel Vizcaya said, "The Balls are very contradictive": a strict, normative understanding of gender categories is necessary for the Balls to succeed, yet they succeed only in the gap between the ideal and the embodied. Balls remain useful, interesting, and important only as long as the people on the runway are "almost but not quite the same" as what counts in their world as an ideal man or woman.

Most of the male-to-female transsexuals in Newark do not take the final, surgical step toward becoming a woman. They seem to relish the transformations in their bodies that result from hormone therapy, but they do not give up their penises—and this decision is not always attributed to the cost of surgery. With them, the hidden penis, tucked back between the legs, functions as the "almost . . . but not quite" that creates the space between act and reality, the same space that makes self-understanding and ultimately self-respect possible.

I resist the trend to see all African American cultural expressions as univocal modes of resistance. bell hooks, for instance, approached the Ballroom Scene in this mood and then found herself disappointed, even angry, about the quality of resistance manifest there.[19] Michel de Certeau makes an important distinction between a "strategy" and a "tactic," a distinction which can help retrieve the genuine resistance of the Ballroom Scene without losing sight of the many other "contradictive" things that are going on simultaneously and with the same level of invested energy. Unlike a "strategy," which requires having a place of one's own on which to stand, "the place of a tactic," says de Certeau, "belongs to the other. A tactic insinuates itself into the other's place, fragmentarily, without taking it over in its entirety, without being able to keep it at a distance."[20] The Ballroom Scene is thus, among other things, a tactical display of resistance.

The Everyday Violence of Gay Life in Newark

According to the members of the Houses, Newark is an especially homophobic city. Religiously and socially conservative racial/ethnic communities managed to keep homosexuality out of the public arena for a long time. Gay pride activities and grassroots organizing, for example, are relatively recent phenomena in Newark. As one gay Newark native put it: "It was AIDS that finally forced gay men out of their closets." Yet with or without activism, gay bashing has remained a disturbingly common occurrence in the city, and, on a daily basis, the streets of Newark are the stage for routine gay-baiting of a less physically violent sort.

Both the Houses of Greater Newark and the Harlem Houses Jennie Livingston filmed took shape in the age of AIDS, and they have been profoundly influenced by it. (This is not apparent in *Paris Is Burning* because the film was made quite early in the AIDS pandemic.) New Jersey is home for 6 percent of the adults in the United States who have AIDS and 9 percent of the children; only New York, California, Florida, and Texas have more AIDS cases. There are twenty-one counties in New Jersey, yet Essex County (where Newark is located) has nearly one-third of all the state's cases. Fifty-three percent of New

Jersey people with AIDS contracted the HIV virus through intravenous drug use, yet there are very few "drug detox beds" available for uninsured people in Newark. Hospice beds are also scarce for people with no insurance. One of the greatest worries of many Newark residents with full-blown AIDS is that of finding a place to die with dignity. Recently, new drugs have dramatically lowered the death rates from AIDS, but some suspect this might be only a pause in the spread of HIV/AIDS. Transmission of the HIV virus can be attributed to homosexual sexual practices in about 14 percent of the Newark cases, yet AIDS in Newark is still assumed to be a gay disease.[21] Homophobia thus acts like a scrim, hiding the city's inhumanity from itself.

AIDS has had an enormous impact on the Houses of Greater Newark. When Bernie Jourdan, mother of the House of Jourdan, was asked by a friend, "How many people have you lost?" he was shocked to hear himself list "fifteen or twenty" names.[22] All of the Houses in Newark have lost members and some have lost many within a short period of time. But the discourse about AIDS in the Houses is tricky. It swallows the key words—the noun "AIDS," and the verb "to die"—as well as contextual terms like "funeral" and "wake." Such fear-laden words are rarely uttered by members of the Houses; it is almost as if they had been banned. Many people in the Houses, perhaps most, no longer attend memorial services of any kind.

Angel Vizcaya, like most of the mothers and fathers, feels himself to be in emotional overload because of AIDS: "I don't know, for me it's . . . it can get real personal. You know? . . . We've been going to too many of them [funerals] for the same reason, because of the same disease [AIDS]. . . . A lot of times I don't go . . . because it makes me deal with my own personal issues."[23] Angel, one of the "elders" of the Houses of Greater Newark, has just turned thirty and he is HIV positive. He does not have AIDS, yet he says he is no longer able to do what he used to do as a House mother: for example, pull kids off the streets and get them involved in his House. Now, he says, it is time to take care of himself.

Although he was born a Catholic, Angel does not currently belong to any religious group, nor does he have any regular religious practice, but he does light candles and burn incense in his home. People who live with the HIV virus or with AIDS frequently express anger at the Christian churches. Almost every person in the Houses interviewed by the Newark Project staff has reported painful rejection by the Catholic or Protestant church he or she attended as a child, and, in the age of AIDS, they have learned not to expect too much from Christianity. For example, House members laugh about the friends who "get saved" as part of their dying process. A person "gets saved" when a previously rejecting family claims the body and takes it home for a "proper" church funeral, one which silences homosexuality and erases AIDS. This type of avoidance is very different from the silencing of key words that prevails in the Houses. In the Houses, people do not dare to say the words because they are too powerful; in the churches, ministers refrain from saying them because they find them shameful.

Bernie Jourdan has spoken eloquently, almost theologically, about the power of the HIV virus:

It's like a guest from hell! And you invite these things because you're doing things you know you shouldn't be doing . . . or, you did things that you didn't know about . . . at the time. . . . And, it's like a vampire, it sucks the living soul out of a person, and it's devastating to you. . . . I hate it so much! I actually hate it![24]

The ambivalence in Bernie Jourdan's account of his experience of AIDS, his vacillation between an understanding of the disease as a guest he was morally remiss to have invited in, and a smooth vampire whose evil intent could not have been detected in advance of the attack, reproduces in his own psyche the public ambivalence about whether people with AIDS are criminals or victims. Bernie Jourdan is caught in this place, and the larger society is too. One thing that is happening at socially conscious balls, such as the Fire Balls, is the deliberate reconfiguring of persons with AIDS as neither victims nor criminals. This reconfiguration happens via the drama of the runway. For example, one of the runway events for the '97 Fire Ball was "Safe Sex Commercial as a House." The prize was $500. Under other circumstances, religious institutions might be expected to recognize the humanity of people with AIDS, and empower them to protect themselves and others.

The 1998 Fire Ball included a category called "Memorial Runway" sponsored by the Drew University Newark Project.[25] Angel Vizcaya was the first to mount the runway and he caused quite a sensation. He wore a fabulous, red taffeta dress with an outsized Southern-belle-style skirt. Halfway down the runway assistants unwrapped the skirt to reveal a feather encrusted hoop that doubled as a birdcage. It contained several live white doves. Angel retrieved one of the birds and then struck a pose with the bird held aloft, its wings flapping. Angel's brother had died from AIDS the week before the Fire Ball, and he poured his grief and his pressing need to transcend suffering, if only temporarily, into this startling runway performance.

Religion, Identity, and Transcendence

It has traditionally been religious institutions that have helped people to "imagine the society of which they are members and the obscure yet intimate relations they have with it."[26] In the United States, churches, temples, synagogues, and mosques are usually in charge of ritualizing death and of helping the grieving deal with sorrow and rage, but for those in The Life, the Ballroom must often function as a stand-in for religion. It is not only humor and resistance that animate the Ballroom; there is also a palpable longing for transcendence, for the high that comes from sheer creativity, for the profound satisfaction of turning oneself into such an image of shimmering desire that every eye in the house is drawn to you, for the thrill that comes with winning, for the joy of coming out on top.

Churches and families have frequently betrayed young gay men and lesbian women in search of their identities. The evidence for this is pervasive in the reminiscences of members of the Houses of Greater Newark. Sexuality and gender are foundational to human existence. They are so basic to human life that only social institutions as deeply involved in the formation of identity as the family and the church can be of much help when there are sexual or gender issues to be resolved. When families demand silence in exchange for a gay child's right to remain in the home, and churches require that gay members remain in the closet, they have rendered these persons invisible. They have refused to see them.

Thus much of the action at the Balls is about being seen—not seeing, but being seen. Paradoxically, the significance of being seen is signaled by the repetition of the trope of the invisible eye. The normative white gaze that shapes the entire ball where whites are "looked up to" but not welcome, is one example. The elided photographer in "Voguing—the old way" is another. Yet the most pervasive invisible eye is the one that the performer turns on himself or herself. In the context of a discussion of Franz Fanon's portrayal of postcolonial consciousness, Bhabha notes that the subaltern "desires not merely to be in the place of the white man but compulsively seeks to look back and down on himself from that position."[27] The interesting relationship between this point and Du Bois's understanding of "double consciousness" argues for moving the theory from the former empire to the Newark runway. The space within, which Bhabha calls the "eliptical *in-between,* where the shadow of the other falls upon the self," may be said to produce the constant ambivalence in the mood of the Ballroom runway, detectable in the "almost . . . but not quite" quality of the mimetic performances. Such intimate ambivalence can become a source of humor, and it can lead to bonding with others whose sense of self is similarly constructed around an erasure, a place of invisibility. But this also makes the identity-affirming task of the Ballroom much more difficult.

Identity is always configured dynamically, in human interactions, and the work of identity formation is fluid. Identity ebbs and flows, even transforms in the course of a lifetime. The Ballroom Scene is not an unlikely place to pursue a firmer sense of self. Yet the runway has an intensity, a repetitiousness, and, most of all, a sheer persistence that speaks poignantly of the pull of invisibility on those who seek out its spotlight. The one who walks is seen, and seen again, and seen yet again, but never seen continuously and certainly not seen enough. It may well be that once identity has been configured as invisibility, it is next to impossible to subvert that construct.

Conclusion

While many would acknowledge that racism is the most American of prejudices, Alan Wolfe's 1998 book *One Nation After All* demonstrates that, in Middle America at least, homophobia is the most resistant to change.[28] The intense, creative, and convoluted mimesis of Newark's Ballroom Scene makes sense against a ground of homophobic and racist violence, extraordinary and quotidian, personal and systemic. It appears that, if gay men of color cannot find a way to be themselves in the world, then they will conjure a world in which they can be themselves.

The Ballroom is *many* things. For one, it is a model of society. On the runways the mimetic talents of gay men of color, as well as of a few lesbian and straight women, are engaged in "play" with the "real" and that "real" world is the one in which these same people must live and move every day. Those who walk the runways, explore, desire, defuse, mock, long for, undermine, exaggerate, adulate, diminish, caricature, mourn, and reinforce the "stuff" of the "real" world.

The Ballroom Scene *is* many things. The social map operative in the Newark Balls is Butch Queen normative. In its gay dimension, it is transgressive and liberatory. In its male-dominant mode, it is socially stagnant, even regressive. The Ballroom Scene *is* "contradictive." The white gaze is not welcome in the Ballroom; this is a black scene, or at least one for people of color. Yet that same gaze transformed into the invisible eye might be said to orchestrate everything that goes on at a Ball.

The Ballroom is a free, relaxed space for people who spend too much energy monitoring their disguises. Yet the Balls are very tense. They can quickly become fiercely competitive and even members of the audience may from time to time sense dread beneath the high-energy music, the wild applause, and the excess of good-natured sensuality. A police car with its blue lights spinning in anticipation of trouble is often stationed outside the Ballroom, even though trouble rarely arrives. One Butch Queen with a responsible job in the health care industry, a man who never walks the runways but comes to all the Balls, says that he goes to relax, "to be myself." But he quickly adds, "It is dangerous too." "What do you mean by that?" I ask him. "Nobody at my job knows I'm gay. I could run into someone here. It could all be over for me—just like that," he says, snapping his fingers. In the Ballrooms of Newark, gay men of color celebrate while dancing on the edge of the pit.

Mimesis is the dominant art form of the Ballroom Scene, and it is important not to define it in reductive ways. Gebauer and Wulf suggest that mimesis is "an 'impure' concept in the sense of rational thought, a concept immersed in practice and shot with traces of tradition and power, a variable of history and social relations and therefore not subject to formalization."[29] It is also important not to deny the "contradictive" richness of the Ballroom tradition simply because that stance can appear politically incorrect. It is fashionable these days to look at virtually all aspects of African American culture as sites for resistance, but confining the Ballroom Scene to such a limited discursive space would deny the full humanity of the persons who currently embody that tradition and sort out their lives in relation to the runway. It would force an unnatural cleavage between politics and desire, anger and yearning, the pain of rejection and the life-saving perspective that being marginalized may provide.

Notes

1. Jacques Lacan, *The Four Fundamental Concepts of Psychoanalysis* (London: Hogworth Press, 1977), 99.

2. Jennie Livingston, *Paris Is Burning*, cited in Henry Louis Gates, Jr., *The Signifying Monkey: A Theory of Afro-American Literary Criticism* (London: Oxford University Press, 1988).

3. Karen McCarthy Brown video interview with Angel Vizcaya, December, 1997.

4. Census data from "CensusCD 1.1 Summary Newark, N.J.," February 2, 1998.

5. Peter Savastano interview with Bernie Jourdan, March 23, 1996.

6. Michael Taussig, *Mimesis and Alterity: A Particular History of the Senses* (New York: Routledge Press, 1993), xiii–xiv.

7. Program, Fire Ball Part IV (Newark, New Jersey), October 25, 1997.

8. Karen McCarthy Brown video interview with Angel Vizcaya, December, 1997.

9. Ibid.

10. Peter Savastano is a Ph.D. candidate at Drew University and the administrator of The Newark Project. I have learned a great deal from the remarkable oral histories that he has done with gay men in Newark.

11. Karen McCarthy Brown video interview with Armand Genesis, November 2, 1997.

12. Ibid.

13. See Judith Butler, *Gender Trouble: Feminism and the Subversion of Identity* (New York: Routledge, 1990), and bell hooks, "Is Paris Burning?" in *Black Looks: Race and Representation* (Boston: South End Press, 1992).

14. Karen McCarthy Brown video interview with Angel Vizcaya, December, 1997.

15. Ibid.

16. Ibid.

17. Roger N. Lancaster, "Guto's Performance: Notes on the Transvestism of Everyday Life," in *The Gender/Sexuality Reader*, ed. Lancaster and Micaela di Leonardo (New York: Routledge, 1997), 562–566.

18. Homi K. Bhabha, *The Location of Culture* (New York: Routledge, 1994), 86.

19. See hooks, "Is Paris Burning?"

20. Michel de Certeau, *The Practice of Everyday Life* (Berkeley: University of California Press, 1984), xix.

21. Census data from "CensusCD 1.1 Summary Newark, N.J.," February 2, 1998.

22. Peter Savastano interview with Bernie Jourdan, March 23, 1996.

23. Karen McCarthy Brown video interview with Angel Vizcaya, December, 1997.

24. Peter Savastano interview with Bernie Jourdan, March 23, 1996.

25. The Drew University Newark Project, in operation since 1993 and currently funded by the Ford Foundation, combines ethnographic research on religious life in the city of Newark with field-based education initiatives, and also with community organizing and social action. I first connected with the Houses through The Newark Project. In addition to Peter Savastano, I have also worked closely with Eugenia Lee

Hancock, a Drew Ph.D. candidate, on research connected to the Houses of Greater Newark.

26. Emile Durkheim, *The Elementary Forms of the Religious Life*, trans. Karen Fields (New York: Free Press, 1995), 227.

27. Bhabha, 60.

28. See Alan Wolfe, *One Nation After All* (New York: Viking, 1998).

29. Gunter Gebauer and Christoph Wulf, *Mimesis: Culture, Art, Society*, trans. Don Reneau (Berkeley: University of California Press, 1992), 3.

9 "The Church's Closet"

Confessionals, Victorian Catholicism, and the Crisis of Identification

Patrick R. O'Malley

> The Protestant has freedom in his mien, it burns in his look, it is stamped on his brow, it is written in the fire of his unquailing eye. You can tell at a glance the Papist who has gone willingly to the CONFESSIONAL, for the practices of the dark den of the Confessional have left him a broken, crushed, degraded being.
>
> —CANON STOWELL, *Lecture at Leeds*

> The priests use the Confessional to obtain the secrets of the individual, the household, or the State. They use it to corrupt, pervert, and enslave their victims—to satiate their own lust, avarice, ambition, and malice. It is the Church's closet for pry, intrigue, and "ambiguous familiarity."   —*The Oxford and Roman Railway* (1871)[1]

The anonymous writer of *The Oxford and Roman Railway*, one of the many tracts published in the 1860s and 1870s by the militantly anti-Catholic Protestant Evangelical Mission and Electoral Union, situates the Catholic practice of private auricular confession, and its increasing appeal to the Ritualist flank of the Church of England, at the center of a series of transgressions against the dominant British social order. The tract imagines the insidious clutches of the confessional as moving in ever wider circles as it first controls "the individual," then "the household," and finally, "the State," extending its corruptive influence from personal ethics to the integrity of the family structure to the nation as a whole. The threat that the confessional poses, according to the tract, is not only theological in its ramifications; it is a sexual threat to the individual and a political threat to the nation. It enslaves the state as it perverts the conscience, and ambition and lust, intrigue and "ambiguous familiarity" function in tandem. Most fundamentally, however, the practice of auricular confession achieves its simultaneously treasonous and seductive goals through the veil of secrecy. The confessional functions as a "closet" in the imaginations of such Protestant polemicists as the author of *The Oxford and Roman Railway* precisely insofar as it confounds knowledge; even the sexually charged "familiarity" of the confessional is necessarily "ambiguous," remaining just outside the possibility of certainty. It represents an epistemological crisis that is central to an understanding of the development of the religious and sexual categories of knowledge that would come to be articulated in the course of the latter half of the nineteenth century.

I bring the quotation from *The Oxford and Roman Railway* together with that of Hugh Stowell's *Lecture at Leeds* in order to demonstrate the disparity in their epistemological conceptions. Although earlier controversialists such as Canon Stowell might assert that the Catholic is easily identified by sight, the equally anti-Catholic rhetoric of "the Church's closet" links national, sexual, and religious anxieties to suggest that the Papist or Ritualist poses a central threat to the very notion of stable systems of identification, systems grounded in the structures and applications of language itself. The cultural fantasy of Catholic linguistic deviance takes on at least two forms as the century progresses. On the one hand, Charles Kingsley, for example, locates in Catholic rhetoric a recognizably effeminate and sexually transgressive ambiguity. On the other, the attacks on the confessional and the imagined conspiracy of silence that surrounded Catholic ritual and practice posit that true Catholic language could never be known, that it would always be hidden under the veil of secrecy or—more threateningly—of apparently normative Protestantism. In both cases, the deviance of Catholic language is constructed as both the mask and the mark of the wide-flung Catholic transgressions against the dominant social, sexual, and national orders.[2] That is, Catholic linguistic deviance is threatening precisely insofar as it is obfuscatory, either through the secrecy of the Seal of the Confessional or through the ambiguities of irony itself. In the course of the nineteenth century, as Catholics enter the social and religious spheres of English life, the anxiety engendered by the Catholic's ability to pass takes on a new urgency because it is through the perversions of language that the deviances of Catholicism are imagined to pass through, and into, Protestant language and culture.

I

Taken by many evangelical Protestants as the paradigmatic site of illicit language, it was the confessional—and the sexual license that was imagined to take place within its confines—that seized the anti-Catholic imagination throughout the nineteenth century. In 1851, for example, a London press published a tract with the aggressive title *The Confessional Unmasked, Showing the Depravity of the Priesthood, Questions put to Females in Confession, Perjury and Stealing Commanded and Encouraged, andc., andc.* The bulk of the author's attack on Roman Catholicism, through a critique of the anonymous confession, relies upon a narrative of sexual deviance and coercion. The tract thus condemns the sheer comprehensiveness of the confessor's license to ask questions related to sexual matters, since the very articulation of the possibility of sexual deviance is taken as productive of that deviance itself.[3] Noting the questions that might be posed to the confessant, the author of the tract—listed only as "C.B."—asks with dismay, "After reading this, who would marry a frequenter of the confessional?"[4]

Yet it is not only the subversion of the confessant's morals that such a controversialist as "C.B." is concerned with; rather, the tract constructs the confessional itself as the *site* of sexual deviance. Thus it quotes the eighteenth-century Catholic theologian Pierre Dens's instruction, in a chapter entitled "On Just Causes for Permitting Motions of Sensuality," that *[j]ust causes of this sort are the hearing of confessions [and] the reading of cases of conscience drawn up for a Confessor. . . . The effect of a just cause is such that any thing from which motions arise may be not only lawfully begun, but also lawfully continued: and so the Confessor receiving those motions from the hearing of confessions, ought not on that account to abstain from hearing them, but has a just cause for persevering, providing however that they always displease him, and there arise not therefrom the proximate danger of consent.*

The *Confessional Unmasked* then offers the following gloss on Dens's teaching:

Thus it appears to be a matter-of-course, that hearing confessions is a just cause for entertaining sensual motions. Dens explains "sensual motions" to be, "Sharp tingling sensations of sensual delight shooting through the body, and exciting to corporeal pleasure." Now, if a lady appears modest, the Confessor is instructed that "that modesty must be overcome, or else he is authorized to deny her absolution." . . . Only think of allowing a wife or daughter to go alone to confession to such beastly sensualists, or of permitting such hideous monsters to enter their sick chamber, especially when they are recovering.[5]

As shocking as this attack on a bedridden young woman might be, the threat of singular (and heterosexual) seduction initiated by—or indeed within—the confessional swiftly gives way to the spectacle of a virtual orgy of indiscriminate sexual partnerings: "any Confessor may absolve a novice, a nun, or a lay woman, a priest, a friar, or a monk, though they be all guilty of committing fornication one with the other."[6]

The deviance of auricular confession lies not only in the fact that priests might seduce young women (or each other) within the secret confines of the confessional but also in that the anonymity of the encounter means that women might tell things to priests that their husbands do not know. Thus, the confessional might prove to be a space that challenges the ultimate authority and control of a man over his wife, and of the law over the citizen. For example, "C.B." observes that although a woman might confess to her priest that she had committed adultery, having been absolved of the sin, she is not, under Catholic law, obligated to tell others of her crime against the nation and male authority, even under oath, just as her confessor is required to conceal her identity: "Yea, if the crime may truly be concealed . . . a woman can deny with an oath, and say, I did not commit the crime, in the same way that the accused can say to his judge, not legitimately interrogating, I did not commit the crime, understanding that he did not so commit it, that he is bound to manifest it to him."[7] The dangers of "Catholic language" to English sexual hierarchies are thus multiple. On the one hand, the woman, believing that she is confessing to the priest (that is, that she is producing her own discourse), ends up seduced by the priest's own language (learning, for example, about sins that she would otherwise never have contemplated); on the other, this scene of seduction simultaneously unmans her husband, undermining his role as the guardian of his wife's sexuality.[8]

This anxiety around the Catholic threat to English values through the secretive power of the confessional—its resistance to co-optation by the legal and social structures of both sexual normativity and national control—continues in evangelical circles throughout the century. Indeed, the connection between Ritualism more broadly (or Roman Catholicism itself) and sexual deviance becomes a staple of the evangelical attack as the century progresses. In 1871, the Evangelical Mission and Electoral Union's tract *Dr. Pusey's Insane Project Considered* presents a panoply of individuals seduced by the attractions of Ritualism: "The Ritualistic clergyman in harlequin dress goes through a variety of evolutions, whilst his silly admirers, consisting of male duennas, aged ladies, big boys, and tall school girls, also change posture, genuflect, stoop down, face about east, or look west, aping as far as allowed these very interesting and expressive attitudes."[9] While the tone of the anonymous tract is here rather facetiously patronizing, its insistence upon the suggestion of confused gender identities (from "male duennas" to "tall school girls") is expressive of the deep cultural link in the evangelical imagination between religious absurdities (including here all of the physical motion of the Catholic liturgy) and the violation of sexual norms.

Published in 1851, *The Confessional Unmasked* appears at the moment of greatest anxiety over the encroachment of Catholicism into English territory. Six years earlier, on October 9, 1845, John Henry Newman, formerly the vicar of St. Mary's, the University church at Oxford, was received into the Roman Catholic faith. Thirty-four years later, he was made a cardinal by Pope Leo XIII. Newman had been one of the most prominent and articulate proponents of the so-called Oxford Movement, an attempt to bring certain rituals (including auricular confession, the veneration of the saints, theologies of the Real Presence of Christ at the Eucharist and of apostolic succession, and such symbols as the crucifix, candles, and colorful ecclesiastic vestments) back into Anglican religious practice. Begun in 1833 as a series of meetings of Anglican men concerned with the directions of the national church, the Oxford Movement was also popularly known as the "Tractarian Movement" (after the affiliated polemical series called *Tracts for the Times*) and was considered the vanguard of the broader "Ritualism" increasing in many parts of the Established Church. While several other well-known Oxford Movement figures, including John Keble and Edward Bouverie Pusey (both, like Newman, fellows at Oriel College), remained within the Anglican Church, Newman's ultimate rejection of his earlier arguments that a High-Church Anglicanism could combine the best aspects of both Protestantism and Catholicism (the *"via media"*) and his embrace of the Church of Rome itself was a stunning confirmation to evangelical Protestants of the dangers of Ritualist Anglicanism. As polemicist Walter Walsh would later write, in *The Secret History of the Oxford Movement*, "The Tractarian Movement had only been in existence a very short time when people began to suspect it as being in reality a Romeward Movement."[10] Or, in the more dramatic words of the midcentury essay "The Three Priests," "The distinction between the Popery of Rome and the Popery of Oxford is only the difference between prussic acid and arsenic; they are both equally deadly, and are equally to be abhorred."[11]

But if prussic acid and arsenic are indistinguishable in their fatal effect, how are they, after all, to be distinguished from healthful ingestions? That is, how can the Catholic—sexually deviant and degraded as he or she might be—be identified? This crisis was further highlighted by the 1850 authorization by Pope Pius IX of the reestablishment of the Catholic hierarchy in England for the first time since the Reformation. Thus, the moderate Reverend Newland describes the dominant, centrist Protestant attitude toward Rome before the so-called Papal Aggression of 1850 in vividly supernatural imagery: "They [his parishioners] were quite innocent of Popery, they had heard of it no doubt, and hated it of course, but none of them knew exactly what Roman Catholics looked like, and whether Jesuits were not to be known by their horns and hoofs."[12] The Oxford Movement, the Papal Aggression, and the sheer attention paid to Catholics in the aftermath of the Aggression made this fantasy of Catholic distinctiveness, for which Newland seems rather nostalgic, impossible for an increasing section of the Church of England, even as the evangelical Protestant attack on Romanism (and its supposedly craven seductees from within the body of Protestantism itself) continued unabated through the entire century.

The terms of that attack, however, began to change as the anxiety over the possibility of identifying the Catholic infiltrators in the midst of Protestant England heightened. In 1851, among the illustrations of panic around the Papal Aggression, one cartoon (figure 9.1) suggests that those very demonstrations of resistance—and parliamentary opposition—have thwarted the imagined attempt by the Roman Church to annex England openly as a Catholic nation. Caricaturing Nicolas Wiseman, the new cardinal of Westminster, as the proprietor of a failed business venture, the cartoon features the caption "Selling Off!!!" and images of banners above a tawdry shop proclaiming "Must be Cleared in a Few Days" and "Alarming Failure!!!" The cartoon likewise provides signs representing the excesses of Roman Catholicism, presented here as theatrical props or baubles meant to entertain women and children; thus, it announces the sale of "hair shirts in great variety," "a prime lot of wax ends" and "several winking pictures." The overt destruction of English Protestant values, the cartoon suggests, has been foiled, although a more sinister, surreptitious co-optation is suggested by the display of signs specifically advertising the wares of the failed Romanist venture to "Puseyites" and "Tractarians." In the very center of the cartoon is the

FIGURE 9.1. "Selling Off." From *Punch, or The London Charivari* (London, 1851).

image of a rather despondent-looking Wiseman handing a pair of ecclesiastical slippers to a Jewish peddler, his deviancy marked by his hunched back and servile posture, large hooked nose, and prominent lips. On the one hand, the presence of the Jewish dealer serves to mark the degradations to which the failed papal venture has stooped in its attempt to pawn off its undesirable products; on the other, it warns of a clandestine alliance between the Catholic hierarchy and the Jews of England in their efforts to subvert English Protestant values. If Catholic paraphernalia and idolatry will not enter the British social economy through the Ritualists, the Jews will manage to proliferate them.

By 1877, *Punch*'s image of Catholic aggression has moved from overt to covert. A cartoon of that year (figure 9.2) presents a prosperously obese John Bull dragging a Catholic cleric by the ear from the house of matronly

235

FIGURE 9.2. "A Wolf in Sheep's Clothing." From *Punch, or The London Charivari* (London, 1877).

Britannia: "Whenever you see any of these sneaking scoundrels about, Ma'am," John Bull announces, clutching his walking stick like a weapon, "just send for me. *I'll* deal with 'em, never fear!!" Here, the anonymous "sneaking scoundrel" is likely a Ritualist Anglican (rather than a Roman Catholic), because he holds in his hand the scandalous *Priest in Absolution*, the tract published in the 1870s instructing Anglican clerics on the protocols of the confessional and attacked by evangelicals as a method of secretly implanting sexually explicit ideas into the minds of the confessants. Significantly, however, the cartoon suggests that there is little difference between Ritualist and Roman versions of Catholicism, except that the former is merely a mask for the latter. The cartoon is, in fact, captioned "A Wolf in Sheep's Clothing," suggesting that the supposedly innocuous Protestant façade of the Ritualists is merely the cover for the importation (into good English homes) of the Romanist practices and sexual transgressions detailed in the *Priest in Absolution.*

But by presenting the Catholic threat as being manifested in the garb of a Protestant minister, *Punch* suggests not that the transgressions of Romanism are old news but, rather, that Catholics have found more effective methods of infiltration: it is precisely because the Catholic is invisible that the insidious influence of Catholicism can be everywhere. Indeed, the cartoon takes another step in its illustration of the extent of the Catholic conspiracy, for the cleric escorted out of Britannia's home by the upright and quintessentially English Mr. Bull is stereotyped almost precisely as a Jew. With his stooped shoulders, cringing posture, prominent, hooked nose, protruding lips, and swarthy, unshaven face, this man's features are remarkably close to those of the Jew in the 1851 cartoon (even to the position of his arms and the implication of a slightly effeminate, ineffectual grasping of his long fingers). But whereas the 1851 image presented the Jew as an accomplice of the Catholic Wiseman, here the Catholic priest seems himself to be a Jew. Or rather, the cultural fantasies of Jewish and Catholic infiltration are so similar in their outlines that the stereotype of the Jew can stand in for that of the Catholic.

The same anxiety is evident in such claims as those by the former Catholic priest Dr. Giovanni Giacinto Achilli, who announced as early as 1847 that "it is well that you should tolerate Roman Catholics even as you tolerate Jews, and even idolatry. But mark this difference: the Papists alone are they who seek to return to injure you—Rome urges them to it, nay makes it a matter of obligation—of conscience to do so. Rome is, therefore, to you an enemy who makes war within your very house."[13] The Catholic is thus more harmful than the Jew, not simply because of the imagined organized conspiracy against English values but also because the Catholic functions "within your very house," from the inside as an unrecognized infiltrator. For Achilli, the stereotype of the Catholic *as* Jew fails in that it ignores the greater insidiousness and virulence of the Romanist. The danger, Achilli claims, is not only that the Catholic hierarchy—unlike individual Jews—is intentionally destructive of English Protestantism but, rather, that the very resistance of the Catholic to social recognition makes that destruction all the easier. It is an attack not from a recognizable outsider but from an unknown and unknowable insider.

II

In December of 1863, the crisis called the Papal Aggression was thirteen years old, and the Oxford Movement and Newman's conversion were even further in the past. Yet it was in that year that Charles Kingsley, signing himself "C.K." in a review of Froude's *History of England*, returned to the same conjunction of national, sexual, and religious deviance that had characterized the attack on Catholicism by *Punch* and its contemporary Protestant controversialists. "The Roman religion had, for some time past," asserts Kingsley, "been making men not better men, but worse. . . . From the time that indulgences were hawked about in [the Pope's] name, which would insure pardon for any man, '*etsi matrem Dei violavisset*' [even if he had violated the mother of God], the world in general began to be of that opinion."[14] Taking as his example an accommodation for the almost unthinkable sexual transgression of the rape of the Virgin Mary herself, Kingsley launches his polemic against the Roman Catholic Church in the language of extreme sexual violence. Although the sheer enormity of the deviances from supposedly normative sexual practice quickly lessens, Kingsley continues to take as exemplary instances of the Catholic abuse of power those historical circumstances that, while intimately related to the history of England itself, likewise show a relevance to his underlying message of the sexual anarchy of Romanism:

A deed might be a crime, or no crime at all—like Henry the Eighth's marriage of his brother's widow—according to the will of the Pope. . . . And the shadow did not pass at once, when the Pope's authority was thrown off. Henry VIII evidently thought that if the Pope could make right and wrong, perhaps he could do so likewise. Elizabeth seems to have fancied, at one weak moment, that the Pope had the power of making her marriage with Leicester right, instead of wrong.

All of the turbulent sexual maneuvering of the English Reformation and its aftermath thus become, for Kingsley, the effects of a vestigial Catholicism.

Although deviant sexuality is for Kingsley the stigmata of the Papist, deviant language—never far from sexual transgression, it seems—is the Catholic's defining characteristic. Kingsley thus quickly moves from the general to the specific: "Truth for its own sake, had never been a virtue with the Roman clergy. Father Newman informs us that it need not, and on the whole ought not to be; that cunning is the weapon which Heaven has given to the saints wherewith to withstand the brute male force of the wicked world which marries and gives in marriage."[15] Alluding rather sarcastically to Christ's famous assertion, related in all three of the synoptic Gospels, that "when they shall rise from the dead, they neither marry, nor are given in marriage; but are as the angels which are in heaven" (Mark 12:25),[16] Kingsley specifically attacks the Roman Catholic practice of celibacy, a practice that Newman had adopted for himself while within the Church of England. The terms of Kingsley's broadside against both Newman and the Catholic Church are telling; for Kingsley, it seems, "brute male force" is the natural— and indeed desirable—norm for human sexual relations. The facetious tone of the attack seems to place the critical implications of the phrase into the mouths of such Catholic orators as Newman, who are presented as rather prissy in their opposition to good Protestant sexual values.

The *ad hominem* attack startled Newman, who immediately shot off a letter to the editors of *Macmillan's Magazine* (in which Kingsley's review had appeared.) A week later, Kingsley himself wrote a note to Newman identifying himself as the "C.K." of the review and standing by its assertions, noting that

it was due to a sermon by Newman that he "finally shook off the strong influence which your writings exerted on me; and for much of which I still owe
you a deep debt of gratitude."[17] The increasingly hostile letter-writing cam-
paign that followed was collected by Newman and published as a pamphlet;
Kingsley responded in early 1864 by publishing his own tract, entitled
"What, Then, Does Dr. Newman Mean?" Finally, in response, Newman published his *Apologia Pro Vita Sua*, in pamphlets issued from April to June of that
same year. The *Apologia* remains one of the most articulate and comprehensive defenses of a specifically English Catholic faith—and indeed conversion—against the charges of hypocrisy and deceit.

In "What, Then, Does Dr. Newman Mean?" Kingsley repeatedly constructs Newman as a seducer of young men, a seduction accomplished
through the power of rhetoric:

*What, then, did the sermon mean? Why was it preached? To insinuate that a Church
which had sacramental confession and a celibate clergy was the only true Church? Or
to insinuate that the admiring young gentlemen who listened to him stood to their fel-
low-countrymen in the relation of the early Christians to the heathen Romans? . . . I
know that men used to suspect Dr. Newman—I have been inclined to do so myself—
of writing a whole sermon, not for the sake of the text or of the matter, but for the sake
of one single passing hint—one phrase, one epithet, one little barbed arrow which, as
he swept magnificently past on the stream of his calm eloquence, seemingly unconscious of all presences, save those unseen, he delivered unheeded, as with his finger-
tip, to the very heart of an initiated hearer, never to be withdrawn again.*[18]

Kingsley makes Newman's oratory into the arrow of Eros, piercing the hearts
of the "admiring young gentlemen" who flock to hear him. It is language
that seduces here, rhetoric that takes physical form as the transgressive and
phallic arrow, literally penetrating the bodies of Newman's male listeners.[19]

More importantly, however, Newman's "insinuation" is, for Kingsley, a
dodge, a violation of the manliness of straightforward English rhetoric.
This demonization of the seductive power of Catholic oratorical skill is
evocative of the anti-Catholic structures of the English Gothic novel. In

Charles Maturin's *Melmoth the Wanderer*, for instance, Monçada notes of a monk that his attractive power over younger men is related to his feminine "dissimulation":

[M]y own experience has never failed in the discovery, that where there was a kind of feminine softness and pliability in the male character, there was also treachery, dissimulation, and heartlessness. . . . [I]f there be such a union, a conventual life is sure to give it every advantage in its range of internal debility, and external seductiveness. . . . This man had been always judged very weak, and yet very fascinating. He had been always employed to ensnare the young novices.[20]

Just as Monçada links this emasculating yet seductive fascination to the monastery, so too does Kingsley point to the celibate clergy that Newman advocates just before he alludes to the "admiring young gentlemen."[21] In each case, the community of men in the absence of heterosexual union is portrayed as both a great sexual danger and, to such impressionable persons as the "young novices" (Maturin) or "young gentlemen" (Kingsley), an irresistible attraction. Like Maturin, Kingsley ultimately discovers the "truth of Catholicism"—the erotically charged "one little barbed arrow"—"unheeded" beneath the cover of rhetorical brilliance. Kingsley continues to make the connection between Newman's oratorical power and its unmanly effect, not only on the orator's own insinuating language but also on the young men who find themselves seduced by his habits:

Now how was I to know that the preacher, who had the reputation of being the most acute man of his generation, and of having a specially intimate acquaintance with the weaknesses of the human heart, was utterly blind to the broad meaning and the plain practical result of a sermon like this, delivered before fanatic and hot-headed young men, who hung over his every word? That he did not foresee that they would think that they obeyed him, by becoming affected, artificial, sly, shifty, ready for concealments and equivocations?[22]

Kingsley notes that Newman himself claims that the true Christian will be seen by the world as "artificial," and "wanting in openness and manliness,"

PATRICK R. O'MALLEY

because the Christian must always practice a certain degree of dissimulation with regard to the state. It is Kingsley who can see the "broad meaning and the plain practical result" that he rather facetiously remarks must have eluded the orator himself, an orator famous (on the one hand) for his brilliance, and yet (on the other) for his rather feminized "intimate acquaintance with the weaknesses of the human heart." As in *Melmoth*'s description of the fascinating monk, Newman's seductiveness is here linked to his internal debility. Like the monk, his effect is "to ensnare the young novices" in both religious dissent and sexual ambiguity.

Newman himself seems to realize the sexual stakes involved in Kingsley's attack on Catholicism. In the *Apologia*, he notes that in 1840, five years before his conversion, he wrote that "we Englishmen like manliness, openness, consistency, truth. Rome will never gain on us, till she learns these virtues."[23] In this formulation, Newman, like Kingsley, aligns "manliness" with straightforward rhetorical strategies, opposing that manliness to the feminized and presumably duplicitous Rome. Indeed, Newman makes of the escalating conflict between the two writers a sort of contest of manliness and sexual virtue: "Now these insinuations and questions shall be answered in their proper places," he notes in the preface to the *Apologia*; "what I insist upon here is this unmanly attempt of his, in his concluding pages, to cut the ground from under my feet."[24] And he complains in a letter to Alexander Macmillan, the publisher of Kingsley's review, that

I, on my side, have long thought, even before I was a Catholic, that the Protestant system, as such, leads to a lax observance of the rule of purity. . . . [But] I should be committing a crime, heaping dirt upon my soul, and storing up for myself remorse and confusion of face at a future day, if I applied my abstract belief of the latent sensuality of Protestantism, on à priori reasoning, to individuals, to living persons, to authors and men of name.[25]

Newman thus attacks Kingsley's insinuations with his own, responding to a cultural linkage between Catholicism and sexual irregularity with an attempt to displace that sexual anxiety onto English Protestantism. In constructing

242

Catholicism as a vital—and indeed natural—part of English society, Newman must first, it seems, defend not its theology but its manliness.

III

The accusation of dissimulation—indeed of unmanliness—that Kingsley lodges against Newman, and that Newman likewise casts back at his accuser, is first and foremost an epistemological issue, a question of linguistic passing in which essential meaning is buried under a quickly shifting set of rhetorical façades. Kingsley's charge of untruthfulness, as he expands it in "What, Then, Does Dr. Newman Mean?" is fundamentally a charge against a particular *style*: "If he would (while a member of the Church of England) persist (as in this sermon) in dealing with matters dark, offensive, doubtful, sometimes actually forbidden, at least according to the notions of the great majority of English Churchmen; if he would always do so in a tentative, paltering way, seldom or never letting the world know how much he believed, how far he intended to go . . . what wonder if the minds of men were filled with suspicions of him?"[26] In fact, what Kingsley ultimately discovers to be most dangerous about Newman's prose is not that it is heretical but, rather, that it confounds the possibility of a single interpretation, that it subverts the apparent stability of language itself: "A hasty reader might say, that herein is an open justification of equivocation and dishonest reticence. But he would be mistaken. The whole sermon is written in so tentative a style, that it would be rash and wrong to say that Dr. Newman intends to convey any lesson by it, save that the discovery of truth is an impossibility."[27]

The heart of Kingsley's text is not so much accusations of untruthfulness as it is a relentless series of questions about *meaning*, from "What, then, did the sermon mean?" to the title of the tract itself, "What, Then, Does Dr. Newman Mean?"[28] On the one hand, this ambiguity is a recognizable threat to English manliness: "In proportion as young men absorbed it into themselves," Kingsley warns, "it injured their straightforwardness and truthfulness."[29] On the other, the real danger lies in the fact that Newman's rhetoric escapes easy categorization, that its ambiguity is a slippery hook on which to hang a charge either of heresy or of sexual dissidence.

This obsession with the epistemological crisis of language, with the inability of an interpreter to know the stable truth of language's meaning, is similar to the obsession with the confessional, the Catholic Church's "closet." What is so frustrating for the authors of such tracts as *The Oxford and Roman Railway* and *The Confessional Unmasked* is that all of the fantasized sexual deviance of the confessional remains—due to the seal of the confessional—resistant to stable structures of knowledge. For "C.B.," this epistemological crisis is mirrored in the very tropes of language. Pointing out that Catholic commentators have allowed the conscious deception of the state or of a husband under certain circumstances, *The Confessional Unmasked* further notes that those commentators have defended the practice on the basis of a scriptural trope: "When in danger of death, it is lawful to use a metaphor which is common in Scripture, where adultery is taken for idolatry."[30] The scriptural conjunction of sexual and religious deviance provides a biblical analogue for the tract's own linkages, but it is the possibility that the structures of language itself might provide cover for those deviances that seems especially to frustrate "C.B.": "We suppose," he glosses in a rather sarcastic footnote, "this is what in Papal logic would be termed a *mixed* metaphor!"

This transposition of the fantasized deviances of Roman Catholicism onto the deviance of language likewise forms one of the primary bases of Walter Walsh's late-century attack on Newman, the Oxford Movement, and Catholicism in general. Walsh accuses Newman of—of all things—*irony*, noting that Newman himself described his use of irony as "when matter-of-fact men would not see what I meant. This kind of behavior was *a sort of habit* with me."[31] Walsh notes that "'irony' is defined in our dictionaries as 'a mode of speech in which the meaning is contrary to the words,' and as 'dissimulation' for the purposes of ridicule. But surely, when those to whom this irony was addressed, as in this instance, did 'not see' the irony, but took the falsehood for truth, they were nothing better than wilfully and shamefully deceived by Newman."[32] For Kingsley, that ironic deception was unmanly; for a late-century English polemicist such as Walsh, writing precisely in the aftermath of the Wilde trials, the relationship between irony and sexual deviance may very well have taken on more definite contours. Irony is, for Walsh as it was for Wilde's accusers, a type of passing, a deception through which, in Walsh's text, Catholic meaning masquerades as Protestant rhetoric.

Indeed, if irony is a "sort of habit" for Newman in the sense of an accustomed action, it seems also, in the rhetoric of his critics, to take on a sartorial image, to be metaphorically related to the "habit" of the Catholic orders. Thus, *The Oxford and Roman Railway* observes that "we think that, if Englishmen resume their Protestantism, the day will not be far distant when such men as Pusey and Wilberforce will be estimated by all at their proper value—and when 'the garments' that now 'deceive' will be rent from off their unhallowed persons, and their irreligious blasphemous characters will stand unmasked."[33] For the Mission and Electoral Union, "Protestantism" is evangelical Protestantism, and the nominal Protestantism of the Ritualists is a type of sectarian and rhetorical cross-dressing that masks their true identities as Catholic infiltrators. Like the "Wolf in Sheep's Clothing" of *Punch's* contemporary cartoon, the Anglo-Catholic here is deadly first and foremost because he cannot be recognized.

Similarly, for Walsh, the "Secret History of the Oxford Movement" is dangerous to good, English Protestant values not because the rituals of Catholicism manifestly degrade the Catholic (as Canon Stowell claimed) but because it is secret, because it introduces Catholicism into England through dissimulation. Thus Walsh quotes a remarkable 1850 letter of the Reverend William Maskell, vicar of St. Mary's Church, a letter written, he ominously informs his reader, "shortly before [Maskell's] secession to Rome:"

Take, for example, the doctrine of Invocation of Saints; or, of Prayers for the Dead . . . or, of the reverence due to the blessed Virgin Mary; or, of the Propitiatory Sacrifice of the Blessed Eucharist; or, of the almost necessity of Auricular Confession and Absolution, in order to the remission of mortal sin—and more might be mentioned than these. Now, let me ask you; do we speak of these doctrines from our pulpits in the same manner, or to the same allowed extent, as we speak of them one to another, or think of them in our closets? Far from it; *rather, when we do speak of them at all, in the way of public, ministerial, teaching,* we use certain symbols and a shibboleth of phrases, well enough understood by the initiated few, but dark and meaningless to the many. *All this seems to be, day by day and hour by hour, more and more hard to be reconciled with the real spirit, mind, and purpose of the English Reformation, and of the modern English Church, shewn by the experience of 300 years.*[34]

At the end of the nineteenth century, this midcentury confession reemerges as proof positive that the real threat of Catholic theology and ritual lies in the fact that it is passed off on innocent Protestants under the cover of rhetorical dissimulation. And once again, the Catholic Church's "closet" appears, that locus of "true" and potentially corruptive Catholicism hidden from the sight and understanding of the many.

Once more associating Catholics with Jews, the striking term "shibboleth" here marks an irony of identity and identification. Taken from the Hebrew word by which Jephthah distinguished the Ephraimites from the Gileadites in the Book of Judges, it becomes in English usage the designation for the linguistic separation of British citizens from foreigners. Thus the second edition of the *Oxford English Dictionary*, noting that the term comes to mean "a word used as a test for detecting foreigners, or persons from another district, by their pronunciation," cites as evidence the 1873 edition of John Earles's *Philology of the English Tongue*: "The TH with its twofold value is one of the most characteristic features of our language, and more than any other the Shibboleth of foreigners."[35] Yet in the Reverend William Maskell's letter, the shibboleth, the very mark of foreignness, becomes a metaphor for infiltration, for undetectable resistance to social and religious norms. Catholicism has no "most characteristic feature" in the arguments of Maskell and Walsh but, rather, a series of "closets." The very symbol of recognizable otherness becomes, in the rhetoric of Catholic infiltration, the mark of unrecognizability.

What Walsh calls irony and Kingsley names dissimulation is, however, not only a style of self-presentation but also, it turns out, a reading strategy. "I found him," Kingsley asserts of Newman, "by a strange perversion of Scripture, insinuating that St. Paul's conduct and manner were such as naturally to bring down on him the reputation of being a crafty deceiver. I found him—horrible to have to say it—even hinting the same of One greater than St. Paul."[36] Kingsley's designation of Newman's analytic technique as "perversion" is a very complicated one in mid-nineteenth-century England. It was the dominant term used by evangelical polemicists for Anglican converts to Rome, implying as it does a turning away from the truth rather than toward it. For instance, Peter Maurice, chaplain of New and All Souls Colleges at Oxford, announced in 1851 that "the sum total of the perverts from Oxford to Rome, up to the first week in April, 1851, is ninety-six—sixty-five of them being ordained ministers of the Anglican Church."[37] This usage apparently reached its apogee in the mainstream press in the mid-1840s, precisely the time of greatest anxiety regarding the conversion of several prominent Oxford Movement figures. The index to the *Times of London*, for example, files seventy-six columns about the conversion to Catholicism of one or more notable persons under the heading of "perversion" between 1830 and 1902. There are an additional fifty-seven columns filed under "Perverts to Rome" between 1843 and 1859, eight in October of 1845—the month of Newman's conversion—alone.

It is certainly true that it is important to historicize this use of the word, taking into account that Freud's localization of "perversion" as a specifically sexual neurosis had not yet been written;[38] yet by midcentury, it could—if necessary—be used with the full force of its sexual potential in the interests of anti-Catholic polemicists. In 1850, Bishop Wilberforce attacked the notion of Ritualistic sisterhoods on the grounds that "I object . . . absolutely, as un-Christian *and savouring of the worst evils of Rome*, to the *Vows* involved in such a context in the statement as 'She is for ever consecrated to the service of her heavenly Spouse.' I object to the expression itself as *unwarranted by God's Word and savouring of one of the most carnal perversions of the Church of Rome.*"[39] And *Dr. Pusey's Insane Project Considered* in 1871 described the "perversion" of the new Catholics as a type of masochistic bondage: "If you except certain 'English perverts,' some of whom go to Rome, and delight to rub their necks against rusty chains, and others who believe in lying pictures and winking images, I verily believe that at this hour she [the Roman Catholic Church] has comparatively few who are ignorant enough and besotted enough to be her sincere and cordial members."[40]

In fact, the *Oxford English Dictionary*'s first two definitions of *perversion* are "The action of perverting or condition of being perverted; turning the wrong way; turning aside from truth or right . . . spec. change to error in religious belief" and "A disorder of sexual behavior in which satisfaction is sought through channels other than those of normal heterosexual intercourse." The *OED* lists citations for the first definition through 1877; the first listed usage of the second, in a medical dictionary of 1892, certainly predates Freud. Here, it specifically means homosexuality: "A passion for the sex to which the sufferer belongs, instead of the normal inclination to the opposite sex."[41] The latter half of the century thus saw the emphasis of *perversion* move specifically from one to the other of those two culturally linked spheres of social organization, religious and sexual deviance.

This very shift in meaning points to the instability of such a centrally categorizing term as *perversion* in the latter half of the nineteenth century. It represents a crisis in meaning that complicates knowledge of what the categories of sexual deviance and Catholicism actually were, as well as how they are to be distinguished from each other. In the same tract in which he decries the tremendous number of "perverts" to Rome, Peter Maurice appeals to his Protestant audience to keep the universities free from this Romanizing influence: "Oxford and Cambridge are, as it were (speaking the language of metaphor), the two Eyes of our Church and Nation, which ought to be wide awake to the best interests of the whole body politic as well as ecclesiastic, and not in disunity."[42] For Maurice, the visual splendor of Catholic ritual, liturgy, and aesthetic production is literally blinding, hypnotizing the "eyes" of Oxford and Cambridge, the protectors of a linked notion of church and state, into sleep. But Maurice's anxiety is not merely concern for the stability of the nation but also an assertion of the need for recognizable epistemological categories. If Catholics are allowed to corrupt the university system, that system will no longer be able to function as the eyes of the nation and church, because it will have lost its vision, its ability to discern and to know. And in fact, the very articulation of his fears forces Maurice to use "the language of metaphor" attacked by his fellow controversialists as the rotten core of Catholicism's deviant use of language.

Maurice's fear of Catholic integration is thus a crisis intimately related to Kingsley's interpretive crisis; if Catholics are once again part of English society itself, how can they be distinguished from "normative" Protestants? If an orator can assert that he is using "irony" to propagate one (Catholic) message under cover of another (Protestant) surface meaning, how is the "true" Catholic to be discerned? If the eyes of the church and state are seduced into sleep, how is the threat of Catholic infiltration even to be seen? If Protestantism is constructed as the only normative faith and Catholicism a "perversion" of that faith, both in the history of religious development and in the history of personal conviction, what is a "true" Catholic at all?

Newman makes his own forays into the question of Catholic identity, beginning to formulate in the *Apologia* a notion of innate English Catholicism. It is true that throughout the *Apologia*, Newman's notion of Catholicism wavers between what might be called "constructivist" and "essentialist" versions of what sectarian conviction means. On the one hand, in the introduction to the chapter describing his increasing tendencies toward Rome, he asks, "For who can know himself, and the multitude of subtle influences which act upon him?,"[43] as if personal identity is the sum of external constructive forces. Yet later in the same chapter, he writes of identity as if it were something innate and fixed, if not always fully understood: "It must be added, that the very circumstance that I have committed myself against Rome has the effect of setting to sleep people suspicious about me, which is painful now that I begin to have suspicions about myself."[44] His antagonism toward Roman Catholicism is thus gradually revealed in the text of the *Apologia* as the very mark, produced by a sort of panic, of his deep sense of identity with Rome itself, an identity that, for Newman, is described in the language of forbidden desire: "In spite of my ingrained fears of Rome, and the decision of my reason and conscience against her usages, in spite of my affection for Oxford and Oriel, yet I had a secret longing love of Rome the Mother of English Christianity."[45] Ultimately, his public conversion to Catholicism is not described as a change in faith but as an Augustinian discovery of his true home: "I was not conscious to myself, on my conversion, of any change, intellectual or moral, wrought in my mind . . . but it was like coming into port after a rough sea."[46] And, finally, in an appeal to his Protestant readership, he argues that Catholicism is somehow built into the very identity of certain persons: "Be large-minded enough to believe, that men may reason and feel very differently from yourselves; how is it that men, when left to themselves, fall into such various forms of religion, except that there are various types of mind among them, very distinct from each other?"[47]

I have used the terms *constructivist* and *essentialist*, of course, since they currently serve as the dominant categories for our understanding of sexuality, as well as for such other epistemological structures as race and sex.[48] Since Foucault's famous assertion that 1870 marked the transformation of the organization of knowledge about sexual practice from the "sodomite" as "temporary aberration" to the "homosexual" as "species,"[49] critical attention has been continually paid to the ways in which a concept of sex as a series of acts was superseded or conjoined with a notion of sexuality as identity, whether produced medically, psychologically, or juridically.[50] Key to the English development of an essentialist notion of sexual identity is the work of John Addington Symonds, himself an admiring critic of Renaissance Catholic artistic production and a prolific poet, critic, and literary historian. The similarities between Newman's *Apologia* and Symonds's own confessional account of his life in his *Memoirs* are telling. Newman describes his intimations of Catholic truth as an uncanny "ghost," which repeatedly appears in eerie presentiments;[51] Symonds describes two linked dreams that he relates to his growing understanding of his "inversion," that of a corpse on his bed and that of a beautiful young man kissing his forehead.[52] Whereas Newman describes his conversion as a kind of resurrection after the death of his Anglicanism,[53] Symonds notes of his 1858 meeting with a lower-class chorister, Willie Dyer, that "from that morning I date the birth of my real self."[54] Although Symonds declares his disaffection with orthodox religious practice of any type, he links Anglo-Catholicism with homosexual affectation in his description of his companions at Balliol College at Oxford: "Urquhart, a Scotchman of perfervid type, developed a violent personal affection for me. He had High Church proclivities and ran after choristers. . . . Vickers was a man of somewhat similar stamp. In their company I frequented antechapels and wasted my time over feverish sentimentalism."[55] Symonds, like Newman, structures his notions of identity around "types," where, for example, Urquhart's "High Church proclivities" seem to be almost identical to his proclivities for young boys.

Symonds is more subversive, however, in *Sexual Inversion*, primarily written by Havelock Ellis but much indebted to Symonds's own contributions. As the anonymous "Case XVIII," Symonds argues against a notion of sexual identity that constructs the invert as necessarily feminized: "He is certainly not simply passive and shows no sign of *effeminatio*. He likes sound and vigorous young men of a lower rank from the age of twenty to twenty-five."[56] While Symonds's concern that homosexuality be separated from "*effeminatio*" demonstrates his own investment in masculine priority, his appearance as a case study in Ellis's book is itself important. Not only does "Case XVIII" (among several other cases) argue that the homosexual cannot be identified by sight, it further provides a disturbing confusion of categories. Whereas Newman's *Apologia* explains how the prominent Anglican theologian may very well be a Catholic *in potentia*, Symonds's "Case XVIII" implicitly hints that the eminent sexologist might himself be a homosexual case study. Just as anti-Catholic polemicist Maurice warned that the admission of Catholics to Oxford or Cambridge would blind the eyes of the nation, making it unable to detect the Catholic threat within, so too does "Case XVIII" argue that the eyes of the nation can no longer be relied upon to find the "invert." And, indeed, Maurice's fear can be said to have been realized with the Universities Tests Act of 1871, which opened Oxford and Cambridge to Catholics just one year after Foucault's watershed date for the invention of the "homosexual."

In fact, Havelock Ellis's preface to *Sexual Inversion* suggests that the construction of a minoritized homosexual identity in the latter half of the nineteenth century is itself in part based on the construction of a minoritized English Catholic identity in the preceding few decades. Ellis attributes to the Catholic Church the greatest credit for the development of knowledge around sexual deviance:

This secrecy [around sexual deviations] has not always been maintained. When the Catholic Church was at the summit of its power and influence it fully realised the magnitude of sexual problems, and took an active and inquiring interest in all the details of normal and abnormal sexuality. Even to the present time there are certain phenomena of the sexual life which have scarcely been accurately described except in ancient theological treatises.[57]

Ellis likewise describes his own inquiry in the language of Catholic theology, translated into the realm of science: "We want to know what is naturally lawful under the various sexual chances that may befall man, not as the born child of sin, but as a naturally social animal, what is a venial sin against nature, what a mortal sin against nature."[58] As the Reverend Maskell's 1850 letter indicates, the whole question of mortal as opposed to venial sin—and the necessity of confession to resolve it—needed to be imported into England surreptitiously, beginning in the "closets" of the proto-Romanist Anglicans. Both Newman and Symonds construct essentialist confessional tracts, tracts that not only suggest the parallelism of Catholic and homosexual identities but also point to their subversive power—and assimilability—through passing. The English Catholic and the English homosexual, these tracts argue, are already part of Britain itself; it has just been impossible to see them.

IV

The introduction to *The Oxford and Roman Railway* notes that "several gentlemen connected with the University of Oxford projected no less than 'ninety' Lines, all, however, conducting to the same Terminus—'The House of the Strange Woman.'" The allusion to the strange woman of Proverbs points to a particularly Gothic moment of Scripture, a moment linking seduction to death.[59] Proverbs asserts that wisdom must have the power "to deliver thee from the strange woman, even from the stranger which flattereth with her words; which forsaketh the guide of her youth, and forgetteth the covenant of her God. For her house inclineth unto death, and her paths unto the dead" (Proverbs 2:16–18). The rhetoric of the "strange" indicates the foreignness of this seductive yet fatal woman, in *The Oxford and Roman Railway* aligned with the feminized Rome of Catholicism, since the root of the word "strange"—like the French cognate *étranger*—itself is derived from the Latin *extraneus*, meaning external or foreign.

The language of *The Oxford and Roman Railway* relies upon the metaphor of the tract's own title to establish the trajectory from Oxford to Rome (and thus to the house of the strange woman) as itself propelled with the force and unidirectionality of the new locomotive systems. But "lines" are not only the lines of the railway but the lines of literature as well. The fundamentally literary nature of the Evangelical Mission and Electoral Union's attack on Roman and Anglo-Catholicism is made clear from the fact that this same introduction appears on the inside cover of *Dr. Pusey's Insane Project Considered* (1871), with, however, the substitution of "Tracts" for "Lines." While "Tracts" continues the railroad trope with its auricular similarity to "tracks," it is more specifically a reference to *Tracts for the Times*, of which the ninetieth was Newman's infamous historicization of the Thirty-Nine Articles, which sought to prove that they were consistent with the teachings of the Catholic Council of Trent. If these "lines" lead inexorably to Rome, they also lead just as inexorably back to Oxford, to the very heart of England. And if Walter Walsh can assert that "the Tractarian Movement" was ultimately "a

Romeward Movement," the title of his own attack on the Tractarians demonstrates that it is, as well, an "Oxford Movement." The notion of "perversion," that false turn, ultimately is a double-edged sword, for with the growing power of the Ritualists—and indeed the Romanists—within England, the imagined horrors of Catholicism can no longer be safely displaced onto the Continent. Indeed, the title of *The Oxford and Roman Railway* itself marks that inescapable fact. Published in 1871, the name is taken almost directly from the name of the controversial and never-completed Oxford and Rugby Railway of the late 1840s. But the clever twisting of a recent event is telling; in some ways, Rome is as close as Rugby, the heart of the public school system, just as Oxford is the heart of the university system. The foreign terrors represented by the strange woman herself have come home to England. As in the case of the *Punch* cartoon of John Bull expelling the Anglican priest from the home of Britannia (a cartoon published in the same year as *The Oxford and Roman Railway*), the crisis of Catholic identity has reached a climax of sorts. It is no longer possible to distinguish the foreign from the domestic, the dangerously Catholic from the safely Protestant. While it cites the passage from Canon Stowell's *Lecture at Leeds* that I have used as my second epigraph, the tract's anxiety about the infiltration of Catholics into the heart of English society marks Stowell's description of the immediately recognizable Catholic as an already threatened epistemological model.

Indeed, the prolific controversialist Reverend John Cumming ends his own apocalyptic call to arms, *Ritualism, The Highway to Rome*, with the image of Britain as a fortress besieged not from without but from within: "And now, I believe, the Papal Aggression of 1850 was bold and perilous, but it was open. The Papal Aggression of 1867 is the Pope in the garb of a Protestant minister, and within a Protestant place of worship. The Aggression of 1850 was outside; the Aggression of 1867 is inside the citadel."[60] For Cumming, the danger of Anglo-Catholicism is once again an epistemological threat: it is no longer possible to *know* the Catholic since he can wear Protestant clothing, just as Kingsley saw a threat in the veiling of Newman's Catholic message in Protestant words. Catholic language—itself devious—and Catholic bodies—themselves deviant—nonetheless do not provide the manifestations necessary for epistemological certainty; they cannot be distinguished, and thus cannot be known. And for that reason, in the fretfully blinded eyes of the evangelical polemicists, they are all the more dangerous.

Notes

1. Cited in *The Oxford and Roman Railway*, 3d ed. (London: Protestant Evangelical Mission and Electoral Union, 1871), 8. Canon Hugh Stowell began preaching widely against Catholicism in the 1830s and was active into the early 1860s. He died in 1865.

2. Although in this paper I am largely concerned with the threats to British masculinity posed by Roman Catholicism, it should also be noted that there is a parallel discourse devoted to the dangers to English womanhood that Romanism presented. Typically (as in an 1851 *Punch* cartoon depicting an English girl at the portal of a great Catholic structure dominated by a lascivious monk), that threat is explored through the invocation of the semiotics of the Gothic, particularly the Gothic of Ann Radcliffe.

3. In itself, of course, this presages Foucault's argument that "the transformation of sex into discourse . . . the dissemination and reinforcement of heterogeneous sexualities, are perhaps two elements of the same deployment: they are linked together with the help of the central element of a confession that compels individuals to articulate their sexual peculiarity—no matter how extreme." See Michel Foucault, *The History of Sexuality*, vol. 1, trans. Robert Hurley (New York: Vintage Books, 1978), 61.

4. C.B., *The Confessional Unmasked, Showing the Depravity of the Priesthood, Questions put to Females in Confession, Perjury and Stealing Commanded and Encouraged, andc., andc.* (London: H. Allman, 1851), 39.

5. Ibid.

6. Ibid., 34

7. Ibid., 21, quoting Liguori.

8. This is, of course, yet one more example of the pattern of the production of masculine relations triangulated *through* the figure of the woman that Eve Kosofsky Sedgwick elucidates in *Between Men: English Literature and Male Homosocial Desire* (New York: Columbia University Press, 1985).

9. No Surrender [pseud.], *Dr. Pusey's Insane Project Considered* (London: Protestant Evangelical Mission and Electoral Union, 1871), 30.

10. Walter Walsh, *The Secret History of the Oxford Movement* (1897), 3d ed. (London: Swan, Sonnenshein and Co., Ltd., 1898), 81–82.

11. "The Three Priests," in *Sword and Trowel*, ed. C. H. Spurgeon, (London: Passmore and Alabaster, May 1868), 203–204.

12. Rev. Henry Newland, *Three Lectures on Tractarianism*, 6th ed. (London: Joseph Masters, 1869), xii.

13. Giovanni Giacinto Achilli, "The Address of the Rev. Dr. Achilli, Formerly, Romish Priest . . . Delivered at Cheltenham, on Thursday, September 2, 1847" (Glasgow: S. and T. Dunn, n.d.), 6.

14. Cited in John Henry Cardinal Newman, *Apologia Pro Vita Sua*, ed. David J. De-Laura (New York: W. W. Norton and Company, 1968), 297. Newman himself collected and published the rather frantic correspondence between Kingsley and himself that took place in January 1864.

15. Cited. in Newman, *Apologia*, 298.

16. Compare Matthew 22:30 and Luke 20:34–35; Luke's account is only one that not only relates that the angels and the resurrected dead do not marry but that holy people on earth should not do so either: "But they which shall be accounted worthy to obtain that world, and the resurrection from the dead, neither marry, nor are given in marriage."

17. Cited in Newman, *Apologia*, 299–300.

18. Charles Kingsley, "What, Then, Does Dr. Newman Mean?" (1845), in Newman, *Apologia*, 316.

19. Oliver S. Buckton has written a compelling account of Kingsley's own sexual obsessions and the way that they have shaped critical opinion of the *Apologia* and of Newman. See his "'An Unnatural State': Gender, 'Perversion,' and Newman's *Apologia Pro Vita Sua*," *Victorian Studies* 35:4 (1992). I am more interested in examining the rhetorical and ultimately literary traditions at play in the cultural fantasy of this linkage between religious and sexual deviance as it was already constructed *before* the Newman-Kingsley controversy.

20. Charles Maturin, *Melmoth the Wanderer*, ed. Douglas Grant (Oxford: Oxford University Press, 1989 [1820]), 110.

21. James Eli Adams makes *fascination* one of the central terms of his analysis of Victorian modes of masculinity, noting for example, that "like D'Aurevilly's dandy, Marius [the Epicurean] fascinates, and that uneasy compound of desire and suspicion elicits the inherent tension in Victorian constructions of the gentleman. . . ." See Adams, *Dandies and Desert Saints: Styles of Victorian Manhood* (Ithaca and London: Cornell University Press, 1995), 194.

22. Kingsley, "What, Then," 317.

23. Newman, *Apologia*, 105.

24. Ibid., 6.

25. Ibid., 302.

26. Kingsley, "What, Then," 318.

27. Ibid., 334.

28. There is a complicated relationship between text and body here, as Newman himself notes: "He asks what I mean; not about my words, not about my arguments, not about my actions, as his ultimate point, but about that living intelligence, by which I write, and argue and act" (Newman, *Apologia*, 11). Through Kingsley's rhetoric, Newman himself becomes a text to be read and interpreted.

29. Kingsley, "What, Then," 318.

30. Cited in C.B., *The Confessional Unmasked*, 21, quoting Liguori.

31. Newman, *Apologia*, 48, cited in Walsh, *Secret History*, 269; italics added by Walsh.

32. Walsh, *Secret History*, 269–270.

33. *The Oxford and Roman Railway*, 16.

34. Cited in Walsh, *Secret History*, 44–45; italics in Walsh.

35. Cited in the *Oxford English Dictionary*, 2d ed., s.v. "shibboleth."

36. Kingsley, "What, Then," 316–317.

37. Peter Maurice, D.D., *Postscript to the Popery of Oxford: The Number of the Name of the Beast* (London: Seeleys, 1851), 19.

38. See, e.g., Buckton, "An Unnatural State," 361.

39. Quoted in *Walsh, Secret History*, 180–181, italics in Walsh.

40. No Surrender [pseud.], *Dr. Pusey's Insane Project Considered*, 10.

41. *Oxford English Dictionary*, 2d ed., s.v. "perversion."

42. Maurice, *Postscript*, 6.

43. Newman, *Apologia*, 81.

44. Ibid., 111.

45. Ibid., 133.

46. Ibid., 184.

47. Ibid., 195.

48. Eve Sedgwick challenges the dominance of this particular paradigm, proposing instead a model of "minoritizing" and "universalizing" identity structures: "I am additionally eager to promote the obsolescence of 'essentialist/constructivist' because I am very dubious about the ability of even the most scrupulously gay-affirmative thinkers to divorce these terms, especially as they relate to the question of ontogeny, from the essentially gay-genocidal nexuses of thought through which they have developed." See her *Epistemology of the Closet* (Berkeley: University of California Press, 1990), 40. Nonetheless, the essentialist/constructivist terminology has remained dominant. Further, because in this project I am particularly interested in the question that Sedgwick poses as the basis of phylogeny ("How fully are the meaning and experience of sexual activity and identity contingent on their mutual structuring with other, historically and culturally variable aspects of a given society?"), I am maintaining the historical usefulness (if not the political progressivism) of the "constructivist/essentialist" distinction.

49. Foucault, *History of Sexuality*, vol. 1, 43.

50. There are simply too many articles and books on this subject to produce any sort of comprehensive list of even the most influential. In addition to Foucault's *History of Sexuality* and Sedgwick's *Epistemology of the Closet*, a few of the most relevant to the questions I am raising in this essay are Richard Dellamora's *Masculine Desire: The Sexual Politics of Victorian Aestheticism* (Chapel Hill and London: University of North Carolina Press, 1990); David M. Halperin's *One Hundred Years of Homosexuality* (New York: Routledge, 1990); Thomas Laqueur's *Making Sex: Body and Gender from the Greeks to Freud* (Cambridge: Harvard University Press, 1990); Jonathan Goldberg's *Sodometries: Renaissance Texts, Modern Sexualities* (Stanford: Stanford University Press, 1992); Ed Cohen's *Talk on the Wilde Side: Toward a Genealogy of a Discourse on Male Sexualities* (New York and London: Routledge, 1993); and Christopher Craft's *Another Kind of Love: Male Homosexual Desire in English Discourse, 1850–1920* (Berkeley: University of California Press, 1994).

51. Newman, *Apologia*, 99 and 114.

52. John Addington Symonds, *The Memoirs of John Addington Symonds*, ed. Phyllis Grosskurth (New York: Random House, 1984), 77.

53. Newman, *Apologia*, 121.

54. Symonds, *Memoirs*, 104.

55. Ibid., 109.

56. Quoted in Symonds, *Memoirs*, 287–288; in the *Memoirs*, the case is erroneously listed as Case XVII.

57. Havelock Ellis and John Addington Symonds, *Sexual Inversion* (London: Wilson and Macmillan, 1897), viii.

58. Ibid., ix.

59. The *Oxford English Dictionary* notes that the phrase "the strange woman" came to mean "harlot" in English because the adjective was derived from two different Hebrew words, *nokriyah* and *zarah*, "both of which have the sense 'not one's own (wife)'" (*Oxford English Dictionary*, 2d ed., s.v. "strange").

60. Rev. John Cumming, D.D., *Ritualism, The Highway to Rome, Lecture I: Ritualism— What is It?* (London: James Nisbet and Co., 1867), 30–31.

10 Moses' Wilderness Tabernacle

Miriam Peskowitz

Tuesday morning at 10:25 we board an old school bus at the Orientation Center, and our tour of the New Holy Land begins. Six of us climb aboard and settle into green vinyl seats sized for children. I sit next to Felicia. We slide around on the seats, giggling as we angle for the most comfortable positions. She was my best friend in high school, although honestly, it's been years since then. Of all my friends, she's got the most vacation time, and takes it, and for reasons I'm not sure I understand, when I posed the idea of visiting a biblical village in northwest Arkansas, she jumped at the chance. She's a banker and doesn't do stuff like this real often.

I wish immediately for a cold bottle of water. Late June here gets hot.

The New Holy Land is built on and landscaped into the grounds of the Great Passion Play. It is run by the Elna M. Smith Foundation, Elna being the late widow of the infamous and also late Gerald L. K. Smith. One way to describe the New Holy Land is as a biblical theme park with more than thirty outdoor exhibits. The New Holy Land replicates parts of ancient Palestine, ancient Israel, and Judah over a patch of Ozark hill. Brochures announce proudly that it contains the world's only complete full-scale life-size reproduction of Moses' Tabernacle in the Wilderness. Visits to the New Holy Land are organized by a two-and-a-half-hour tram ride with intermittent stops at attractions. The monuments and scenes that dot the windy road through the hills narrate the specific kind of Christian story that the New Holy Land builders wish to promote. Along the way are several attractions at which the bus stops and visitors meet a local tour guide. Each guide dresses as a scriptural figure or a composite character that fits the site, be it "Moses' Wilderness Tabernacle," the "New Testament Village," or "A Walk with Peter Along the Sea of Galilee." For the most part, the guides speak in the first person and slip in and out of being their character. Visitors too, are supposed to slip in and out, to shuttle back and forth between being ourselves now and living among the ancients. But mostly, we are to be inspired by visual contact with this past.

For a few minutes we busy ourselves with sunglasses, and I do a check. The woman across the aisle wears huge red ones, the kind you get from Pearl. The man next to her sports thick silver-wire rims, and I can't see farther back without twisting too obviously. Ours are more urbane. Felicia's pulling on those hip undersized frames everyone I knew was wearing that summer. A recent splurge means my eyes are protected by some oversized black Jackie-O's.

The bus driver's name is Patrick. He chats into the microphone, fidgets with dials, and fixes his cap. At ten-thirty on the dot he closes the bus door, flips the ignition, and starts a story he will repeat throughout the day. His is a large soft voice that reminds me of Johnny Ozark, a guy I knew in San Francisco anarchist circles, a long time ago, when we all took on new names depending on where we lived or where we were from or who we wanted to be. The motor revs loudly and the bus creaks across the parking lot. We're on our way.

"This is a replica of the Eastern Gate, of the Golden Gate in Jerusalem," Patrick tells us as he drives beneath it. "It's a freestanding wall. By that I mean it's constructed with no mortar between the blocks. These blocks and pillars are just stacked one on top of the other. They're not mortared together. Just sitting here." He tells us that in the 1600s the Muslims blocked off this entrance—in the real Jerusalem—with bricks. But now the gate is open again. "Legend has it that these are the gates through which Jesus will return at the millennium." At 10:25 we boarded a bus that at 10:30 descended through time and traveled across space. After we roll under the Eastern Gate, Patrick points out the various replicas on each side of the narrow road.

At five miles an hour we reach the Canaanite altar. "They would build round altars like these. They called them high places. They would sacrifice animals. Scripture tells us to tear down the high places. Ergo, they're gonna tear down about half of that thing to show those altars were destroyed. Actually, this is a replica of one found in the Valley of Kinom. There's only one left."

In slow motion we watch the altar go by. Sure enough, stones from one side have been roughly removed. Farther down the road are bread ovens, tents, even two donkeys with crosses on their backs. "Jerusalem donkeys," says Patrick, "like what Jesus rode." A few moments of silence while we look, and then he confides, "You know, our terrain is a lot like the terrain in the Holy Land. We've got a lot of soil like they've got, we've got a lot of the limestone bluffs and cliffs like they've got. One thing we've got that they don't have, that's all of this beautiful vegetation."

A minute later the bus slow-brakes to a full stop and Patrick pulls the lever that opens the door. We have arrived at Moses' Wilderness Tabernacle and are ready to meet the Priest.

At 10:25 we boarded. At 10:30 we moved through the Gate. Eight minutes later we are in a spot that vacillates between being the desert wilderness of Sinai and the busy temple-city of

Jerusalem. Eight minutes on the bus and we've arrived at Exodus 25:19, where God gives Moses a message to the Israelites, that they should bring offerings to the Tabernacle.

A large man greets our group with a jovial smile. He's got broad shoulders and is paunchy in front. White linens drape his body from head to toe. Wide pants are covered by a long robe wrapped with a sash that hangs low, near where his hips would be were he a woman. A small white floppy hat sits atop his head and a not-yet-but-almost-gray beard makes him look older than he probably is. He walks backward while he talks. Our group follows him along the white fabric fence that forms the Tabernacle's south side.

Felicia falls in toward the rear, listening to other people's conversations that she tells me about later. She is a quiet provocateur of opinion and insight. I find a place near the guide but not too close. A microrecorder hums in my bag. It needs to hear him without his hearing it. I haven't asked permission, can't figure out how without dragging unwanted attention to my presence here. I want nothing other than to look like the ordinary, usual kind of visitor.

"Ever seen a Tabernacle?" the Priest asks happily. "The name means 'dwelling place.'" He translates slowly. "That's exactly what this is. God's dwelling place. This is where the Jewish nation came for about 480 years of their history for the Lord God Almighty. Aside from one detail, everything else I show you will be true to the biblical record. It will be exactly the right size, the right shape, the right design. . . ." He speeds up, "Right color, right function, right position." His speech grinds to a halt: "and one hundred percent wrong material."

The New Holy Land guides continually point out where the replicas might be a bit off from something imagined as the genuine real thing. Distinguishing between layers of architectural truth and degrees of reconstructive accuracy lets them acknowledge the possibility and limitation of human knowledge. They straddle the desire to produce something that makes visitors feel as if we are really there, the knowledge that this is not the real thing but an invocation of biblical truth, and the belief that the real thing itself is only and always symbolic. Time and again guides call attention to the gap between the replicas' verisimilitude and the truth. They note what research can tell them and what is impossible to know. Brochures and guides remind viewers that the replicas they see are based on the most advanced philological and archaeological research. I know the archaeological reports and articles they are relying on, and hence, know that when they make this claim they are not lying. Really, they are returning the science of biblical archaeology to its roots as a witness to biblical truth, a science set to magnify biblical truth by rendering it visual.

Far from undermining the power of this place to simulate—and to stimulate—attending the gap between an imagined real thing and what visitors see only emphasizes the commitment to the inerrancy of biblical truth and the truth of that inerrancy. By noting that some details are incorrect, the guides emphasize the accuracy of other elements. Clear knowledge of what something is—and what it isn't—is part of the attraction. Besides, many visitors are "Bible Study" regulars and know scriptural details better than the back of their hand. At each stop they query the guides. This is part of the fun they have while visiting, since responding to the replicas demonstrates how closely they know their Bible. I share in this. I match the replicas to my knowledge of the excavated material culture of Israel, Palestine, and the Golan Heights, marveling at the similarities and noting the disparities. Part of the pleasure is the chance to test one's knowledge against the experts, a walk-along game show, if you like.

It's 10:50 A.M. on a Tuesday, but we are no longer sure of the year.

The Priest continues.

"In order to understand this place properly, take yourselves back in time about thirty-five centuries. About that time, with the establishment of the Tabernacle, Jewish families began coming here once a year, bringing a sacrifice for their sins. They would be led by their spiritual leader, the man with the blessing.

"He comes here. He has in his arms a very special little lamb. He's been raising this lamb in his home for about a year. Since that time it has become a very precious and beloved member of his family. He's gonna take it right inside and sacrifice it for all the sins his family has committed in the previous year. See, without the shedding of blood there can be no remission for those sins.

"He makes his family wait outside here by the large gate. He presents that lamb. He's met by a priest such as myself As priest I do not allow him or his lamb inside until that lamb passes two important tests. Test number one: I'll examine the lamb, make sure there are no marks, defects, or blemishes. It has to be perfect. If it's going to be paying for someone else's sins it can't have any of its own. Just like if you're going to be paying someone else's debts you can't be broke yourself Does that make sense?"

For some time now we have been standing by the brilliant purple banner that curtains the Tabernacle's entrance. Purple for God's royalty, we're told. The thin white lines running through it signify purity. Scarlet's for sacrificial blood, and a small light blue patch at the center stands for a glimpse of heaven. The Priest is enjoying himself. The vowels and soft consonants of his words hang together flawlessly as he travels up and down a spectrum of tones.

"After that first test we go to the second test, with a live demo.

"I'll ask him: 'Do you love this lamb?'

"If you don't love it's not a sacrifice at all. He does love this lamb. This lovely lamb has lived with his family for a year before he brought it here to Jerusalem. The lamb's been in his home for a year. Imagine this pet at the year's end. The family starts to love the lamb." Our group of six is imagining ourselves as if we were an ancient Israelite man and his lamb. We hear the bleats, feel the oily wool. From the calm quiet of our hillside morning we enter the hustle and bustle of pilgrim families trying to get sacrifice right.

"The man loves the lamb so I'll escort him and his lamb inside to the killing tables. I'll take you all in shortly, but, uh, let me explain something important about this place first. This is the only entrance. It faces the eastern sky toward the morning sun. That's very significant. See, as the sun rises in the morning it passes over this Tabernacle here. It traces a line right down the middle, a line that runs from the world of sin out here to the throne of God in there. That's an important path because every one of us is going to have to travel it eventually. Every one of us at the end of our lives will meet God. We've got to get ready. The Tabernacle is nothing more than a map. It shows us the right steps to take along that journey towards God's throne. Now in Christianity this route is called the path of conversion, the plan of salvation. Everything I show you in here will be a necessary element in the salvation experience.

"Normally I couldn't allow you to see any of this stuff. Beyond the curtain here is the Court of the Priests. It's holy ground. Reserved only for Priests, and on special occasions that spiritual leader I mentioned earlier. But I kind of like you folks, so I'm gonna give you a shot at it. I'm gonna ask you a question. If you give me an honest answer, I'll be inclined to let you in."

A second or two separates these words from the next. The Priest leans over to lift the curtain that suspends us from the Court. In midmotion he stops and straightens himself out. His next question moves toward us in a lower, rougher voice.

"Do you love Jesus Christ?"

An uncertain not-quite-silence grabs hold of our group. For a moment no one responds. Then someone mumbles. One man offers a very timid assent. We all seem to shuffle, looking simultaneously straight ahead and at the dusty ground. Are the others surprised, as I am? What's Felicia going to do? I get nervous and wish myself into further invisibility.

This question I remember from school days. "Are you Christian? Do you believe in Jesus?" A true and positive answer makes a difference. A negative answer shatters the boundaries of comfort. Saying no transforms you into the kind of person that other children's parents say is not quite like us. "I can't be close friends with someone who doesn't love Jesus like I do," said a girl to me in eighth grade as our friendship waned.

Felicia's standing next to me. What's her reaction to this test, to these boundaries of difference? Dissociation? Curiosity? Shock? She too grew up in a Jewish family, but otherwise not surrounded by Jews. And here we are in the middle of America. We've never prepared for a moment like this.

The Priest raises his voice.

"C'mon. What's the matter? Are you ashamed of it? Afraid somebody's gonna hear you?"

Only those in the priesthood of believers can enter the Tabernacle's Courtyard. He needs us to answer yes so that he can announce us a priesthood of believers and allow us to move past the banner and inside. We need to say yes so the tour can continue. Our yes is an integral part of the plan.

The Priest's once jolly body and beard turn angry. He creates a sound that soars in volume and fullness.

"Say it like you mean it folks: DO YOU LOVE JESUS CHRIST?"

And in a split, unthinking second our group sends him a loud, resolute, and unified YES! which he catches with "Much . . ." and as our "s" ends its final hiss we hear his ". . . better" finish it all off. "Much better." Our answer pleases him. His smile returns and the narration moves ahead.

"Well, since you said yes Scripture tells me that makes you a royal priesthood. And as priests you're well qualified to step on any old patch of holy ground you want. So, come right on inside."

He lifts the curtain again. This time he keeps it pulled high enough for us to walk under. As we file past him he chides one of the women, picking up their earlier conversation. "No wonder nobody goes to your church anymore!" I lag to the other side. I'm skittish and I don't want to walk too close.

My heart pounds with the fear of being caught in the lie. I don't really love Jesus, not in that way, although I've just said out loud that I do. Then my anxiety mixes with pleasure. My body verges on an explosive but repressed giggle that grows as I realize the pleasure of passing. Is it really this easy?

Do my words matter? My yes means different things in different worlds. In the New Holy Land vision of Christendom words mean and matter. This mattering is a key part of a commitment to the possibility that certain words are inerrantly true. Words are vehicles of affirmation and faith. If people say they love Jesus, they do. In my world words are there to be played with, traced in conversation, sculpted in writing, tossed about with more or less intent. Words mean things but not necessarily what we think or want them to. Words in my world are less predictable and controlled. They circulate from person to person, overflow from radios, billboards, newspapers, books, and T.V.'s, so many that we hear few, retain fewer, and believe even less. Here, yes is a singular moment, sometimes memorable and reliable, sometimes not. It can be perfect truth, an expediency to get from one place to the next, a syllable that fades quickly as new ones take its place, a sincere affirmation, a connector between the pleasures of putting other words together in interesting and intriguing ways.

By the time I float back into the consciousness of the tour, we have walked through the courtyard and are inside the Holy of Holies. Our Priest is finishing a discussion of the clothing worn by the mannequin priests inside the life-sized display cases. "And the Priest comes in and sees that light and he first presents his incense to it. He prays for his people, in the Jewish manner. And he takes that cup of blood and sprinkles it toward the ark. Although you would expect that to make a big mess, well, remember we're dealing with God here, and he works a little differently sometimes. Every tiny speck is drawn right up into the light. I know that is a hard subject, but it is an ancient Jewish concept, by the way. I have met some that doubted its truth, but, I know it is. When I came to God years ago seeking mercy and forgiveness, he brought me into his light too, so that all my darkness could be dispelled."

Was my pass insincere? When I first considered this, I thought saying no would have been impossible. I imagined biblical stonings and hecklings, and the discomfort I would feel. I feared being put back on the bus and sent home, or at the very least, being made to wait in the hot sun till the others finished their tour. This would reverse, ironically but perhaps just as cruelly, the ancient Temple's restrictions on Gentiles entering. On later reflection, and knowing more about the theology of this place, this fantasy is doubtful. Far from an incursion to be removed, a live Jewish body is a prize. The presence of living Jews visiting would demonstrate the power of the New Holy Land. Then again, I never tested it out, nor did I ask later about the protocol, so I don't really know what this guide, this group, might have done.And here's the trap, I realize: Why am I worrying about impersonating a modern Christian when a man stands before me, dressed up in white garments, impersonating an ancient Jew? Shouldn't we both be laughing?

Was my momentary passing as a Christian a social crime, by whatever sets of standards social crimes operate? Are the current rules of religious and ethnic identity such that what one is is what one is, and such that performances of being something else are not allowed? Under what stringent notions about identity was mine an attempt to pass? By certain standards, professing a love for Jesus Christ is not a pass or a masquerade. It is the means by which one becomes a Christian. In this logic, I was not a Jew passing as a Christian, but became a Christian.

But we're not all having a good laugh. When I return to his talk the Priest is ending this part of his discussion. "Now that's Tabernacle from Jewish eyes. Any Jews here? No? Christians? Why didn't you say so to begin with?"

The four questions are tossed in a quick staccato. They don't make much sense. If we've already told him that we love Jesus Christ, then how could any Jews be present? Did he not believe my affirmation? Can he sense something? Does he know I'm passing (if that's in fact what I'm doing)? Do the others? If we all just told him that we loved Jesus Christ, then he knows we are all Christians and his question is redundant. Is there something he can see that gives me away? Not hair or eye color, not the tones of my skin, but things more learned: a stance, a way of looking out at the world, some habit or ritual I would know if I went to church, and to the right kind of church at that?

"Now that's Tabernacle from Jewish eyes," and here his performance of a Jewish Priest ends. He turns directly to us. "I want to ask you one more time: Do you really love Jesus Christ?"

People say yes again, but without much enthusiasm. I join in, mouth the words, but I am drained and dissociative and I want to leave. The air is hot, despite the outsize outdoor fan that circulates air our way. My throat is parched. Passing no longer feels like much fun.

"Are you sure?" he presses. I'm sure that folks answered something, but I cannot remember. The tape recorder stowed in my hand bag offers only silence until the Priest comes back with "Oh, good. Because He's your lamb. Your sacrifice."

Who owns these identities—ancient Jew, modern Jew, Christian? What grounds for claiming an identity are in place and at work, at any given moment, as we make judgments about who is really what they are, as we make decisions about authenticity and inauthenticity, about realness, passing, performance, and play? How are these identities bounded? is the question, since without boundaries the question of who owns each character becomes moot because the boundaries often supply the preconditions for claims to ownership.

Given the racial discourse of this country, and the way that race is imagined as linked to biology, physiology, skin color, and physical phenotype, we are used to thinking about passing through the lens of what is visible and visual. Most often when the subject is religion, questions of passing, authenticity, assimilation, and realness are linked to these terms. The conceptual and discursive linking of racial terminology with religious identity has a long, if relatively unacknowledged, history in the United States, a longer and more pervasive one in Europe. But of course, despite the dominant discourse, physiology has never completely secured the notion of race. Discourses of the visual have never been quite secure with the boundaries and the crossings, and with the instances in which identities are less than visible. Hence the recurring conversational topics: Did you know so and so is Jewish, can you tell? So and so is black, through his mother's side, did you hear that rumor? Is he gay, I can't tell. Did you know so and so is Latina, through her Brazilian father?

In much contemporary discourse, passing is discussed as assimilation, as a phenomenon of ethnicity, possible because one looks or doesn't look a certain way, enabled by the surprises of genetics, nutrition, learned social habits, surgery, skin and bone alteration, speech therapy, and more. The expressions and presentation of self done without strict recourse to clear markers are rarely part of the way we discuss identity, despite the fact that these less-than-clear expressions are the unexpressed conditions for the anxieties that produce the discussions in the first place. If we all "knew" what everyone "was," and were all content with these forms of knowledge (and their uses) we wouldn't need to raise these questions and talk about them, would we? In other words, the possibility that someone whom some would consider something is not acting like or expressing himself or herself as that something—this is the pervasive concern that sets in motion the desire to define the boundaries of that something.

This tense moment at Moses' Wilderness Tabernacle raises these questions. As the heroine of Nella Larsen's 1929 novel *Passing* says, "It's funny about 'passing.' We disapprove of it and at the same time condone it. It excites our contempt and yet we rather admire it. We shy away from it with an odd kind of revulsion, but we protect it." Admiration, disgust, and protection. What do we do with identities that cannot clearly be known, that defy the comforts of our reliance on visual knowledge? Over dinner one night a friend tells me of his cousins who are African-American in Charleston, and white when they visit relatives up north. In *The Black Notebooks: An Interior Journey* (1997), Toi Derricotte describes how questions about religion are used to ferret out her visually invisible but apparently still unsettling, racial identity. "Are you Catholic?" a real estate agent finally asks her, in a desperate search for a clue. In a situation where her skin tones make people uncomfortable and uncertain, Derricotte momentarily wishes for a sign of clarity, for the racial equivalent of a necklace with a cross or a star of David, those things that people wear to announce religious identities that otherwise are potentially unseeable. These limits of the visual are where much of the critical literature on passing falters. If passing, as Elaine Ginsberg writes, "is about specularity: the visible and the invisible, the seen and the unseen," these terms collapse when facing religion-based identities.[1] In all the competing discourses, religious identities are not necessarily grounded in "putative visibility," despite the history of attempts to link religious identity to racial discourse, and using that failed logic, make religion visual and visible to all.

Reflections on this phenomenon become more complicated here at the intersections of American Christians and Jews. Historically in Jewish traditions, Jewishness is a function of biology and a result of physical reproduction, somehow unexplainedly genetic, passed on from mother to child, and in more recent traditions, from father to child (although the possibility for nonbiologically-based conversion does exist). These traditions imagine religion as part of physical and biological reproduction. In most forms of American Christianity, religion is not imagined as inherently biological and reproductive, hence the need for physical initiations like baptism, and/or verbal affirmations, depending on the denomination and church. Words and other enunciations take on greater significance for questions of being and not being. Being Christian is explicitly verbal, not visual, and not physically inherited. These are very different ways of enacting religious identities.

Our bus tour through the New Holy Land began at 10:30. It is now nearly noon. The Priest ends his talk and people pepper him with questions. He offered concepts and stories and theology. The visitors want details. In the Bible, did they move the Tabernacle, and how many times? How many workers did it take? Was it solid gold or plated? When the questions peter out the Priest ushers us back across the sandy courtyard. He lifts up the banner for us to pass under, and walks us along the sidewalk at the Tabernacle's north wall, where we will wait to be taken to the New Testament Village. I am thirsty and hot. Much later, I learn that at the bus stop I stood not five feet away from a drink machine. But for now there is nothing in sight. Felicia and I have been silent with each other. We are in Judea, about to step into an open-air tram with blond wood exterior and blue-cushioned seats, cooled by Arkansas breezes. We are on our way to Galilee, really a copy of the artistically rendered domestic dwelling at the reconstructed Talmudic Village at Qatzrin. In this landscape, it is no longer a monument to nationalist expansion as it is in occupied Golan/Syria/Israel. No, it is new, natural, and real part of this Arkansan place, weathering at the edges as *if* it had always been here, and belonged.

Notes

1. Elaine K. Ginsberg, introduction to *Passing and the Fictions of Identity*, ed. Ginsberg (Chapel Hill: Duke University Press, 1996), 2.

Contributors

Michael Bronski is the author of *The Pleasure Principle: Sex, Backlash, and the Struggle for Gay Freedom* and *Culture Clash: The Making of Gay Sensibility*. He has written extensively on gay and lesbian culture, sex, AIDS, and politics.

Karen McCarthy Brown is Professor of Anthropology of Religion in the Graduate and Theological Schools of Drew University. She is author of *Mama Lola: A Vodou Priestess in Brooklyn* and *Tracing the Spirit: Ethnographic Essays on Haitian Art*, and the founder and director of Drew's Newark Project, an educational endeavor that combines field-based learning with community advocacy work.

Brad Epps is Professor of Romance Languages and Literatures at Harvard University. He has published numerous articles on modern literature, film, and art from Spain, Latin America, Catalunya, and France, and is the author of *Significant Violence: Oppression and Resistance in the Narratives of Juan Goytisolo*. He is currently preparing a book on gay and lesbian issues in Latin America, Spain, and Latino cultures in the United States.

Judith Halberstam is Professor of Literature at the University of California, San Diego, where she teaches queer theory, gender studies, film, and literature. Halberstam is the author of *Female Masculinity* and the coauthor with Del LaGrace Volcano of *The Drag King Book*. She is currently working on a book about queer subcultures.

Peter Hitchcock is Professor of Literary and Cultural Studies at Baruch College and the Graduate School and University Center (GSUC) of New York. His books include *Dialogics of the Oppressed* and *Oscillate Wildly: Space, Body, and Spirit of Millennial Materialism*. Recently he edited a special issue of *South Atlantic Quarterly* on Michael Bakhtin.

Daniel Itzkovitz is Assistant Professor of English at Stonehill College and Lecturer on History and Literature at Harvard University. He is currently working on a new edition of Fannie Hurst's novel *Imitation of Life*.

Patrick R. O'Malley is Assistant Professor of English at Georgetown University, where he teaches courses on the nineteenth-century novel and gothic literature. He is working on a project entitled *Skeletons in the Cloister: Catholicism, Sexual Deviance, and the Haunting of English National Identity*.

Miriam Peskowitz is Visiting Associate Professor of Jewish Studies at Emory University. She is the author of *Spinning Fantasies: Rabbis, Gender and History*. Her essay is part of a work-in-progress entitled *Travels in the Holy Land*.

María Carla Sánchez is an Assistant Professor in the Department of English and Comparative Literature at San Diego State University, where she teaches nineteenth- and twentieth-century U.S. literature. She is currently at work on a book about race and print culture in the antebellum period.

Linda Schlossberg is an Andrew W. Mellon Post-Doctoral Fellow in the Humanities and Assistant Professor of English at Haverford College. She is writing a book about hunger and identity in the Victorian era.

Sharon Ullman is an Associate Professor of History at Bryn Mawr College. Her first book, *Sex Seen: The Emergence of Modern Sexuality in America*, looks at conflicting public representations of sexuality in early-twentieth-century America. Her current work is on "brainwashing" in 1950s America.